The Frugal Potluck Cookbook

Crowd Pleasing Recipes for All Occasions

Hillbilly Housewife

RS Net Design

ISBN: 979-8-5106-6691-5

Contents

Introduction

Gathering to visit with family, friends, church community or really for any other reason is always a good excuse for a potluck. What's not to love about sharing a meal and it's nice to share the workload.

As a passionate cook and recipe developer, I love tasting different dishes. A potluck is my favorite kind of meal, and it never fails to inspire me to come up with something new in my own kitchen after.

Throughout this little cookbook I'm sharing some of my favorite potluck recipes for any occasion with you. There are dishes ideal for hot summer days. They will keep for a while in the heat. Then there are others I wouldn't serve unless I knew I could chill them. And of course there are plenty of recipes that call mostly for pantry staples. We all know how it goes. Potlucks seem to sneak up on you, and some of the best ones are spontaneous. Except for a few ingredients (looking at you prosciutto), the ingredients are frugal and the recipes affordable to make.

At the beginning you'll find my best general tips and suggestions, but don't miss the ideas and anecdotes sprinkled throughout the book.

Please enjoy any of these recipes at your next potluck!

Warmly,

Susanne – The Hillbilly Housewife www.HillbillyHousewife.com

Thank you for downloading my book. Please be kind and review it on Amazon. Thanks!

How To Host A Potluck

Hosting a potluck can be a lot of fun. It takes a little planning and preparation to make everything go off without a hitch. By following a few simple guidelines, you'll greatly increase your chances of a successful potluck and, more importantly, spend a lot less time on organizing and going back-and-forth with the other participants.

Decide on a Location

Most of the time this will be predetermined. You may have a potluck at work, or at church. Even then, you may have a choice of rooms to use, or at the very least some flexibility on where you set up.

Walk the location. Think back on some potlucks that have worked well and some that haven't. What can you implement to set yourself up for success?

Things I consider when choosing a location are how easy it will be to walk around and get the food and where do I have outlets. Everything else you can usually work around. It doesn't hurt to check on where the closest sink is for doing dishes, and if there's a fridge on the premises to store food before you eat and leftovers after.

Create A Sign-Up Sheet Or Assign Dishes

My best advice is to plan your potluck well ahead of time. Yes, sometimes the most amazing ones are very last minute and thrown together, but as a rule, you want to give people a little time to prepare.

What to bring to a potluck is an important decision. Some of us have a handful of favorite recipes that we rotate through. Others may need a little extra help or encouragement. And then of course there are always participants best put in charge of drinks, ice, or chips. And that's okay.

The better you know your fellow cooks, the easier it will be to assign certain dishes or types of dishes. If you don't know your participants well, I recommend a sign-up sheet.

With a sign-up sheet you want to be specific, or you'll end up with three different rice dishes, four potato salads, a bunch of desserts and little else.

Start by determining how many people will participate. Create your main categories like meat, sides, salads, and sweets for example. Add several spots under each category, and request that each participant include what dish they plan on making. This will encourage your fellow potluckers to mix things up and avoid duplications.

Send Out Reminders

As the organizer, it's your job to make sure everyone is ready for the potluck. You don't want to be obnoxious, but it's helpful to send out reminders to sign up for the potluck and then two or three reminders leading up to the potluck. I like to do one a week or so before the event to give everyone plenty of time to grocery shop and one the day before.

Get organized ahead of time by collecting emails or cell phone numbers on the sign-up sheet. Let your participants know the emails or text messages are coming.

Keep it fun and stay flexible. Things happen. People change their minds. That's okay. Being organized helps you manage any last-minute hiccups with grace.

Be Prepared

Last but not least, make sure you are prepared for any eventuality. For me, that usually means having a few extra serving spoons and dishes on hand. I double check on electricity, outlets, and bring a cooler full of ice.

Last but not least, I make sure I include a time buffer or have someone on standby to go run to the store to grab whatever else we may need. There always seems to be something. The person in charge of napkins decides to make a batch of broccoli salad instead. Or the one who promised to bring drinks doesn't show up. It happens. Don't make a big deal about it. Send someone to the store to grab what you need and enjoy yourself. Life's too short to hold potluck grudges.

Potluck Food Safety

The last thing you want is for someone to get a case of food poisoning as a result of your potluck. Thankfully, there are some simple precautions you can take to keep bacteria from growing, mainly by not giving food the time to go bad and keeping it at the appropriate temperature.

Pass these tips along to your fellow potluck contributors and encourage them to implement them. None of this is hard, but it does take a little planning ahead.

Keep It Short

One of the best safety measures you can implement is keeping the time that the food sets out short. Don't go over two hours, ninety minutes is even better. This gives everyone time to set up, eat and enjoy each other's company, and call it done.

Hot Food Hot - Cold Food Cold

It's important to keep hot food hot and cold food cold. Encourage participants to bring their crockpots or use warmers to keep hot dishes at a safe temperature.

The same goes for cold items, especially things like seafood or salads with a mayonnaise dressing. Have a couple of coolers on hand, or ask participants to bring a second larger bowl and ice to keep the item cold. Use stoves and refrigerators available on site to keep everyone's dish cold until it's time to eat.

When In Doubt - Throw It Out

Last but not least, take your grandmother's advice and throw food out if you are in doubt at all about how long it has sat out or if it's still safe to consume. It's always better to be safe than sorry. While I hate to waste food as much as anyone, I don't want anyone to get sick.

As the potluck organizer, this is one of your most important responsibilities. And aside from a little cleanup, your last one. Don't feel bad about wasting food. Nothing's worth getting food poisoning over.

A Few Tips And Ideas On What To Bring To A Potluck

I thought we'd wrap this section of tips and advice up with a few more ideas on what to bring to a potluck. Think of it as the dos and don'ts of potlucks. After that we'll get to the fun part, the recipes.

Be Prepared

Bring your own serving utensils and anything else that may be needed. If you need an outlet, check with the host ahead of time. If you have an extension cord, bring it just in case.

Keep It Simple

A potluck isn't the best time to try a new recipe for the first time or make something too exotic or spicy. Another good tip is to make something that can be eaten off a plate. If you know someone is in charge of bringing paper plates, make sure your dish can be served on those. If you do decide to make a dish best eaten out of a bowl, bring enough disposable cups or bowls for everyone along with spoons.

Another good tip is to look through the sign-up sheet or ask the host if there's anything that's missing. Maybe this is the time you bring some chips or pretzels, or maybe you're the person in charge of soda.

Be Time Conscious

Show up on time and make sure your dish is hot and ready (or chilled to perfection) by the time everyone will eat. It doesn't always work out, but do your best to not cause a delay.

Clean Up After Yourself & Help Out

Putting on a potluck can be a lot of work. Do what you can to help out during setup and don't leave until after cleanup. At the very least, make sure you take everything back you brought and clean up after yourself.

Go Vegetarian

Traditionally, a lot of potluck dishes include meat. If you know there will be vegetarians present, why not highlight a vegetable dish? Or keep it simple and bring a platter of cut up raw veggies with a dip. Bonus points if you make the dip a vegan hummus.

I'm sure there are lots of folks who appreciate this lighter and healthier addition. Tortilla chips and salsa are another fun addition or look through the recipes below for more inspiration.

Antipasti Pasta Salad

Let's start things off with a fun twist on the favorite pasta salad. I love this for potlucks and family gathering because unlike mayonnaise-based pasta salad, this one can sit out for a while. It eats like a meal and is frequently dinner on a warm summer evening.

Ingredients:

- 3/4 lb. short twisted pasta, such as campanelle
- 2 jarred roasted red peppers, drained and cut into 1/2-inch strips
- 8 large pitted green olives, sliced crosswise
- 1/2 small red onion, thinly sliced lengthwise
- 4 oz. fresh mozzarella or bocconcini, cut into 3/4-inch pieces
- 2 oz. thinly sliced salami, slices halved or quartered if large
- 2 tablespoons red-wine vinegar
- 4 teaspoons extra-virgin olive oil
- 1 cup lightly packed fresh parsley leaves
- Coarse salt and ground pepper

Directions:

Cook the pasta in boiling salted water according to the package directions. Once pasta is tender, reserve 1/2 cup pasta water. Drain the pasta.

After draining, pour the pasta back into the pot and stir in olives, onion, mozzarella, peppers, salami, oil, vinegar and reserved pasta water. Season with salt and pepper. Stir until combined and garnish with parsley.

Serve at room temperature.

Bacon Chipotle Deviled Eggs

I have yet to attend a potluck that doesn't include deviled eggs. Take your version up a notch and impress the other participants with the addition of chipotles and bacon. They add a lot of flavor and interest to a dish everyone is familiar with.

Ingredients:

- 12 hard-cooked large eggs
- 1/4 cup cooked bacon, finely chopped, plus additional 2 or 3 tablespoons for garnish
- 1/2 cup light sour cream
- 1/3 cup mayonnaise
- 1 tablespoon adobo sauce (from canned chipotle peppers)
- 2 canned chipotle peppers in adobo sauce, very finely chopped
- 1/2 teaspoon ground chipotle chile pepper
- 1/2 teaspoon smoked paprika

Directions:

Slice all the eggs in half, lengthwise. Carefully scoop out the yolks and mash them in a medium sized bowl. Mix in the sour cream, mayonnaise, adobo sauce, smoked paprika, chipotle peppers, chile pepper, and 1/4 chopped bacon. Mix until all ingredients are combined.

Spoon the mixture into the egg whites and garnish with bacon.

Cover and refrigerate until ready to serve.

Baked Macaroni and Cheese

What's a potluck without a dish of mac and cheese? Here's my favorite tried and true recipe. There's nothing fancy about this recipe. Just plain good. Easy enough for a weeknight dinner and a great go-to for the holidays and potlucks.

Ingredients:

- 5 cups cooked macaroni
- 2 eggs
- 4 cups cheddar cheese, shredded
- 2 cups mozzarella cheese, shredded
- 3 cups milk
- 5 tablespoons butter
- 1/2 teaspoon salt
- 1/2 teaspoon pepper

Directions:

Preheat the oven to 350F.

Cook the macaroni and drain.

Mix together the macaroni, milk, mozzarella cheese, 3 cups cheddar cheese, butter, salt and pepper in a bowl. Pour the mixture in a casserole dish.

Beat eggs in a separate bowl and mix into the casserole dish.

Cover the casserole dish with aluminum foil and cook for 45 minutes.

Remove the aluminum foil from the dish and add a layer of cheddar cheese over the top and bake for another 15 minutes.

Baked Ziti

Here is another great weeknight dinner recipe that doubles as a perfect potluck dish. After all, who doesn't love a nice plate of ziti? Keep a pound of ground beef in the freezer and a couple of other pantry staples on hand and you're ready to make this at the drop of a hat.

This is also a great dish to make and take to a sick friend, a grieving neighbor, or new parents bringing a baby home from the hospital.

For more dishes like this check out my Make And Take Meals cookbook.

Ingredients:

- 1 pound lean ground beef
- 1 pound dry ziti pasta
- 2 (26 oz.) jars spaghetti sauce
- 1 1/2 cups sour cream
- 1 onion, chopped
- 6 oz. mozzarella cheese, shredded

- 6 oz. provolone cheese, sliced
- 2 tablespoons grated Parmesan cheese

Directions:

Preheat the oven to 350°.

In a large pot, boil the ziti pasta in salted water. Boil for 8 minutes then, drain.

Brown the ground beef and onions in a skillet over medium heat. When ingredients are browned, add the spaghetti sauce and allow it to simmer for 15 minutes.

Grease a large baking dish. In the bottom of the greased pan, layer it with half of the ziti pasta, provolone cheese, sour cream, half of the sauce mixture, the rest of the pasta, mozzarella cheese, and the rest of the sauce mixture. Top it with parmesan cheese and bake for 30 minutes.

Black Bean and Corn Salsa with Cilantro Lime Dressing

Let's switch things up a little bit with another delicious salad that makes for an amazing side dish - particularly during the warmer summer months.

I'll be honest. Like many of the recipes in this book, I don't just make this for potlucks and cookouts. I make a batch of this salad at least once a week throughout the summer for lunches or dinners. It goes great with pretty much any piece of grilled meat or fish.

Ingredients

Salsa:

- 2 cans black beans, drained and rinsed
- 2 jalapeno peppers, finely minced
- 1 very large red bell pepper, diced
- 3 cups cooked, fresh sweet corn kernels
- 2 cups tomato, diced
- 1 1/2 cup green onion, chopped

- 1 3/4 cup red onion, diced

Lime Cilantro Dressing:

- Zest of 1 very large lime
- 3/4 cup fresh lime juice
- 2/3 cup cilantro, chopped
- 1 1/2 tablespoons garlic, finely minced
- 2 tablespoons extra virgin olive oil
- 1 tablespoon ground cumin
- 1 teaspoon kosher salt

Directions:

In a large bowl, mix together all the salsa ingredients then, set aside.

In another bowl, stir together the lime juice, lime zest, salt, cumin, garlic and olive oil. Once mixed together, stir in the cilantro and pour over vegetables. Toss to coat all the ingredients.

Cover and refrigerate for 2 hours before serving.

Black Olive, Feta and Watermelon Salad

Ready for another salad recipe that will make your potluck contribution stand out from the crowd. Try this watermelon salad with black olives, feta cheese, and lots of fresh herbs. It is sure to brighten up all the other casseroles and crockpot dishes.

Ingredients:

- 4 cups watermelon, cut into 1 inch cubes
- 1 small red onion, cut into thin half-moon slices
- 1/2 cup pitted oil-cured black olive
- 1/2 lb. feta cheese, cut into 1 inch cubes
- 2 -3 limes, juice of
- 1 cup whole flat leaf parsley
- 1/4 cup chopped fresh mint
- 3 tablespoons extra virgin olive oil
- 1/8 teaspoon fresh ground black pepper

Directions:

In a bowl add the lime juices to the onions, and set aside.

In another bowl, mix together the watermelon cubes, and feta cheese cubes with the mint, black olives, olive oil, parsley, and pepper.

Once mixed completely add the lime juice mixture and onion then, toss the mixture to combine completely.

Refrigerate until ready to serve.

Broccoli Salad

Who doesn't love this perennial favorite? There are certain events that I'm not allowed to show up without a double batch of this salad.

A word of caution. Be careful with dishes like this and other mayonnaise-based salads. Don't let them sit out, especially not in the heat. I recommend sticking to indoor events and removing any leftovers after two hours.

Ingredients:

- 8 slices bacon, crisp-cooked, drained and crumbled
- 7 cups chopped fresh broccoli florets
- 1/2 cup sunflower seeds
- 1/2 cup raisins
- 1/4 cup finely chopped red onion
- 1 cup mayonnaise
- 3 tablespoons sugar
- 2 tablespoons vinegar

Directions:

Mix together the raisins, onions, mayonnaise, sugar and vinegar. Once completely combined, add the chopped broccoli until broccoli is coated. Cover for a minimum of 2 hours. When ready to serve, remove from the refrigerator, mix in the bacon and sunflower seeds. Serve immediately.

Chili Con Carne

This isn't your regular pot of chili. The meat makes all the difference. Get some good beef chuck and cut it into small bite-sized chunks. We like the hot sausage in this dish. If you're not a fan, try using chorizo, or any pork sausage. Even ground breakfast sausage or plain ground pork will work. If you don't eat pork, use ground beef or turkey.

Ingredients:

- 2 pounds beef chuck, cut into 1/2-inch cubes
- 8 ounces hot Italian sausage, casings removed
- 1 large onion, chopped
- 4 cloves garlic, minced
- 2 jalapeños, seeded, finely chopped
- 2 14.5-oz. cans diced tomatoes
- 1 15.5-oz. can black beans, drained and rinsed
- 1 15.5-oz. can dark red kidney beans, drained and rinsed
- 1/2 cup beer

- 2 tablespoons vegetable oil
- 2 tablespoons chili powder
- 1 tablespoon plus 1 teaspoon cumin
- 2 teaspoons dried oregano
- 1 teaspoon salt
- 1 teaspoon pepper

Directions:

In a skillet, warm the oil over high heat. While sautéing the beef, season it with salt and pepper. Sauté until browned. Once beef is browned, transfer it to a slow cooker.

Repeat the same steps with sausage and add to the slow cooker.

In the skillet, sauté the garlic, jalapeños and onions together for 2 minutes. Add the cumin, oregano and chili powder to the skillet and sauté for 1 more minute. Transfer all the sautéed ingredients to the slow cooker.

Pour the beer into the skillet and allow it to boil. Stirring every once in a while and pour into the slow cooker.

In the slow cooker, stir in the tomatoes, kidney beans and black beans. Cover and cook on low for 7 hours.

Serve hot.

Chicken Pot Pie

This may not be the first dish you think about when you're looking for something to make for a potluck, but it's always a big hit. I love how quickly it comes together. I make the pie crusts ahead of time and store them in the fridge.

Depending on how many people you are feeding, you may want to make and bring two of these. Add a serving spoon and you're good to go. No need to cut. Let everyone help themselves.

Ingredients:

- 2 pie crusts (top and bottom)
- 2 (10 1/2 ounce) cans cream of potato soup
- 2 cups cooked chicken, cut into bite sized chunks
- 1 (16 ounce) bag frozen mixed vegetables
- Salt and pepper

Directions:

Preheat the oven to 375°.

In a large bowl, mix together the chicken, cream of potato soup, mixed vegetables, salt and pepper.

Place the bottom pie crust in a baking dish.

Pour the mixture in the bottom pie crust and top with the top pie crust. Pinch the sides all the way around. Bake for 60 minutes.

Corn Bread Salad

There are certain events that won't be complete without someone from my family bringing corn bread salad. Yes, it's that essential. It's also just plain good and always a big hit. After all, what's not to love about cornbread covered and soaked in the delicious flavors of beans, corn, tomatoes, onion, and of course bacon.

Ingredients:

- 1 (8 1/2 oz.) package corn muffin mix
- 10 slices bacon, crisp-cooked, drained, and crumbled
- 2 (15 1/2 oz.) can pinto beans, rinsed and drained
- 2 (15 1/4 oz.) can whole kernel corn, drained
- 3 cups coarsely chopped tomatoes
- 1/2 cup sliced green onions
- 1 cup chopped green pepper
- 2 cups shredded cheddar cheese
- 1 (1 oz.) envelope ranch dry salad dressing mix

- 1 (8 oz.) tub sour cream
- 1 cup mayonnaise

Directions:

According to the package, prepare the corn muffin mix to make cornbread. Allow to cool, then crumble and set aside.

Mix together the sour cream, salad dressing mix and mayonnaise in a small bowl.

Layer the crumbled cornbread in a baking dish. On top of the corn bread layer, add an even layer of 1 cup cheese. Spread half the dressing on top of the cheese. On top of the dressing layer it with beans, corn, 1 cup of cheese, bacon, tomatoes, sweet pepper, and the other half of dressing.

Cover and refrigerate for at least 4 hours.

Couscous with Chicken and Orange

If you have the time, bake a chicken the day before and use the meat. It's a little more economical that way. But to be honest, this is what I make when I don't have a lot of time, but I want to bring a dish that will stick to your bones.

This also makes an amazing meal during the hot summer months when you don't want to cook. I've even made this on road trips before (minus the pistachios).

Ingredients:

- 1 cup shredded rotisserie chicken
- 1 cup couscous
- 1 navel orange, peeled and coarsely chopped
- 1/3 cup pistachios, toasted and coarsely chopped
- 2 teaspoons red-wine vinegar
- 2 teaspoons extra-virgin olive oil
- 2 tablespoons chopped fresh mint leaves

- Coarse salt and ground pepper

Directions:

Add couscous and 1 cup boiling water in a medium size bowl. Cover and let sit for 5 minutes. Once tender, fluff couscous with a fork.

In another bowl, mix together the chicken, mint, orange, oil, pistachios and vinegar. Season the mixture with salt and pepper. Toss couscous with the chicken mixture until coated completely.

Easy Shredded Chicken Enchiladas

Here is a wonderful baked dish that works equally well when you're having friends over to watch the game or as your contribution to a potluck.

What I love about dishes like this is that you can make them work to feed four, or as part of a potluck that feeds twenty or more. When I make this for dinner, I serve it with sour cream and/or guacamole.

Ingredients:

- 1 lb. boneless skinless chicken breast
- 12 corn tortillas
- 1 (10 oz.) can enchilada sauce
- 1 (8 oz.) can tomato sauce
- 1/4 cup chopped onion
- 1 tablespoon Worcestershire sauce
- 2 teaspoons chili powder
- 1 teaspoon oregano

- 1 teaspoon paprika
- 1 teaspoon garlic powder
- 1/2 teaspoon cumin
- 1/2 teaspoon black pepper
- 3 cups shredded cheese
- Oil olive

Directions:

Preheat the oven to 350°.

Boil chicken breast in water. Rinse and shred with a fork.

Combine the shredded chicken with onion and garlic. Mix in the Worcestershire sauce, tomato sauce, paprika, oregano, chili powder, cumin and black pepper.

Heat oil in a separate skillet.

Fry tortillas for 10 seconds on each side and drain on a paper towel.

Pour the enchilada sauce in a baking dish to coat the bottom. Spoon the meat mixture into each tortilla to fill it. If desired, add onions, cheese and olives in the tortillas. Fold up tortillas and place them in the pan seam side down. Pour the rest of the enchilada sauce over the prepared tortillas and top it off with cheese. Bake for 20 minutes. Serve warm.

Garlic Chicken Bites

Let me warn you about these chicken bites. Once you taste one, you don't want to stop. They are delicious and with the garlic and seasonings they make your house smell amazing. Just thinking about them makes my mouth water.

I bake them as close to potluck time as possible and then wrap them in paper towels and aluminum foil to keep them as warm as possible. They still taste good at room temperature, but are best fresh from the oven. They make a great kid-friendly dinner too.

Ingredients:

- 2 boneless skinless chicken breasts, cut into bite size pieces
- 1/2 cup olive oil
- 4 cloves garlic, minced
- 1/4 teaspoon pepper
- 1/2 cup breadcrumbs
- 1/4 teaspoon cayenne pepper

Directions:

Preheat the oven to 475°.

Mix together the garlic, olive oil and black pepper in a small bowl.

In a shallow dish place the chicken and pour the mixture over the top. Cover the dish and allow the chicken to marinate for 30 minutes.

After 30 minutes, drain.

Mix together the cayenne pepper and bread crumbs. Roll the chicken in the bread crumb mixture to coat.

In a single layer, place the chicken on a baking sheet and bake for 10 minutes.

Glazed Meatballs

You've probably been wondering where the meatball dish is, right? After all, there is some unwritten rule that you can't have a potluck without meatballs in some sort of sweet and tangy sauce. Here's my favorite version and one of two reasons for me to buy jellied cranberry sauce.

(The other is thanksgiving. It's not complete without the sauce you can slice. What can I say? It's family tradition.)

Ingredients:

- 1 (16 oz.) can jellied cranberry sauce
- 1 (12 oz.) bottle chili sauce
- 2 (2 lb.) bags cocktail meatballs, 1-inch in size
- 1/4 teaspoon cayenne pepper
- 1 teaspoon ground cumin

Directions:

In a saucepan, mix together the chili sauce, cranberry sauce, cayenne pepper and cumin. Stirring occasionally, cook the mixture over a medium heat until the cranberry sauce mixture is smooth. Stir in the meatballs until coated.

Cook for 30 minutes on medium low heat. Serve warm.

Green Bean Casserole

No, you didn't switch cookbooks. While perfect for any holiday table, green bean casserole is also always a welcome addition to a potluck. It goes with just about everything and almost everyone loves it.

Here's a bonus tip. If you have a favorite holiday casserole dish, or something everyone asks you to bring to a family gathering or dinner, make it for a potluck too.

Ingredients:

- 2 (14 1/2 oz.) cans French-style green beans
- 1 (2 7/8 oz.) can French-fried onions
- 1 (10 3/4 oz.) can condensed cream of mushroom soup
- 3/4 cup milk
- 1/8 teaspoon pepper

Directions:

Preheat the oven to 350°.

In a bowl, mix together the milk, cream of mushroom soup and pepper. Once combined, stir in 2/3 cup of French fried onions and green beans.

Pour the mixture into a casserole dish.

Bake for 30 minutes.

Remove from the oven and stir the mixture. Add the remaining French fried onions over the top and bake for an additional 5 minutes.

Serve hot or cold.

Homemade Oven Fries

We love these oven fries around here. I make them for dinner with burgers or anything from the grill all the time. If you have the space, or a convection oven, you can easily double this recipe.

These fries taste best hot and fresh out of the oven. Perfect if you live closeby or are hosting a potluck at your house. Even having access to an oven on-site to reheat them works. I wouldn't make these for a work potluck where you bring your food in the morning and don't eat until about lunch time. These fries don't taste that great after they've sat for a while.

Ingredients:

- 3 medium unpeeled baking potatoes
- 2 cloves garlic, minced
- 2 tablespoons lemon juice
- 2 teaspoons olive oil
- 1 teaspoon dried oregano
- 1/4 teaspoon salt
- 1/4 teaspoon pepper

- Cooking spray

Directions:

Preheat the oven to 400°.

Cut each potato into 8 wedges, lengthwise.

In a large bowl, mix together the olive oil, garlic, lemon juice, oregano, salt and pepper. Toss the potato wedges in the mixture to coat.

Grease a baking sheet and place potato wedges skin side down on it.

Bake for 45 minutes.

Kale & Squash Risotto

This is my go-to recipe when I know we'll be feeding vegetarians. Serve the parmesan cheese on the side and you have a vegan dish.

This is also one of the healthier potluck recipe contributions. But don't let that fool you. It's delicious and goes well with all sorts of other potluck fare. Or make a batch for lunch, or a light dinner at home.

Ingredients:

- 4 cups vegetable broth
- 1 1/2 cups Arborio rice
- 1/2 cup dry white wine
- 1 medium butternut squash, peeled and diced (about 4 cups)
- 1 bunch curly kale, stems removed, cut crosswise into 1/2-inch strips
- 2 green onions, diced small
- 2 tablespoons extra-virgin olive oil
- 2 garlic cloves, minced

- 1 teaspoon fresh thyme, leaves
- Coarse salt and ground pepper
- Grated Parmesan, for serving

Directions:

Preheat the oven to 400°.

In a cast iron or heavy ovenproof skillet with a tight-fitting lid, heat oil over medium-high. Add green onion and cook, stirring occasionally, until soft, about 3 minutes. Add thyme and garlic and cook until fragrant, approximately 1 minute. Add rice and cook, stirring frequently, until opaque, about 3 more minutes; season with salt and pepper. Add wine and cook, stirring, until completely absorbed, about 2 minutes. Add broth and squash then bring to a boil. Stir in kale. Immediately cover and transfer to the oven.

Bake for 20 minutes or until most of the moisture has been absorbed and the rice is tender. Top with parmesan just before serving.

Kielbasa with White Beans and Tomatoes

Here's another dish that's an entire meal in one pot. For a potluck this goes a long way. If you're making it at home, it easily feeds six, especially if you serve it over rice.

What I love about this is that aside from the smoked kielbasa sausage, everything in this recipe is shelf-stable. And the sausage lasts in the fridge for a long time. This is one of my go-to pantry meals, perfect when I don't have time to run to the grocery store.

Ingredients:

- 1 lb. smoked kielbasa, sliced 1/2 inch thick
- 1 (16 oz.) can great northern beans, drained
- 1 (14 1/2 oz.) can peeled diced tomatoes
- 2 garlic cloves, minced
- 1 small onion, chopped
- 1/2 teaspoon dried oregano
- 1/2 teaspoon dried rosemary, crushed

- 1/2 teaspoon dried basil
- 1-2 tablespoon oil

Directions:

Over medium heat, heat up the oil in a large skillet and cook the kielbasa until browned. Remove kielbasa from the skillet and set aside.

Add onions to skillet and cook until transparent. Reduce heat to low. Add the garlic, rosemary, oregano and basil to the onion and cook for 1 minute. Add the tomatoes, white beans, and kielbasa to the mixture. Bring to a boil and simmer for 10 minutes.

Lasagna Roll-Ups

These are so much fun and always a big hit because it's a different twist on lasagna. It's a little extra work to make them, and let's be honest, it's going to get a little messy, but give it a try.

If you're brave, make it with the kids and let them spread the sauce mixture and roll up the noodles. Before becoming a teenager who avoids the kitchen at all cost (when she's not starving), my daughter loved helping with this dish.

Ingredients:

- 8 lasagna noodles, cooked and drained
- 3 cups chopped cooked chicken
- 2 cups Prego Spaghetti Sauce
- 1 cup Ricotta cheese
- 1/4 cup grated Parmesan cheese
- 1/4 cup crumbled feta cheese
- 1/4 cup milk
- 1/8 teaspoon white pepper

Directions:

Preheat the oven to 375°.

Spread 1 cup of spaghetti sauce in a baking dish.

Mix together milk, chicken, pepper, and cheeses in a medium sized bowl. Spread 1/2 cup of the chicken mixture on each lasagna noodle and roll it up. Place the lasagna rolls seam side down in the baking dish.

Top with the remaining 1 cup spaghetti sauce, cover and bake for 30 minutes. Serve warm.

Melon Balls with Prosciutto and Mozzarella

How about something fresh and light, perfect for a summer potluck, or even a brunch-type event. I've always loved the combination of melon and prosciutto. The salt and sweet play well together. The mozzarella gives this dish a little more substance and interest.

Because of the prosciutto and mozzarella balls, this isn't the most frugal dish in the book, but worth a try, especially when you can find a good deal on the prosciutto.

Ingredients:

- 1 cantaloupe or honeydew melon, or 1/2 of each
- 1/4 lb. thinly sliced Italian Prosciutto di Parma
- 1 8-ounce container of fresh cherry-size mozzarella cheese, each cheese ball cut in half
- A lemon for squeezing

You'll also need:

- Party toothpicks or bamboo skewers

- Melon Baller

Directions:

Split the melons and remove the seeds. Scoop the melon into balls using a melon baller. In a bowl, place the melon balls and sprinkle lemon juice over them to coat.

Wrap a strip of prosciutto around each melon ball and pierce it with a toothpick to hold and add a piece of mozzarella on top of the toothpick. Serve immediately.

Mozzarella Sticks

Who doesn't love mozzarella sticks? They've long been one of my favorite appetizers to order on the rare occasion that we go out to eat. I thought why not see if I could make them myself.

It took a little trial and error, but I came up with something that works well at home. Since then, they've also become a favorite for any type of finger-food situation including having people over to watch the ballgame and of course potlucks.

Ingredients:

- 1 lb. mozzarella cheese, cut into 3/4 inch x 3/4 inch strips (or you can use string cheese and cut each in 2 half)
- Eggs
- 1 tablespoon milk
- 1 cup Italian style breadcrumbs
- 1/4 cup flour
- 1 cup vegetable oil

Directions:

Heat oil in a skillet over medium heat.

In a bowl, whisk together the milk and eggs.

Roll each piece of cheese in the flour, then dip in the egg mixture and roll in bread crumbs. Dip the coated cheese stick in the egg mixture and roll in breadcrumbs again.

Add cheese sticks to the hot pan and cook for 1 minute on each side. Drain the oil off the cooked mozzarella sticks on paper towels.

Serve with dipping sauce.

Oriental Coleslaw

By now you know that I prefer to make salads without mayonnaise for cookouts and potlucks. Here's another fun spin on everyone's favorite - coleslaw.

The ramen noodles give the salad some crunch and great texture. And they are cheap. All in all this is a fun potluck addition that's easy to prep ahead of time.

Ingredients:

- 1 (16 oz.) package shredded cabbage with carrot (coleslaw mix)
- 1 (3 oz.) package chicken-flavored ramen noodles, broken up
- 4 green onions, thinly sliced
- 3/4 cup slivered almonds, toasted
- 3/4 cup sunflower seeds
- 1/3 cup vinegar
- 1/2 cup salad oil
- 1 tablespoon sugar

- 1/8 teaspoon ground black pepper

Directions:

In a bowl, mix together the coleslaw mix, ramen noodles, almonds, sunflower nuts and green onions.

Cover and refrigerate until ready to serve.

In a jar with a lid, mix together sugar, vinegar, oil, pepper and ramen noodle season pack. Screw on the lid to the jar and shake. Refrigerate until ready to serve.

When ready to serve shake dressing again and pour over coleslaw mixture and toss to coat.

Orzo Pasta Salad

Pasta salads are always a welcome addition to a potluck. Why not mix things up with a flavor-packed and mediteranean inspired Orzo Pasta Salad?

This is a great frugal salad if you grow your own herbs. You can grow them in a sunny kitchen window, on a patio, and of course in the garden. They add a lot of flavor and nutrition to all your meals.

You can substitute dried herbs for fresh if needed. Use one tsp of dried herbs for each tbsp of fresh herbs.

Ingredients:

- 1 1/4 cups dried orzo
- 8 oz. feta cheese, cubed or coarsely crumbled
- 1/2 cup pitted Kalamata olives, chopped
- 1 cup roma tomatoes, chopped
- 1 tablespoon snipped fresh flat-leaf parsley
- 1 tablespoon snipped fresh basil
- 1 small clove garlic, minced

- 1/2 teaspoon snipped fresh oregano
- 1/3 cup olive oil
- 3 tablespoons lemon juice
- Salt and ground black pepper

Directions:

According to package direction, cook the orzo and drain. Rinse it off with cold water and drain again.

Transfer the pasta to a bowl with a lid and chill for 2 hours.

Combine the tomatoes, basil, olives, parsley and feta to the chilled pasta.

In a jar with a lid, add lemon juice, oregano, olive oil and garlic and shake to combine. Once dressing is well mixed, pour it over the pasta mixture and toss to combine. Season the pasta salad with salt and pepper.

Cover the salad and refrigerate for a minimum of 2 hours before serving.

Parmesan-Artichoke Crostini

This recipe is a lot of fun. I first made it when we had friends come over. Fair warning, this isn't for everyone and some people have some very strong opinions about artichokes. That said, this is a great dish for the vegetarian / vegan crowd and something different from your usual potluck fare.

Ingredients:

- 1 jar (6 1/2 oz.) marinated artichoke hearts, drained, rinsed, and patted dry
- 8 slices (1/4 inch thick) baguette
- 1/4 cup shredded Parmesan cheese, plus more for garnish
- 2 tablespoons olive oil
- 1 tablespoon chopped fresh parsley
- Coarse salt and ground pepper

Directions:

Preheat the oven to 350°.

To make the crostini, brush the baguette slices with oil on both sides. Layer an even amount of salt and pepper on both sides. Place on a baking sheet and bake for 12 minutes, turning over half way through. Allow the crostini to cool.

While the Crostini is cooling, chop the artichokes. Put the artichokes in a bowl and mix in the parsley, Parmesan, and tablespoon oil. Scoop even amounts onto the crostini.

Party Pinwheels

This recipe is more of a formula or an idea. It works great as is, but feel free to replace the chicken with your favorite sandwich meat. Salami works great for example.

The cheese is interchangeable as well. I've used laughing cow cheese that I have on hand because it's pantry stable. I've used various cream cheeses, and even homemade farmers cheese. Play around with it and see what you like, or make it based on what you have in the fridge.

This is great for lunch boxes as well (using one tortilla)

Ingredients:

- 9 inch flour tortillas
- 3/4 pound very thinly sliced cooked chicken
- 1 (5.2 oz.) container semi soft cheese with garlic and herb
- 2/3 cup bottled roasted red sweet peppers, drained and cut into very thin strips
- 1/2 cup mayonnaise
- 2 teaspoons milk

- 1/2 teaspoon curry powder
- 2/3 cup lightly packed fresh basil leaves

Directions

In a bowl, mix together the curry powder and mayonnaise and set aside.

In another bowl, mix together the milk and semi soft cheese and set aside.

On half of the tortillas, evenly spread the mayonnaise mixture. With the other half of the tortillas, evenly spread the cheese mixture. Arrange the chicken over all the tortillas. Top with fresh basil and sweet pepper strips. Then, roll the tortillas up, wrap in plastic wrap and refrigerate for a minimum of 4 hours.

Remove the plastic wrap and slice rolls diagonally into 1 inch slices before serving.

Tip:

For a twist try using flavored tortillas, such as spinach, dried tomato and basil.

Pizza Pasta Salad

Here's another family favorite. This pizza pasta salad is always a big hit. It has a lot of flavor and is perfect for the summer months.

If you have leftovers, they store well in the fridge for several. days. If you are not a fan of artichokes, or they aren't in your budget, leave them out or replace them with a different vegetable or pizza topping.

Ingredients:

- 1 lb. short pasta such as bow ties, shells or penne
- 3/4 cup sliced marinated artichoke hearts
- 1/2 cup chopped oil-packed sun-dried tomatoes
- 8 oz. bocconcini
- 4 oz. pepperoni, diced
- 1/3 cup rice vinegar
- 1/4 cup extra-virgin olive oil
- 2 tablespoons chopped fresh oregano
- 1/2 cup shredded fresh basil leaves

- Salt and pepper

Directions:

Add salted water to a large pot and bring water to a boil. Add pasta and cook for 8 minutes then, drain.

Spread drained pasta on an oiled baking sheet and allow to cool.

After the pasta has cooled down, transfer it to a bowl and stir in oil. Once the pasta is well coated in oil, add the sun dried tomatoes, artichoke hearts, vinegar, bocconcini, pepperoni, oregano and basil. Toss to coat and season with salt and pepper.

Refrigerate until ready to serve.

Pudding Fruit Salad

Are you ready for something delicious that's fun to make with the kids? Get some canned fruit, some fresh fruit, and a box of dry vanilla mix and put it all together for a delicious dessert.

This is another great kid-friendly recipe. If you want to get fancy add some whipped topping or whipped cream.

Ingredients:

- 1 (3 1/8 oz.) box dry vanilla instant pudding mix
- 1 lb strawberry, stemmed and quartered
- 1 (29 oz.) can peach slices, undrained
- 1 (20 oz.) can pineapple chunks, undrained
- 1/2 pint blueberries
- 1 bunch grapes
- 1 banana, sliced

Directions:

In a bowl, mix together the vanilla pudding mix, peaches, pineapples and juices from the cans. Mix until all ingredients are completely combined and pudding has dissolved.

Once pudding has dissolved, stir in the grapes, banana, blueberries, and strawberries.

Refrigerate for a minimum of 2 hours before serving.

Radish-Chive Tea Sandwiches

Are you ready to get a little fancy? Think British tea party meets American potluck. If you have a garden, these are a no-brainer in the spring. Otherwise, find some good radishes and fresh chives at the grocery store or farmers market. This is one recipe where dried herbs won't do.

Ingredients:

- 16 1/4-inch-thick baguette slices
- 10 radishes, thinly sliced
- 3 tablespoons minced chives, divided
- 1 tablespoon toasted sesame seeds
- 1/4 cup butter, room temperature
- 3/4 teaspoon grated peeled fresh ginger
- 1/4 teaspoon Asian sesame oil

Directions:

In a bowl, mix together 2 tablespoons chives, ginger, sesame seeds, butter and oil. Season with salt and pepper. Generously spread the chive mixture over each slice of bread and top with radishes. Serve immediately.

Ranch and Cheese Potato Bake

Yes, these potatoes call for an entire bottle of ranch (pay attention to the size) and a pack of shredded cheese. Let's not even talk about the butter. This is an incredibly rich dish and a little goes a long way.

That said, these are some of THE BEST potatoes you've ever eaten and it's perfect for your next potluck. Try it and let me know how you and your fellow potluckers like it.

Ingredients:

- 4 pounds russet potatoes, cut into 1/4 inch cubes
- 2 teaspoons chili powder
- 1 teaspoon salt
- 1/2 teaspoon ground black pepper
- 6 tablespoons butter, melted
- 1 (8 oz.) package shredded Colby-Monterey Jack cheese blend
- 1 (8 oz.) bottle Ranch dressing

Directions:

Preheat the oven to 400°. Grease a baking dish.

Place cubed potatoes in the baking dish and season with salt, pepper and chili powder. Evenly coat the seasoned potatoes with butter. Cover the baking dish with aluminum foil and bake for 1 hour. Remove from the oven.

Mix in the Ranch dressing and cheese and continue to cook for 10 more minutes.

Red Potato Salad

I didn't grow up eating red potato salad. We were very much a yellow potato, mayonnaise, and hard boiled eggs kind of family. I was first introduced to this variation when I worked in a deli during college. I've loved it ever since.

After some trial and error and experiments with sour cream, dill, and a host of other ingredients, this is our favorite version of red potato salad right now. I hope you give it a try.

Ingredients:

- 4 pounds small red potatoes
- 2 celery stalks, thinly sliced
- 1 onion, thinly sliced
- 1 1/4 cups mayonnaise
- 2 tablespoons sweet pickle relish
- 1/3 cup whole-grain mustard
- 2 tablespoons red wine vinegar
- Salt and pepper

Directions:

In a large pot, add potatoes and enough water to cover by 1 inch. Bring to a boil. Once boiling, reduce heat to low, cover and simmer for 30 minutes. Drain water from potatoes.

Halve the potatoes and set them in a large bowl with onion and celery.

In another bowl, mix together mayonnaise, mustard, relish, vinegar, salt and pepper. Add the mayonnaise mixture to the potato mixture. Gently stir. Refrigerate until ready to serve.

Roasted Brussels Sprouts

Let's talk about brussel sprouts. They get a bad rep, mainly because of how they are prepared. I happen to like steamed brussel sprouts, but I understand why they aren't everyone's favorite. These roasted ones though? Out of this world.

Make them for a potluck, fix them for a nice family dinner, and definitely add them to your holiday table.

Ingredients:

- 1 1/2 lbs. fresh Brussels sprouts
- 3 tablespoons extra virgin olive oil
- 1/2 teaspoon dried sage
- 1/2 teaspoon garlic powder
- 1/2 teaspoon salt
- 1/2 teaspoon ground black pepper

Directions:

Preheat the oven to 400°.

Cut the bottom off of each Brussel sprout and halve, lengthwise. Combine oil, halved Brussel sprouts, garlic powder, sage, salt and pepper in a bowl and pour in a baking dish. Roast for 25 minutes. Serve hot or cold.

Roasted Tomato with Cheesy Pasta

Ready for another pasta dish to try for your next potluck? I've got you covers with this simple recipe. I make this all summer long when cherry tomatoes are plenty. Use your own or buy some at the store.

The beautiful thing about cherry tomatoes is that even store-bought ones have a decent flavor. But if you get the chance to make this with homegrown cherry tomatoes, go for it. The flavor is amazing. If you have fresh oregano in the garden, use it. About two tablespoons of chopped fresh oregano leaves will do the trick.

Ingredients:

- 1 pound red and/or yellow grape or cherry tomatoes, halved
- 1 (16 oz.) package dried rotini pasta
- 2 tablespoons white wine vinegar
- 3 cloves garlic, thinly sliced
- 2 teaspoons dried oregano, crushed
- 8 oz. small fresh mozzarella balls
- 1/2 cup snipped fresh basil

- 1/3 cup olive oil
- 1/4 cup olive oil
- 1 teaspoon kosher salt
- 1/2 teaspoon cracked black pepper

Directions:

Preheat the oven to 450°.

In a foil lined baking pan, place the tomato halves cut sides up. Sprinkle the tomato halves with garlic, salt and oregano. Drizzle seasoned tomatoes with 1/4 cup olive oil. Roast the tomatoes in the oven for 20 minutes and set aside.

While the tomatoes are roasting, cook pasta according to package instructions and drain.

Whisk together the vinegar, pepper and 1/3 cup olive oil. Add the pasta to the vinegar mixture and toss to coat. Stirring occasionally, allow the pasta mixture to cool to room temperature.

Add the mozzarella, basil, and tomatoes to the pasta. Toss to coat and serve.

Shrimp Salad

Fair warning. This is something you want to keep chilled and remove from the potluck table after an hour. The good news is that chances are that it will be long gone before it gets to that point. All I'm saying is don't take any risks between the shrimp and the mayonnaise.

I like to get a big bowl of ice to set my serving bowl in when I take this dish to a potluck. I never make it for an outdoor event in the summer.

Ingredients:

- 3 cups cooked shrimp, chopped
- 1 cup celery, diced
- 3 hard-boiled eggs, chopped
- 3/4 cup mayonnaise
- 1/2 teaspoon garlic powder
- 1 teaspoon salt
- 1 teaspoon Worcestershire sauce

- 1/4 teaspoon allspice

Directions:

Mix together the eggs, shrimp and celery in a large bowl.

In another bowl, mix together the mayonnaise, garlic powder, salt, Worcestershire sauce and allspice.

Pour the mayonnaise mixture over the shrimp mixture and toss to coat.

Cover and refrigerate for a minimum of 4 hours. Serve on lettuce leaves.

Spinach Casserole

I keep several boxes of frozen chopped spinach on hand and one of the recipes I use it for is this spinach casserole.

This doesn't make a lot, but it's delicious, rich, and something a little different. Don't expect people to grab more than a spoonful of this casserole, so a little goes a long way.

Ingredients:

- 2 (10 oz.) boxes frozen chopped spinach, defrosted
- 1 large egg
- 1 teaspoon salt
- 1/4 teaspoon black pepper
- 1 small onion, chopped fine
- 1 1/2 cups sharp cheddar cheese, shredded
- 1 can condensed cream of mushroom soup
- 2 cup croutons

Directions:

Preheat the oven to 350°.

In a strainer, squeeze as much extra liquid from the spinach as possible.

Combine all ingredients except for the croutons. Combine well. Pour the mixture into a casserole dish and layer with croutons. Bake in the oven for 40 minutes.

Taco Biscuit Casserole

Ready for one last potluck casserole? I saved one of our favorites recipes for last. This also makes a great weeknight dinner, or take it to a family in need of a hot meal.

The remaining cheese melts into the cooked biscuits at the very end, giving it that extra cheesy goodness. If you don't want to use biscuit mix, replace it with your favorite scratch biscuit recipe. Replace the corn with peppers with regular sweet corn if you can't find it.

Ingredients:

- 1 1/2 lb. lean ground beef
- 1 (1 1/4 oz.) package taco-seasoning mix
- 3/4 cup water
- 1 (16 oz.) can kidney beans
- 1 (11 oz.) can whole-kernel corn with sweet peppers, drained
- 3 1/4 cups packaged biscuit mix
- 1 cup milk
- 3 cups shredded cheddar cheese

Directions:

Preheat the oven to 350°.

Cook ground beef in a large skillet until brown and drain.

Return to the pan, add the taco seasoning mix and water. Add the kidney beans, undrained and add the drained corn. Allow to boil.

Meanwhile, mix together the milk and biscuit mix. Stir moistened and beat for 30 seconds more. On a floured surface, roll out the dough and make 10 biscuits with a 2-inch biscuit cutter.

Spoon the ground beef mixture into a baking dish and top it off with 2 cups cheese. Place the biscuits on top of the cheese and bake for 20 minutes. Sprinkle with remaining 1 cup cheese.

More Hillbilly Housewife Cookbooks

Homemade Mixes – Make It Yourself & Save

Many of the mixes and convenience foods you buy at the store are quick and easy to make at home. Save money and get full control over the ingredients.

Old-Fashioned Cooking - Recipes from Grandma's Kitchen

A collection of my family's favorite recipes that have been past down for generations.

Homemade Bread Recipes

Making your own bread at home is a lot easier than you think. Start with one of the quick breads, or try your hand at the one-hour homemade bread. You can't go wrong with any of these tasty recipes.

Breakfast Casseroles

Jumpstart your morning with these delicious dishes. They are tasty for dinner too (and quite frugal)

You can find all my Kindle Cookbooks at www.amazon.com/author/hillbillyhousewife

About The Author

Susanne, The Hillbilly Housewife has a passion to help families with limited time, money, and energy. Her mission is to share only the very best resources to help parents run their household and raise their families all while squeezing a bit of fun so they end their days with a smile and a grateful heart.

She runs the wildly popular blog www.HillbillyHousewife.com where frugal living is the focus. She believes that if people can live within their means, they can truly enjoy all the blessings God has given them.

Her mission is to provide a well-rounded approach to all areas of keeping a home, and provide a place for her readers to voice their opinions and share recipes and tips with each other.

Manufactured by Amazon.ca
Bolton, ON

NTC's Language Project Books

Por todos lados 1

Development and Production: Elm Street Publications, Wellesley, MA
Composition: Jan Ewing, Ewing Systems, New York, NY
Illustrations: Len Shalansky
Electronic Art: William J. Cataldi, Ewing Systems, NY

ISBN: 0-658-00308-9 (hardbound)
ISBN: 0-658-00088-8 (softbound)

Published by National Textbook Company,
a division of NTC/Contemporary Publishing Group, Inc.
4255 West Touhy Avenue
Lincolnwood (Chicago), Illinois 60646-1975 U.S.A.

Manufactured in the United States of America.

99 00 01 02 03 04 05 QB 9 8 7 6 5 4 3 2 1

Índice

To the Student

You are studying a foreign language—Spanish. And languages are meant to be spoken. But people talk for a reason: maybe to tell a friend about something that's just happened, or to ask about the time a movie starts. Well, ***Por todos lados 1*** also provides reasons for using language—different situations in which you need to speak, read, and write Spanish.

Por todos lados 1 consists of ten projects that relate to topics ordinarily taught in first-year Spanish. You may do them in the order that fits your textbook. Why projects? Because each one has a different goal and includes a different reason for using Spanish. Because you'll have the satisfaction of actually using Spanish to create something. Some of the projects involve:

- Setting up and going to a restaurant typical of a Spanish-speaking area
- Planning mini-Olympic games for the Spanish-speaking world
- Creating a Spanish-language weather report
- Producing a Spanish-language fashion show
- Setting up a health clinic for Spanish-speaking clients
- Making a holiday calendar for the Spanish-speaking world

You'll reach the goals of these projects in many different ways. To make a calendar, for example, you'll research holidays in Spanish-speaking countries. That research could be done on the World Wide Web, if you have access to it. Once on the Web, you can search for information in both Spanish and English! To give a weather report, you'll need to change Fahrenheit temperatures into Celsius because after all, that's what people from most Spanish-speaking countries use and understand.

A resource section of special tools is available in the Almanac in the back of ***Por todos lados 1***. It contains lots of helpful information, including the following:

- A list of the Spanish-speaking countries with their capitals and a monetary unit chart with directions for changing money from dollars to the currencies of various Spanish-speaking countries

- A guide for doing searches on the World Wide Web
- Extra vocabulary related to the projects you're working on
- A metric chart with directions for converting standard U.S. measurements

Por todos lados 1 includes other features to help you. Each project begins with a list of the tasks to be performed. This is a kind of road map showing what you can accomplish. There is even a **Conexiones** (*Connections*) box indicating other subject areas related to this project, such as history, art, technology, or study skills. The **Herramientas útiles** (*Useful tools*) boxes suggest sources for finding information you will need, as well as materials required for each step in the project. This may include worksheets to help you organize and present information.

Worksheets are available from your teacher, and activities that use them have a worksheet icon in the margin of the text. The **Vocabulario útil** (*Useful vocabulary*) boxes include Spanish words and phrases you may need to complete a step in the project.

While you're working through a project, you'll see interesting tidbits of information about Spanish-speaking countries in the **¿Sabías que...?** (*Did you know that ... ?*) boxes. They present interesting facts, such as unique holiday celebrations and what a typical Mexican cheer sounds like, so that you can write your own.

During a project, you will often work with partners or a small group of other students. In Project 6, **¡Presenten su colegio!**, you might make classroom signs, or perhaps videotape important areas of the school for the student guidebook. Occasionally you'll work on your own. You may

see an icon indicating that a task can be done as homework.

While you work with other students on these projects, you will have many opportunities to speak, read, and write Spanish. You may play the role of an exchange student, talk with your host, and later write a thank-you note in Spanish. In Project 4, you will play a game that a group has invented. You may have to read and answer questions in Spanish.

But what if you'd like to add something extra to a project? Maybe you'd like a challenge. In each project, **Un poco más** (*Something extra*) sections provide those opportunities. You can spread your wings and push your Spanish to its limits.

In these projects, Spanish is everywhere; it is necessary and useful. You and your classmates will have the satisfaction of using Spanish in real-life situations and enjoying it.

¡Diviértete!

PROJECT

1

Las presentaciones

For this project, your class will plan a visit to a Spanish-speaking country. You will be working in one of two groups. One group will consist of students from the U.S. who are "visiting" a major city in a Spanish-speaking country. The other group will be the host students. During the course of this project, you will:

- Decide on a city in a Spanish-speaking country to visit
- Write a letter of introduction to one of the new students you're going to meet
- Find the best flight times and fares to your destination (visitors)
- Find ways to pick up your guests at the airport and create a welcome banner (hosts)
- Introduce yourself personally to the new students
- Investigate a site for a group excursion and design postcards from the site
- Write a note to a new friend

¡Buen viaje!

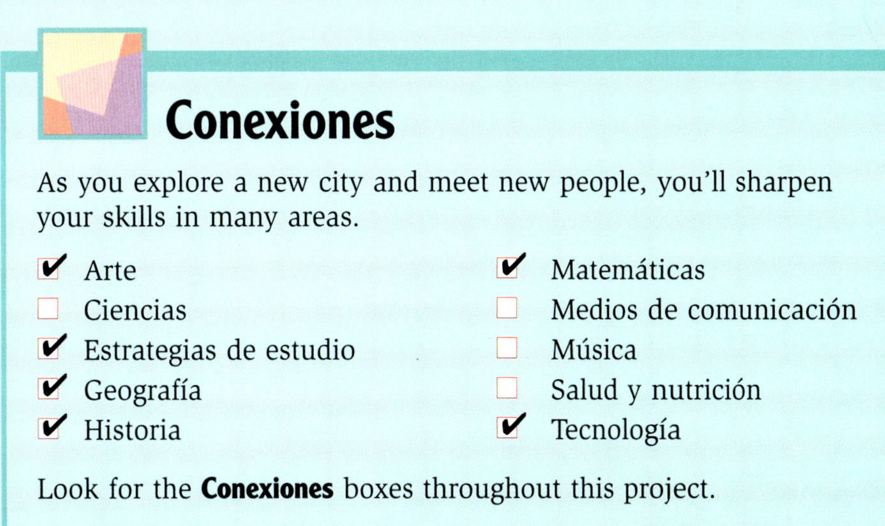

Conexiones

As you explore a new city and meet new people, you'll sharpen your skills in many areas.

- [x] Arte
- [ ] Ciencias
- [x] Estrategias de estudio
- [x] Geografía
- [x] Historia
- [x] Matemáticas
- [ ] Medios de comunicación
- [ ] Música
- [ ] Salud y nutrición
- [x] Tecnología

Look for the **Conexiones** boxes throughout this project.

Warm-up: ¡Vamos a empezar!

Herramientas útiles

- A three-ring binder or folder for each student for compiling a portfolio

A. With two or three other students, create a list of words and phrases in Spanish that you associate with greetings and introductions. Share your ideas with your class and expand your list as you listen to your classmates' ideas. How are Spanish greetings and introductions similar to or different from greetings and introductions in the U.S.?

B. In a group of three or four, discuss what greetings and introductions in the U.S. are like. What are the typical words and phrases people say when meeting someone new? Do people shake hands? How might greetings between two friends be different from those between two business associates?

Hi!

Hey!

How are you?

How do you do?

Hello!

Howdy!

Mornin'!

It's a pleasure to meet you.

Good morning!

c. As you plan and carry out your trip, you'll be putting together a portfolio of your experiences and accomplishments. You'll need a three-ring binder. Begin your portfolio by inserting the list of words and phrases you and your classmates brainstormed. You may want to refer to this list throughout the project.

A Las preparaciones

There are over twenty Spanish-speaking countries, and each has its own distinct geography, attractions, history, and culture. After researching various possibilities, your class will decide on one city to visit on your exchange trip.

Herramientas útiles

- World map
- World Map Worksheet 1.A, pages 1 and 2
- Colored markers
- Maps of Spanish-speaking countries
- Encyclopedias
- Guidebooks for Spanish-speaking countries
- Travel magazines or brochures with photographs of Spanish-speaking cities
- TV programs about selected cities
- Portfolio
- The World Wide Web

1er Paso

El mundo hispano

A. Working in a group of three or four students, see how many Spanish-speaking countries you can name. When you're done, share your list with the class and make a complete list together on the board. Compare your list with the one in the Almanac at the back of this book.

B. Continue working in your group. Each person should have a copy of World Map Worksheet 1.A. Color all the Spanish-speaking countries the same color and label each with its name. Consult your Spanish textbook or the Almanac for help.

Conexiones

- ☑ Estrategias de estudio
- ☑ Geografía
- ☑ Tecnología

C. In your group, choose three Spanish-speaking countries on your map. Think of at least two things you associate with each one. Consider cities, famous people, arts, geographical landmarks, foods, climate, and so on. Record your associations on World Map Worksheet 1.A, page 2, and share them with the class.

País	*Asociaciones*
▶ España:	1. Barcelona 2. los toros
Perú:	1. los Andes 2. las llamas

¿Sabías que...?

In 1492, Spain became the first country in the world to adopt Spanish—**castellano** (named after Castilla, the region in which this language was spoken)—as its official language. The nations that speak Spanish today adopted it as a result of the Spanish conquest of the Americas. The first to adopt it was **La Nueva España**, now Mexico.

2° Paso ¡A empezar!

Your group's next step is to learn something new about a city in a Spanish-speaking country that interests you. On a map, locate a city you'd like to visit in one of the countries you chose earlier and write its name on World Map Worksheet 1.A, page 2. Use some of the resources listed in the **Herramientas útiles** box on page 6 to find out at least five facts that you didn't already know about the city. Record them on World Map Worksheet 1.A, page 2.

¡Investiguemos en el Web!

Look for information about a Spanish-speaking city via the Web. Use the Reference or Travel sections of a Web guide to link to encyclopedias and national or local travel-related sites. Be sure to keep the addresses of sites that are of particular interest. Write them down or use the bookmark feature of your navigation software. This feature is usually accessible from one of your pull-down menus. If any of the terms used here are unfamiliar to you, you can look them up in the Web Search Guide in the Almanac at the end of this book. The Web Search Guide also contains general guidelines for searching the Web.

3er Paso La propaganda

In English, try to persuade the rest of the class that the city you've chosen would be the best destination for a student exchange trip!

A. With your group, prepare a brief but convincing presentation for your class—in English—about your city. Use the information you've gathered and try to include some photographs of the city from guide-books, travel brochures, magazines, or the Web. Use World Map Worksheet 1.A, page 1, to show where the country and city are located.

B. After the presentations, hold a class vote to determine which city is the class favorite. That city will be the destination of your student exchange trip! On World Map Worksheet 1.A, page 1, outline the country your class has chosen in a contrasting color. Add World Map Worksheet 1.A and the information that you gathered about your city to your portfolio.

Los dos grupos

For much of the rest of this project, you will be working in one of two groups. One group will be the host students in the city you've chosen. The other group will be the exchange students visiting from the U.S.

Las cartas de introducción

Before the trip begins, the visitors and the hosts will want to find out something about each other. A short letter can provide a good introduction.

Herramientas útiles

- A self-portrait or a drawing of you and your family
- Portfolio

1er Paso

Lo esencial

Before you write a letter to one of the new students you're going to meet, think about how you want to introduce yourself.

A. Find a partner from your own group (host students or visiting students). In English, brainstorm a list of standard information that should be included in a letter of introduction. Then come up with a list of phrases in Spanish that will help you express this information in your letter. Keep in mind whether you're host students or visiting students.

Standard information	*Phrases*
▶ *name:*	Yo me llamo ___.
hometown:	Yo soy de ___.

B. Share your Spanish phrases with the class and make a list together on the board.

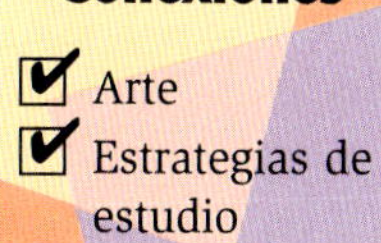

Conexiones

- ☑ Arte
- ☑ Estrategias de estudio

2° Paso La información personal

Make a list of personal information you want to include in your letter, using the topics you brainstormed in the **1er Paso**. If you're one of the host students, you'll need to invent a Hispanic identity: a name, address, and so on.

3er Paso Las cartas

A. Choose an exchange partner from the other group. Write a brief letter introducing yourself to your exchange partner. Include a self-portrait or a drawing of yourself and your family. For help with the format of a Spanish letter, see the example on the facing page and the Almanac at the back of this book.

Vocabulario útil

Querido amigo/Querida amiga	*Dear (male/female) friend*
Tu nuevo amigo/Tu nueva amiga	*Your new friend*
¡Hasta pronto!	*See you soon!*
No tengo hermanos.	*I don't have any brothers (and sisters).*
Me gustan los deportes.	*I like sports.*
Me gusta jugar al/a la ___.	*I like to play [name of game].*
Me gusta tocar el/la ___.	*I like to play the [musical instrument].*

B. Give your letter to your teacher for delivery to your exchange partner. If your exchange partner is a host, put his or her real name on the back so your teacher knows whom to deliver it to. Read the letter you've received and add it to your portfolio. If you have any problems understanding your letter, consult your teacher.

Chicago, el 21 de septiembre

Querido amigo:

Hola. Me llamo Tom. Tengo 14 años. Soy de Chicago, Illinois. Tengo dos hermanos y un perro (estamos en la foto). Me gusta jugar al tenis, leer y nadar. ¡Hasta pronto!

Tu nuevo amigo,

Tom

XXX XXXXX
XXXX XXXXXXX XXXX
XXXX, XX

Sr. Alberto Zamuria-Espinosa
de la catedral vieja 3 cuadras al sur,
media cuadra al lago
Managua, Nicaragua

¿Sabías que...?

In some Latin American countries there are neighborhoods in which houses don't have numbers and streets don't have names, so directions are given in terms of well-known landmarks. For example in Managua, Nicaragua, Lake Managua and the old cathedral are used as reference points. Look at the envelope for a sample address. Can you understand the directions given? (*From the old cathedral three blocks to the south, half a block to the lake.*)

Un poco más

Now see if you can find two people in your group (hosts or visitors) who have something in common with your exchange partner. Survey at least five classmates, sharing information from the letter you received. Be sure to make notes so you can tell your exchange partner later what you found out.

▶ *You:* Mi amigo, Tom, tiene dos hermanos. ¿Tienes dos hermanos?

Group member 1: No, no tengo dos hermanos.

Group member 2: Sí, ¡yo tengo dos hermanos también!

¿Cómo llegamos allí?

Before the exchange trip gets under way, the visitors need to make travel plans, and the hosts need to make plans to receive the visitors.

Herramientas útiles

- Airline flight schedules and fares to the city you've chosen
- The World Wide Web
- Portfolio
- Markers, paper, tape
- Computer with word-processing software

1er Paso

Para los huéspedes: La investigación

This **Paso** is for the visitors. The visitors need to research flight times and fares to make sure they find the best bargains. Work with three or four other students from your group.

A. Using the airline flight schedules and fare lists, find out what flights are available from your hometown (or the nearest airport) to the city you've selected for the exchange trip. Make a list of five different possible dates and times; include the arrival times in the Spanish-speaking city, and record the flight numbers and the names of the airlines.

B. Find out the fare for each of the flights. Use the monetary unit chart in the Almanac section of this book and exchange rates available from newspapers, banks, or the Web to list the prices in both dollars and the currency of the Spanish-speaking country.

Conexiones

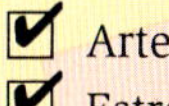

- ✔ Arte
- ✔ Estrategias de estudio
- ✔ Matemáticas
- ✔ Tecnología

2° Paso Para los anfitriones: La llegada

A. This **Paso** is for the hosts. Brainstorm ways of getting to the airport to pick up your guests. Choose the best way to go by taking a vote and then decide what arrangements need to be made. Do you need to rent a vehicle?

B. Now make welcome banners to greet your visitors. Be creative and try to use both Spanish and English on them. Use some of the materials suggested in the **Herramientas útiles** box on page 13. Keep the banners for later use.

3er Paso La decisión

Each visitor reports to the class in Spanish the date, time, and fare of one of the flights his or her group has selected. The teacher writes the information on the board, and the class then decides which flight is the best choice for the whole group.

4° Paso Un álbum

Add your list of flight times and fares as well as the group's final choice of flight to your portfolio.

¿Sabías que...?

There are many different ways to answer the phone in Spanish. In fact, telephone greetings vary from country to country. For example, in Spain, the typical greeting is **¿Diga?** or **¿Dígame?** (literally, *Tell me?*), while in Mexico **¿Bueno?** (literally, *Well?*) is more common. People in Argentina prefer the greeting **¿Aló?**

Un poco más

Work with your partner from the other group. Together, prepare a telephone conversation in Spanish. If you are the visitor, call your host partner. You will need to introduce yourself, ask for your partner, and tell him or her where you're from. Then say where your group is arriving, what the flight number is, and what time and date you are coming. If you're a host, you'll need to answer the phone, greet your caller, and respond to his or her introduction. Then ask when the group will arrive and take down the information your partner gives you. You might need to ask the caller to repeat something.

Vocabulario útil

¿Quién habla?	*Who's calling?*
Soy ___.	*This is ___.*
¿Me comunica con ___?	*May I speak with ___?*
Somos de [*name of city*].	*We're from ___.*
Llegamos al aeropuerto [*name*].	*We're arriving at ___ airport.*
¿Cuándo llega el vuelo?	*When does the flight arrive?*
Llega el [*date*] a la(s) [*time*].	*It arrives on ___ at ___.*
¿Está bien?	*Is that good?/Does that work?*
¡Nos vemos en el aeropuerto el [*date*] a la(s) [*time*]!	*See you at the airport on ___ at ___!*

El encuentro

When the visitors arrive, the hosts greet them at a gathering with the exchange coordinator (your teacher).

Herramientas útiles

- Adhesive name tags or index cards and tape
- Markers
- Welcome banners made in Section C
- Portfolio

1er Paso

Me presento...

At this first meeting, you're going to introduce yourself to the new students. Prepare a name tag to help your new friends learn your name. In addition to your name, add one piece of information about yourself in Spanish that will help stimulate conversation with your new friends, such as your age, whether you have siblings or pets, or the name of an activity that you really enjoy.

Vocabulario útil

Tengo [14] años.	*I'm [14] years old.*
Tengo [una hermana].	*I have [a sister].*
No tengo hermanos.	*I have no brothers (and sisters).*
Tengo [dos gatos].	*I have [two cats].*
Me gusta [jugar al fútbol].	*I like [to play soccer].*
Me gustan [las novelas].	*I like [novels].*

Conexiones

- ☑ Arte
- ☑ Estrategias de estudio

2º Paso ... ¿Y tú?

Working with a partner from your group (host students or visiting students), write at least three questions in Spanish that you want to ask your new friends when you meet.

3er Paso ¡Mucho gusto!

Now it's time to meet your new friends! Don't forget to wear your name tag and bring your questions to the introductory gathering. Hosts should be sure to hang up the welcome banners in the classroom.

A. First, find your exchange partner and introduce yourself in Spanish. If you can't find your exchange partner, ask around.

▶ *You:* Perdón, busco a José. ¿Dónde está?
Student: ¡Allí está!
You: ¿Eres José?
José: Sí, soy yo.

B. Now introduce yourself to at least three other students. Use your list of questions and the information on their name tags to start a conversation with each of them.

¿Sabías que...?

Greetings in Spanish-speaking countries are generally less formal and reserved than the typical handshake in the U.S. For example, when meeting a new person, Spanish-speaking people generally shake hands. When meeting a friend, men may give each other a hug **(abrazo)**, and women may often greet male or female friends with a kiss on the cheek. In some countries, people kiss on both cheeks.

4° Paso

Un álbum

Add your list of questions and your name tag to your portfolio to keep as souvenirs of the first meeting with your exchange partner.

Un poco más

In Spanish, introduce your exchange partner to one of the people in your group with whom he or she has something in common. Use the information from the **Un poco más** activity in Section B on page 12. Give your friend's name and tell your exchange partner what he or she has in common with your friend.

- ▶ Marcos, te presento a mi amiga Jennifer. Jennifer tiene 14 años y le gusta esquiar también.

Planeando una excursión

Along with meeting new people, your exchange trip includes an excursion to a site of interest in the city you've chosen.

Herramientas útiles

- Encyclopedias
- Guidebooks for Spanish-speaking countries
- Travel brochures and magazines
- Blank 3" x 5" index cards
- Colored markers
- Portfolio
- The World Wide Web

1er Paso

El tema

A. To help you decide what type of site you'd like to visit, choose two topics from the following list that interest you.

el arte	la tecnología	la naturaleza	los deportes
la arquitectura	la geografía	la historia	los mercados
las ruinas	la política	la música	el teatro

B. Present your selections to the class and find two or three people who share your interests.

▶ *Student 1:* ¿Te gusta el teatro?
Student 2: Sí, me gusta el teatro.
Student 3: No, no me gusta el teatro.

Conexiones

- ☑ Arte
- ☑ Geografía
- ☑ Historia
- ☑ Tecnología

2º Paso

La investigación

A. Now work with your group of three or four to find a site that reflects one of the areas of interest you've chosen. Use some of the resources listed in the **Herramientas útiles** box on page 19. The site must be in or near the city where the exchange trip is taking place. Based on the information you find, make a list of three reasons in Spanish why you would like to visit the site.

▶ *Topic:* la política

Site: el palacio nacional

Reasons:
1. El presidente vive en este palacio.
   The president lives in this palace.
2. Hay visitas del palacio todos los días.
   There are visits to the palace every day.
3. Está cerca de muchos restaurantes y museos.
   It's near many restaurants and museums.

¡Investiguemos en el Web!

Look back at useful Web sites you located in Section A on page 8. Look for information about specific places, such as museums or monuments, that you would like to visit in your city. Once you're on the Web site, you can look for information about the places you're interested in, links to additional pages within the site, and links to other sites with information about places of interest.

What if you already know a place in your city that you would like to know more about? Enter its name, such as "Prado Museum," in the search function of your navigation software. If you only have a particular theme in mind, for example, historical monuments in Buenos Aires, you could search via the city and theme. *Tip:* If your keyword is a phrase, put it in quotation marks. Remember not to put two words together in quotation marks unless you want to find them together as a phrase on a Web page.

Keywords

name of museum
"[name of city] + [theme]"

B. With your small group, present your site to the class in English or Spanish.

Las tarjetas postales

While visiting your site, you will want to buy and write some postcards to your friends back home.

A. Working with a partner from your group, design two postcards showing the site you've visited. Decorate one side of an index card with an image of the site. On the other side in the upper left corner include the name and a brief description of the place in Spanish (or in English).

B. On your postcard, write a brief message in Spanish to send to another Spanish class in the visiting students' school in the U.S. If you're a host student, be sure to introduce yourself.

C. Include your research and your postcard in your portfolio.

Queridos amigos:

Saludos desde el mercado central de Cuzco, Perú. Hay ropa, comida y arte. Estoy muy contenta aquí, pero ¡los extraño mucho! ¡Adiós!

Un abrazo,

Julia

Queridos amigos:

Saludos de Juanito, el amigo de Julia. Cuzco es muy bonito. A Julia le gusta mucho el mercado. ¡Hasta luego!

Atentamente,

Juanito

Vocabulario útil

Con cariño/Cariñosamente	*With affection/Affectionately*
Un abrazo	*Hugs and kisses*
Atentamente	*Sincerely*
Es muy divertido.	*It's a lot of fun.*
Saludos desde [*place*]	*Greetings from [place]*
Saludos de [*person*]	*Greetings from [person]*
Te extraño./Los extraño.	*I miss you./I miss you all.*

¡Adiós!

The day for the visitors to return to the U.S. has arrived. It's time to say good-bye.

Herramientas útiles

- Colored markers
- Construction paper
- Portfolio

1er Paso

¡Hasta pronto!

On the day of the visitors' departure, say good-bye to the new students you've met during the exchange. Use the phrases below and others you've learned in class. Since this is an exchange trip, you'll see each other again soon!

Vocabulario útil

¡Buen viaje!	*Have a good trip!*
¡Escríbeme pronto!	*Write soon!*
¡Hasta pronto!	*See you soon!*
¡Que te vaya bien!	*All the best!*

2° Paso

El correo

A. After the visitors have returned to the U.S., both groups of students sit down to write notes to their new friends. If you were a visitor, write a thank-you note to your host. If you were one of the hosts, write a note to your guest, giving the date and time of your arrival in the U.S. for the second part of the exchange trip. Use one of the examples on page 23 as a model. The letters to hosts who have chosen a new identity should have their real names on the back so your teacher can distribute the letters.

Querido Juan:

¡Hola! ¿Cómo estás? muchas gracias por tu hospitalidad. Tu casa es muy bonita y tus padres y tu hermana son muy simpáticos.

¡Hasta luego!

Chris

Querida michelle:

¡Saludos desde España! ¿Cómo estás? Yo voy a los Estados Unidos el 12 de octubre. Llegamos a las 4 de la tarde. ¡Hasta pronto!

Un abrazo,

Lupita

B. Give your letter to your teacher, who'll deliver it to your exchange partner. Read the letter you've received. If you need help understanding it, consult your teacher.

3er Paso

Un álbum

Add the letter you've received to your portfolio. Now you have a complete record of your exchange trip! Decorate the cover of your portfolio and give it a title, such as **Mi viaje a** ___. (*My trip to* ___).

PROJECT

2

Un calendario de fiestas hispanas

Using your knowledge of holidays, celebrations, and the cultures of Spanish-speaking countries, you will help make a Hispanic calendar. You'll work in groups and research holidays of a Spanish-speaking country. Your work will be combined with that of other groups to make a yearlong calendar. In the process, you will:

- Research the major legal holidays of one Spanish-speaking country and compare them to the U.S. legal holidays
- Determine what special occasions are observed in your chosen Spanish-speaking country, including when, why, and how they are celebrated
- Pay special attention to one holiday that is common to all Spanish-speaking countries
- Use the information you've gathered to put together a holiday calendar that you can use throughout the year
- Hold a Hispanic celebration

¡Diviértanse!

Conexiones

In the process of making a holiday calendar, you'll sharpen your skills in many areas.

- [x] Arte
- [ ] Ciencias
- [x] Estrategias de estudio
- [x] Geografía
- [x] Historia
- [ ] Matemáticas
- [ ] Medios de comunicación
- [x] Música
- [ ] Salud y nutrición
- [x] Tecnología

Look for the **Conexiones** boxes throughout this project.

Warm-up: Los días feriados en los Estados Unidos

Like every country, the U.S. has its legal holidays as well as other special celebrations. At these times, people in the U.S. commemorate occasions and traditions important to the entire country or to a particular region. Government offices and many businesses may close, and there may be public or private celebrations. Let's take a look at U.S. holidays, which can give you clues to what's celebrated in Spanish-speaking countries.

Herramientas útiles

- Calendar with U.S. holidays
- Folder to use for the calendar project

A. Your teacher will divide the class into groups. Each group will make a calendar for a Spanish-speaking country or region. In your group, use a calendar to make a list of U.S. holidays and give their dates.

B. You may get some of these days off, but do you know what each one celebrates? In your group, discuss in English or Spanish the reason for each holiday and decide which of the following categories each holiday belongs to. Some holidays may fit in more than one category.

- Political—related to government
- Military—related to a war, armed victory, or veterans
- Civil—related to an event or an idea that is neither political nor military
- Religious
- Historical
- Other categories

C. When you've finished, report your findings to the class and discuss your ideas together. Put your notes in your calendar folder.

¿Sabías que...?

The events that a country celebrates and the dates on which they're commemorated can change. The U.S. used to celebrate November 11 as Armistice Day, the day World War I (1914–1918) officially ended. After the Korean War (1953–1956), the name for the November 11 holiday was changed to Veterans' Day in honor of the veterans of all U.S. wars. At present, some states celebrate it and others don't. For some people in the U.S., remembering veterans is now part of the Memorial Day commemoration in May.

Los días feriados de los países hispanos

The Spanish-speaking countries wouldn't celebrate the Fourth of July, of course, but do they have legal holidays like Thanksgiving or Independence Day? You're going to find out!

Herramientas útiles

- Books and magazines about international holidays and Spanish-speaking people and cultures
- Guidebooks for Spanish-speaking countries
- Spanish-English dictionary
- Legal Holidays Worksheet 2.A.1
- Holiday Comparison Worksheet 2.A.2
- The World Wide Web
- Folder

1er Paso ¿Cuáles son los días feriados de los países hispanos?

A. Work with your group to find the major legal holidays of a Spanish-speaking country, using some of the resources listed in the **Herramientas útiles** box. List each day in Spanish with its English translation on Legal Holidays Worksheet 2.A.1 under **El día feriado**. As you do your research, record in English or in Spanish when and why each holiday is celebrated under **La fecha** and **La razón**. Be sure to keep a list of the resources for later use.

B. In your group, categorize the holidays, using the same groupings you did for U.S. holidays—**fiestas políticas, militares, civiles, religiosas, históricas.** Add any other categories that would apply. While your discussion may be in English, use the Spanish names for the holidays and the categories. Record your results under **El tipo de fiesta** on Legal Holidays Worksheet 2.A.1.

Conexiones

- ☑ Historia
- ☑ Tecnología

¡Investiguemos en el Web!

Official agencies of Spanish-speaking countries are a good source of information about holidays in those countries. At the Government, Reference, Travel, or Society and Culture sections of a Web guide, use the keywords to the right to help you in your search about your country.

Keywords

"embajada de ___" (España, Perú, etc.)
consulado
name of holiday
fiestas

C. Now present your findings to the class. While your discussion may be in English, use the Spanish names for the holidays. Be sure to put your worksheets in your calendar folder.

2° Paso

¡Comparen las fiestas!

A. In your group, compare in English how U.S. and Hispanic holidays are alike. Be sure to use the Spanish names for the holidays. Do Americans and Spanish speakers celebrate the same kinds of events? In English, record at least two similarities on Holiday Comparison Worksheet 2.A.2.

B. Now search for differences. What category do most Spanish-speaking holidays belong to? What about U.S. holidays? Do Americans and Spanish speakers celebrate comparable holidays but at different times of the year? Discuss and record at least two differences in English on Holiday Comparison Worksheet 2.A.2.

C. Present to the class, in English, the similarities and differences.

¿Sabías que...?

The start of the New Year is celebrated in many Hispanic countries with parades and festivals. However, different countries have different traditions. In Bolivia, for example, families celebrate with a special dinner of New Year's soup (**picana**). In Mexico, children are given New Year's clay figurines (**tanguyús**) to play with. In addition, someone in each Mexican town dresses up as an old man to symbolize the old year and parades through town, stopping to ask families for alms.

¡En búsqueda de tesoros!

Although you may not get the day off from school, you know that many special days are celebrated throughout the year in the U.S.—Valentine's Day and April Fool's Day, for example. There are also local holidays, such as Patriots' Day in Massachusetts, or Mardi Gras in New Orleans. Every country has such special days. Let's find out about these holidays in the Spanish-speaking world!

Herramientas útiles

- Books, guidebooks, and magazines on international holidays and Spanish-speaking people and cultures
- Spanish-English dictionary
- Special Days Worksheet 2.B
- The World Wide Web
- Folder

Busquemos las fiestas

In your group, research four occasions that are celebrated in your Hispanic country. Gather all the information you can on these events. If possible, find pictures of people and things connected with these celebrations. Use the materials listed in the **Herramientas útiles** box for help. For each occasion, fill in the chart on Special Days Worksheet 2.B.

Vocabulario útil

la fiesta es el [*date*]	*the holiday takes place on ___*
celebrar	*to celebrate*
conmemorar	*to commemorate*

Conexiones

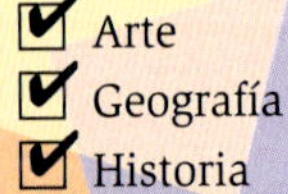

- ☑ Arte
- ☑ Geografía
- ☑ Historia
- ☑ Tecnología

¡Investiguemos en el Web!

How to find holidays will depend greatly on what you've chosen. Most Web guides will not have a category called Holidays, so look under sections labeled Culture, Social, or Society for references. You may also want to refer to the Web pages of consulates and embassies, if you've already found some interesting information there. If you search by holiday name, remember that it's best to use Spanish names. Otherwise you'll be referred to holidays all over the world. Don't forget to bookmark useful Web sites for future reference.

Keywords

fiestas
name of holiday
"wtg-online"

2° Paso La información

Now with your group, get together with another group in the class and share information. Take turns asking each other in Spanish, if possible, the following questions about the special celebrations in your countries.

> ¿Cómo se llama la fiesta? ¿Cuándo es la fiesta? ¿Por qué se celebra (*Why do you celebrate*) esta fiesta? ¿Cómo se celebra esta fiesta?

3er Paso Un cartel para la fiesta

Using the information and visuals you gathered in the **1er Paso**, create a poster in Spanish to advertise one of the special **fiestas** of your country. Include the date, name, and other relevant information and symbols. Make it attractive, and hang it on the wall of your classroom for everyone to see.

¿Sabías que...?

Some festivals in Hispanic countries are closely linked to nature and the seasons. If you were in Peru on the first Sunday of October, for example, you could participate in the **Fiesta de Agua** (*Water Festival*). During this celebration, a parade of horsemen rides into the town of San Pedro de Casta to symbolize the rapid arrival of the spring waters of the Carhuayumac River.

¡Una fiesta en común!

It just wouldn't be July 4 without . . . a picnic at the lake? fireworks? a parade? What would you say? Each U.S. holiday has its own festivities. How do Spanish-speaking people celebrate their holidays? Pick a holiday common to all groups and describe it.

Herramientas útiles

- Legal Holidays Worksheet 2.A.1
- Special Days Worksheet 2.B
- Books on international holidays
- Books on Spanish-speaking people and cultures
- Guidebooks for Spanish-speaking countries
- Spanish-English dictionary
- Folder

1er Paso

¿Cuáles son las fiestas en común?

You know the names, dates, and reasons for your group's holidays. Now you'll discuss what holidays the Spanish-speaking world has in common.

A. As a class, take turns asking each other in Spanish about the holidays celebrated in different Hispanic countries. Refer to Worksheets 2.A.1 and 2.B and follow the model below to find out what holidays are common to all the countries studied. Make a list together.

▶ ¿En Perú también se celebra la Semana Santa?
Sí, los peruanos celebran la Semana Santa. (*or*)

¿En Chile también se celebra el cinco de mayo?
No, los chilenos no celebran el cinco de mayo.

Conexiones

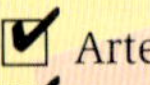

- ✔ Arte
- ✔ Historia
- ✔ Música
- ✔ Tecnología

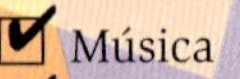

B. Select one common holiday that all groups will investigate. First discuss the possible choices. While your discussion may be in English, use the Spanish names for the holidays. Choose a secretary to list the suggested holidays in Spanish on the board. At the end of the discussion, take a vote. Voters for each holiday raise their hands and count off aloud in Spanish. The secretary records the votes and announces the class choice.

▶ *Secretary:* ¿Cuántos votan por [el Año Nuevo]?
Voters: Uno, dos, etc.
(Repeat for each common holiday.)
Secretary: La selección de la clase es [el Año Nuevo].

2° Paso ¿Cómo se celebra esta fiesta?

A. Now find out how your group's country celebrates the holiday your class has chosen. In your group, use some of the resources listed in the **Herramientas útiles** box to answer the following questions in English. You'll use the answers to prepare a brief report to the class.

1. How is the holiday celebrated? Are there private events with friends and relatives at home? Are there any public events, such as parades, fireworks, and dances?
2. Are any special foods served? Describe them.
3. Are there any special clothes or colors that people wear? What do the clothes or colors represent?
4. What special music or songs are played? Why? Provide examples, if you can.
5. What special places, symbols, or flowers do people associate with this day? Why? Provide examples, if you can.

Un poco más

Write a brief paragraph in Spanish explaining how your group's country celebrates the holiday your class has chosen. The holiday vocabulary in the Almanac will help you.

B. With your group, prepare a short oral and visual presentation in English or Spanish about how your country celebrates this holiday and present it to the class. If your presentation is in English and you have a paragraph in Spanish, include it here (see the **Un poco más** activity on page 33). Include any pictures, drawings, and music you found.

C. After each group has given its presentation, have a class discussion about the similarities and differences in the celebrations.

¿Sabías que...?

Many Hispanic holidays are religious in nature. For example, each country celebrates its patron saint's day and some towns have their own patron saint. Also, many countries hold a festival called **Carnaval** during the week before the 40 days of Lenten fasting begin. Many celebrations of **Carnaval** are theatrical, with participants playing the roles of death, the devil, and other masked figures parading in the streets.

El calendario especial

Now that you have the information you need, it's time to decide on the final details and assemble the Hispanic calendar.

Herramientas útiles

- The materials in your calendar folder
- Tagboard or large pieces of butcher paper
- Art supplies, such as markers, rulers, etc.
- A 12-month calendar covering the current school year

1er Paso

¿Qué símbolo representa cada fiesta?

Using your worksheets and the materials and notes in your folder, consider what you now know about each of the holidays in your Spanish-speaking country—its purpose, the way it's celebrated, and the common colors and symbols that people use for it. With your group, decide how you want to represent each holiday on the calendar. You might draw something or use pictures that you found in your research.

2° Paso

La división del trabajo

You need to make some basic decisions on the actual making of the calendar. How will you divide the tasks?

A. In class, decide how you want to divide the work. Do you want each group to work on one part of the year, creating the grids and representing the holidays for these months? Or do you want each group to have a particular task? Make these decisions with the help of your teacher.

Conexiones

- ✔ Arte
- ✔ Historia
- ✔ Tecnología

B. Next, decide with the class how you want to set up the calendar pages. Be creative. Use the questions below to guide you.

- Where will the name of the month be? across the top? down the side? along the bottom?
- Will all the grids be the same color? different colors?
- Where will the names of the countries or regions be listed? on the cover page?
- What art do you want to include to represent each month?

Remember: **lunes** is the first day of the week on many Spanish-language calendars!

¿Sabías que...?

In Spain and in most of the Catholic Spanish-speaking countries, people celebrate their name days. Each day of the year marks the feast of a particular saint or an important event in the Catholic Church. Saints' days are included on most Spanish-language calendars, and daily newspapers and weather reports will give the day's saint and sometimes briefly tell the story of the saint. To mark the occasion, children named after that saint receive cards, candies, or small gifts. To wish someone a happy name day, simply say: **¡Feliz santo!**

¡Investiguemos en el Web!

Can you find your name day? If you don't find your first name, try your middle name. Having a name day is like having two birthdays a year!

Keywords

"Catholic calendar"
"Catholic Online Saints"

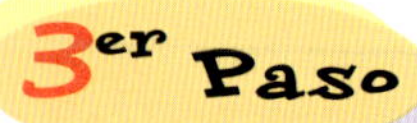

¡A decorar!

A. In your group, divide up the tasks of making the calendar pages, and get to work! Make sure you have all the information you need from the other groups.

B. Assemble your work as a class, making sure everything is in place. After your calendar is created, if you wish, add the name days and birthdays of your group members to your calendar.

C. Display the calendar and admire your handiwork. You've made a resource that you can use all year!

Vocabulario útil

La fiesta ocurre ___.	*The holiday takes place ___.*
preferir	*to prefer*
yo prefiero	*I prefer*
el acontecimiento	*event, happening*
favorito/a	*favorite*

4° Paso

¿Cuál es la fiesta favorita de la clase?

Think about all the different **fiestas** that your class has discussed and decide which one is your favorite. In your group, take turns asking and answering questions, following the model below. When you've finished, determine the favorite **fiesta** of your group. Then take a class vote to determine the favorite **fiesta** of the class. If that celebration appears on your group's calendar, mark it in a special way.

▶ —[*Classmate's name*], ¿cuál es tu fiesta favorita?
—Yo prefiero [la Semana Santa]. ¿Y tú?
—Mi fiesta favorita es [el cinco de mayo].

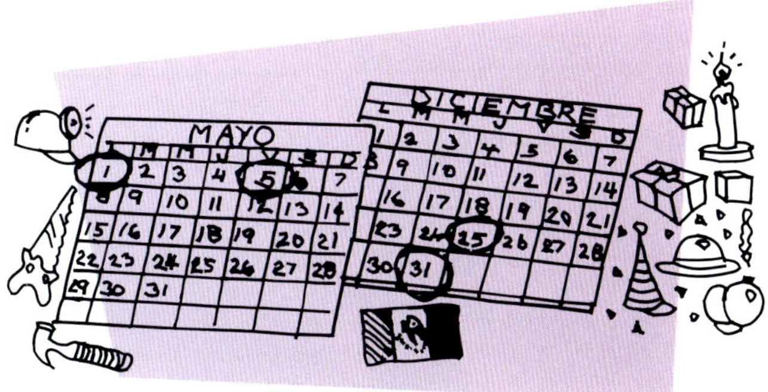

¡Celebremos!

After all the hard work you've done, you deserve to celebrate! Celebrate holidays the way Spanish-speaking people do. Think colors, sounds, and excitement everywhere.

1er Paso

¿Qué fiestas quieren celebrar?

As a class, decide how you want to celebrate and organize the party. Do you want to celebrate the class's favorite holiday (see Section D, **4° Paso**)? Do you want to celebrate the holiday coming up next on the calendar? Or do you want to celebrate a mix of the Hispanic holidays you studied? Discuss the options with your teacher.

2° Paso

La organización

You should now decide on the logistics of this celebration. What do you want to prepare for the celebration? Will you have guests coming to the party? How will you invite them? Where will you hold the party? Will there be food? How will you divide the work? Make sure you use your worksheets and the materials in your folders to help you present the holidays. You might want to choose a volunteer or two to prepare a checklist of what's needed and to supervise the preparation.

3er Paso

¡Diviértanse!

Has everything been taken care of? You are now ready to celebrate and answer questions about the Hispanic holidays. Enjoy!

¿Sabías que...?

From October 31 to November 2, Mexico celebrates **el Día de los Muertos** (*Day of the Dead*). During this celebration, families gather to remember those relatives who have passed away. People clean the family graves and sometimes spend the night at the cemetery to keep the spirits company. Families also build altars in their homes and fill them with the favorite foods and items of the departed, along with the customary **pan de los muertos** (*bread of the dead*) and colorfully decorated sugar skulls.

PROJECT

3

El dormitorio ideal

In this project, you and your group will design your dream bedroom! At the end of the project, your class will award prizes to the best rooms in several categories. As part of this project, you will:

- Choose categories and make prizes for the room competition
- Design the style, color, and décor of your room
- Select appropriate furniture
- Prepare an exhibit and make a presentation of your room
- Hold a design festival and award the prizes

¡Buena suerte!

Conexiones

As you design your room, you'll sharpen your skills in many areas.

- [x] Arte
- [ ] Ciencias
- [x] Estrategias de estudio
- [ ] Geografía
- [x] Historia
- [ ] Matemáticas
- [ ] Medios de comunicación
- [ ] Música
- [ ] Salud y nutrición
- [x] Tecnología

Look for the **Conexiones** boxes throughout this project.

Warm-up: Pensemos en los dormitorios

A. Work with the same group of three or four of your classmates for this entire project. Each group member should bring in at least two photos or drawings of student rooms or bedrooms from magazines, catalogs, books, and so on. In Spanish, describe each of your rooms to your group. Then as a group, write a list of features that you like and dislike in the rooms.

▶ ***Nos gusta(n)...***	***No nos gusta(n)...***
la lámpara alta	**el color negro**
los sillones cómodos	**las camas pequeñas**

B. Now, interview some other members of your class in Spanish to find out which features appeal to them and which don't.

▶ **[Matt], ¿te gustan las lámparas altas?**
Sí, me gustan.
No, no me gustan.

C. In your group, share the information that you've gathered and add it to your list of likes and dislikes.

▶ **A Matt le gustan las lámparas altas.**
A Cristina...

D. Review your list of likes and dislikes. Are there any features that were liked or disliked by more than one student? Circle them on your list and keep the list for reference when designing your room.

¿Sabías que...?

In Spain and in many cities in Spanish-speaking countries, it's common for most families to live in apartments, and rooms tend to be smaller than those in American homes. Few teenagers have their own phone or TV in their bedroom, and most share a room with a sibling. The family congregates in one central room, generally **la sala** or **la cocina** for conversation, recreation, and relaxation. In fact, most families only have one TV and one phone for the family to share.

Los premios

At the design festival, prizes will be given for the best rooms in several categories. Create these categories now so that you'll have a goal in mind as you complete the design of your ideal room.

Herramientas útiles

- Ballot Worksheet 3.A
- Cardboard or sturdy paper
- Scissors, tape, glue
- Computer and word-processing program
- Folder for storing worksheets and creative ideas

1er Paso

Muchas ideas

A. Working in your small group, brainstorm in Spanish three possible prize categories to be used in your room competition. Be creative!

▶ El dormitorio más divertido
El dormitorio con más colores
El dormitorio más original
El dormitorio más moderno

B. For each category, write a short description in English of the criteria that will be used when choosing a winner in that category.

▶ **El dormitorio con más colores:** This room must contain at least three prominent colors in its decor and be bright and cheerful.

Conexiones

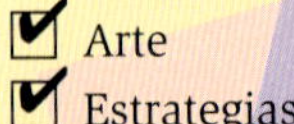

- ☑ Arte
- ☑ Estrategias de estudio

El voto

Share your ideas for categories with your class. Vote as a class to choose four to eight categories to be used in your competition. Copy the categories the class chooses onto Ballot Worksheet 3.A. You'll use this ballot when it's time to vote.

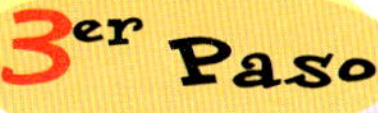

¡Creemos los premios!

A. Divide the chosen categories with their descriptions among the groups in your class. Each group will make prizes to award to the winner of its categories. You may choose to make ribbons, medals, certificates, or trophies. Use the resources in the **Herramientas útiles** box to help you.

B. Put the prizes, the descriptions of the categories, and Ballot Worksheet 3.A away until the day of the competition. File the categories and descriptions in your folder.

¿Sabías que...?

If you were one of the millions of Spanish speakers who inhabit the **selvas** (*jungles*) of Latin America, you probably wouldn't have your own room at all! In fact, most people who live in the jungle regions build their own one- or two-room houses—one room is a central gathering and cooking area, and the other is a group sleeping area.

Las decisiones básicas

Now it's time to begin designing your ideal bedroom. You'll need to make some general decisions first. This is your chance to be creative!

Herramientas útiles

- Cardboard or sturdy paper
- Style Worksheet 3.B
- Magazines showing decorating ideas
- Art books or pictures of artwork from Spanish-speaking countries
- Encyclopedias

El estilo

Working with your group, you'll need to decide on the décor of your room. Do you want it to be traditional? futuristic? Should it have a theme, such as a particular movie, time period, or sport?

A. When you've chosen a style, write a description of it in English on Style Worksheet 3.B.

B. Now consider how you will achieve this look. Will it be with wall-paper? a mural? furniture? On Style Worksheet 3.B, write a general description of ways that your style can be established in your room. When you're finished, put it in your folder. You'll make final decisions later. Make sure you choose specific competition categories.

Conexiones

Arte
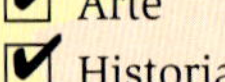
Historia

Un poco más

Choose an influence from a Spanish-speaking country to include in your room's décor, such as a Mayan or Aztec design, or a design showing the influence of the Moors in Spain. Record your ideas on Style Worksheet 3.B with the description of your room. Use the resources in the **Herramientas útiles** box to help you.

2.º Paso Los colores

Now decide which colors will work best with this style. Maybe metallic colors would look great in your space-age room. Or perhaps you'd like bright blues to complement a nautical theme. Refer to the Almanac for a list of colors. Choose colors for the walls (**las paredes**), floor (**el piso**) or floor covering, and even ceiling (**el techo**). Record your choices in Spanish on Style Worksheet 3.B.

3.er Paso Los detalles de la decoración

Finally, decide what kinds of floor, window, and wall coverings you'll use in your room. Use the words for furniture and furnishings in the Almanac to help you. Record your choices in Spanish on Style Worksheet 3.B, and place it in your folder.

Los muebles

Your ideal room wouldn't be complete without plenty of interesting furniture. Keeping in mind the style of your room, design your furnishings!

Herramientas útiles

- Decorating magazines, mail-order catalogs
- Catalogs from furniture and department stores
- Original drawings/descriptions of creative décor
- The World Wide Web

1er Paso

¿Qué y cuántos?

In your group, make general decisions about the furniture you'll want to have in your room. Make a list in Spanish of the items and the quantities. Refer to the list of furniture and furnishings in the Almanac as needed.

▶ 1 cama
2 sillones
1 mesa

2° Paso

Las posibilidades

As homework or in class, look through decorating magazines, store and mail-order catalogs, and the Web to find some of the pieces of furniture on your list. Draw or cut out several options for each item on your list, so that your group has possibilities to choose from.

Conexiones

☑ Arte
☑ Tecnología

¡Investiguemos en el Web!

Many furniture and furnishings stores and companies advertise on the Web. Their ads often include pictures of their products. To locate such Web sites, try using a search engine that has versions for Spanish-speaking countries. For example, if you are using Yahoo!, click on Spain at the bottom of the page and then follow the path: **de compras, Hogar y jardín, Decoración del hogar, Muebles.** Scan the brief descriptions of the selected Web sites and investigate ones that look promising.

3er Paso

¡Los muebles perfectos!

Finally, in your group, choose the furniture items that you feel best complement your room's style. Refer to your list of furniture to make sure that you choose enough items. Save your pictures and drawings of furniture to prepare your room for the competition.

¿Sabías que...?

In Mexico, Central America, and many Caribbean nations, bright colors are the latest style in decorating. Walls or doors may be the deep blue of the sea, often complemented by a bright, sunny yellow. In central Mexico, these are the most common colors present on the regional tiles, or **talavera,** used in decorating kitchens and bathrooms. Ceramics, dinnerware, picture frames, and tabletops are often made of **talavera** too, making it an excellent accessory in decorating.

La presentación del dormitorio

Now decide how you're going to present your room visually during the design festival. Do you want to make a drawing of your room design and label the features in Spanish? Or draw it using a computer drawing program? Do you think a poster with cut-out pictures will work best? Would you like to make a three-dimensional model of the room, such as a diorama? The possibilities are numerous!

Herramientas útiles

- Cardboard boxes
- Scissors, tape, glue, markers, paints
- Computer with drawing software
- Pictures or drawings of furniture

1er Paso

¿Cómo vamos a presentar el dormitorio?

Discover your group's talents and decide how to present your room to your class during the competition. If you're artistic, consider using those talents to make a painting, drawing, or model of your room. If you enjoy working with computers, try out a drawing or paint program. Find a style of presentation that uses everyone's talents.

2° Paso

La creación

Once your group has decided on how to present your room, it's time to get to work! Remember to include in some way all of the decisions that you made earlier on colors, style, and furnishings. Put it all together into a finished visual product, ready for the design festival!

Conexiones

- ✔ Arte
- ✔ Estrategias de estudio
- ✔ Tecnología

¡Preparemos la presentación!

Finally, create short descriptive labels in Spanish for your display. Label the furniture and furnishings, give your room a title, and highlight four or five features that make your room special. Prepare what each group member will say in Spanish for your presentation.

Un poco más

Write a composition or poem in Spanish describing the unique features of your ideal room. You may mount it, and then illustrate it.

¡Todos somos ganadores!

The day of the design festival has arrived! Your room and those of your competitors will be on display. Today you will be both competitor and judge of the design festival!

Herramientas útiles

- Prizes and descriptions of categories
- Ballot Worksheet 3.A
- Your room presentation

1er Paso

Un repaso de las categorías

Before starting the competition, review the categories that you recorded on Ballot Worksheet 3.A by which the rooms will be judged. Each group will briefly read to the class the names and descriptions of its competition categories.

2° Paso

Las presentaciones

Now it's time for the competition to begin! Display your room presentation and have each member of your group describe a few important features of your room to the class. After each group has given its presentation, take turns answering questions about your display and visiting the other displays. Be prepared to ask questions and make comments in Spanish while you visit. Take notes on Ballot Worksheet 3.A as you view each presentation.

Conexiones

Arte

El voto final

It's time to vote for the winners of each category. Each class member votes on each category and gives the completed Ballot Worksheet 3.A to your teacher, who will tally the results.

Los premios oficiales

After the vote, the teacher awards a prize to the winning presentation for each category. Celebrate your victories! Display your group's presentation in the classroom.

Vocabulario útil

¡Felicitaciones!/¡Felicidades!/ ¡Enhorabuena!	*Congratulations!*
el ganador/la ganadora	*the winner*
Los ganadores del premio para el [dormitorio más original] son ___.	*The winners of the [most creative room] prize are ___.*

PROJECT

4

¡Juguemos un juego de mesa!

Using your knowledge of games and Hispanic cultures, you and your group will make a board game. In the process, you will:

- Make up questions and answers in Spanish about daily life
- Research one or more Spanish-speaking countries and make up questions and answers in English
- Write directions for the game
- Design and make a game board
- Test the game board and rules
- Share your game with your classmates

¡Te toca a ti!

Conexiones

In the process of making a game, and depending on what topics you choose for your game, you'll sharpen your skills in many areas, including these:

✔ Arte	☐ Matemáticas
☐ Ciencias	☐ Medios de comunicación
✔ Estrategias de estudio	☐ Música
✔ Geografía	☐ Salud y nutrición
☐ Historia	✔ Tecnología

Look for the **Conexiones** boxes throughout this project.

Warm-up: Hablemos de sus juegos favoritos

You probably have a few favorite games. Why are they your favorites? Some people like short and simple games, while others prefer games that involve more complex strategy. Still others like the excitement of games in which luck is an important ingredient. Perhaps you prefer the physical dexterity and quick thinking that are part of video games. Find out what games you and your fellow group members like to play and why.

A. Form a small group of four to six students. Name your favorite games in English and explain why you like them. Read the **¿Sabías que...?** box to find out the Spanish names of some popular games.

B. In your group, brainstorm any Spanish words and expressions you know that have to do with games.

C. In your group, talk in Spanish about the types of games you prefer to play: for example, board, card, or computer games. The **Vocabulario útil** box and the illustrations that follow will help you.

¿Sabías que...?

Board games are popular in Hispanic countries. Many are probably familiar to you—**las damas** (*checkers*), **el ajedrez** (*chess*), **el dominó**, and **el Monopolio.** Some Hispanic board games have different names, but they often follow rules similar to those that Americans know.

Vocabulario útil

jugar	*to play (a game or sport)*
¿Qué tipo de juegos te gusta jugar?	*What kinds of games do you like to play?*
Me gusta jugar ___.	*I like to play ___.*
Yo prefiero jugar ___.	*I prefer to play ___.*

jugar al ajedrez

jugar a las damas

los juegos de mesa

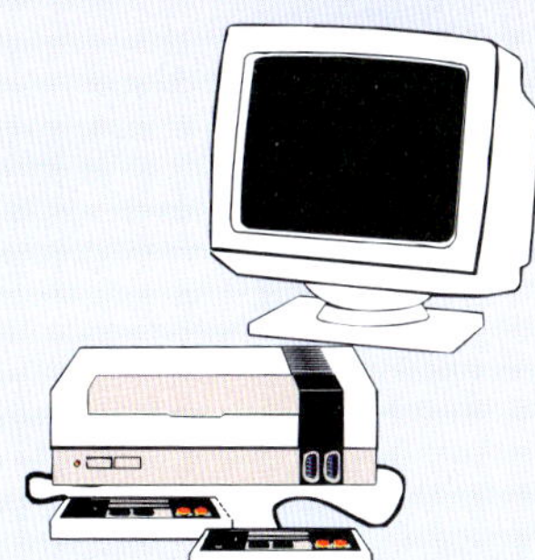

jugar a los juegos electrónicos

hacer crucigramas

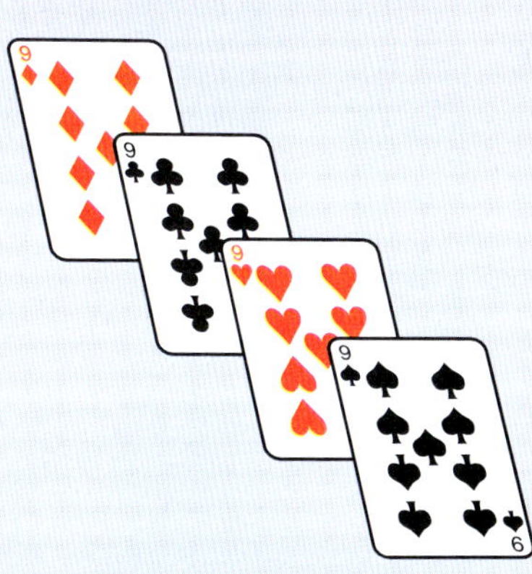

jugar a las cartas

Las preguntas del juego

You've been asking and answering questions in Spanish ever since you started studying the language. You may not realize it, but you can make a board game using those questions and answers—and that's what you're going to do!

Herramientas útiles

- 3" x 5" cards in one color
- Question Worksheet 4.A
- Folder or binder to compile Worksheets and other materials

1er Paso

¿Cuánto saben?

A. What kinds of questions can you ask in your game? Start with everything you've learned to say in Spanish so far. Build on simple questions by adding a phrase, such as **a tu derecha** (*on your right*) or **a tu izquierda** (*on your left*) or ask about someone's family members.

▶ ¿Cómo te llamas?
¿Cómo se llama esa chica?
¿Cómo se llama la chica a tu derecha?
¿Cómo se llama tu hermana?

How many variations of these questions can you come up with? Brainstorm and record a list with your group.

B. In your group, read through the topics under **Los temas** on Question Worksheet 4.A. Check off topics that you know how to ask questions about. If you can think of any other topics, write them under **Otros temas.**

Conexiones

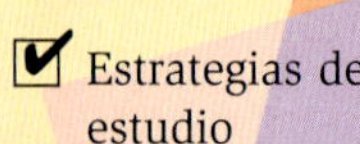

☑ Estrategias de estudio

Las preguntas y las respuestas

Form pairs within your group, and divide the topics among the pairs. Work with your partner to write 5–10 questions and answers in Spanish for each of your topics. Record them on Question Worksheet 4.A. Use the back of the worksheet if necessary. Some questions will have only one possible answer (e.g., **¿De qué color es la nieve?**), while others will have answers that vary (**¿Dónde vives?**).

▶ *Question:* ¿Dónde vives?
Possible response: Vivo en la calle San Miguel, número 15.

Question: ¿Cuántos años tiene tu hermano?
Possible response: Él tiene ___ años.

Question: ¿Cuántos hermanos tienes?
Possible responses: Tengo ___ hermano(s) y ___ hermana(s).
No tengo hermanos.

¿Sabías que...?

Due to the popularity of card games in Spanish-speaking countries, there are several expressions that relate to cards:

- **jugar la última carta** *to play one's last card*
- **poner las cartas sobre la mesa** *to put one's cards on the table*
- **tomar cartas** *to intervene, to come in between*

Seleccionen las preguntas y las respuestas

A. Trade questions with another pair in your group and check each other's Spanish. If you disagree or are unsure about what's correct, see if you can come to an agreement as a group before consulting with your teacher. Work together to make the best possible questions and answers.

B. Get back together with your group and look at the questions and answers that each pair has written. If possible, come up with additional questions and answers. Delete any duplicate questions.

C. Finally, write all the questions and answers on 3" x 5" cards of the same color. Use a separate card for each question and answer. Write the question on one side and its answer on the other.

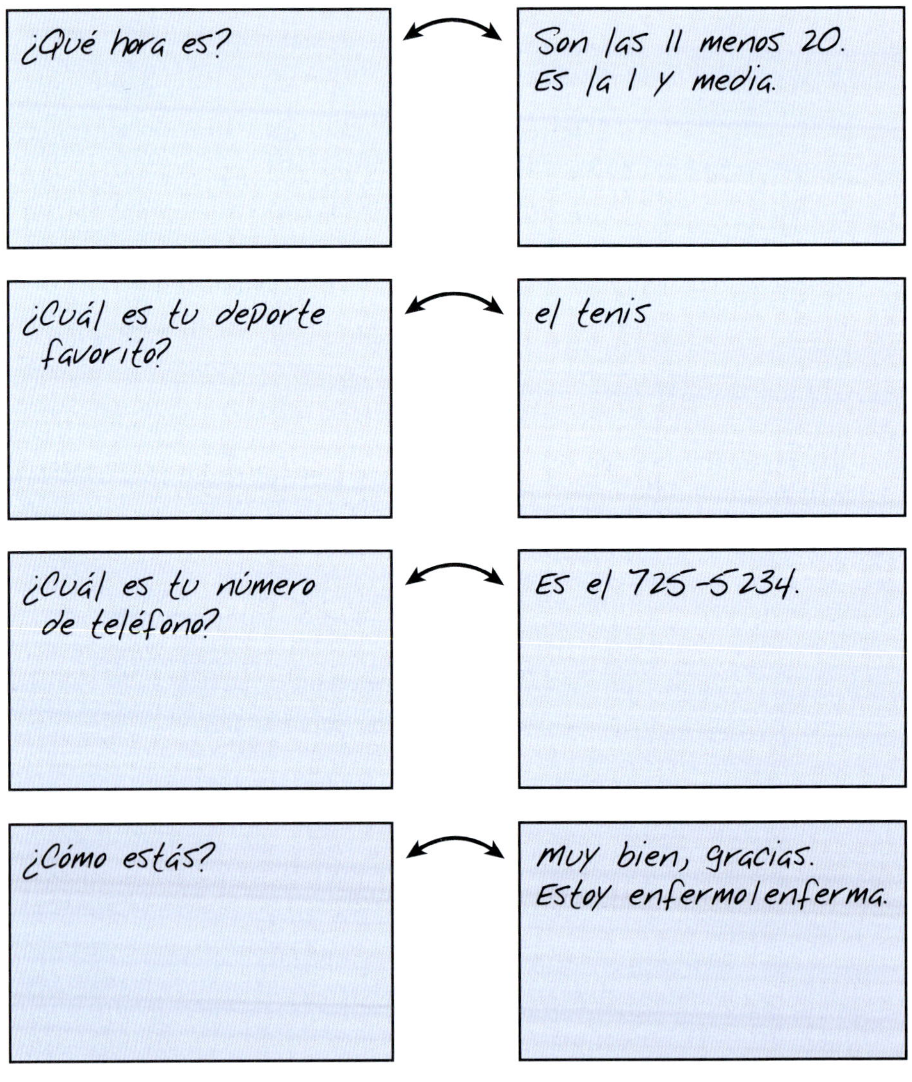

Las preguntas culturales

Keep your game interesting and exciting by preparing questions in English about one or more Spanish-speaking countries.

Herramientas útiles

- World map and maps of Spanish-speaking countries
- Books and magazines about the culture of Spanish-speaking countries
- Encyclopedias and almanacs
- Travel magazines and brochures about Spanish-speaking countries
- 3" x 5" cards in a color different from those in Section A
- Folder
- The World Wide Web

1er Paso

¿Qué tipo de preguntas culturales?

A. In your group, discuss what subjects relating to the Spanish-speaking world seem interesting to you. You may know very little about some of the Spanish-speaking countries, so you might want to do a little research before choosing your topics. Below and on the next page are a few sample topics:

- The geography, history, and/or famous people of a Spanish-speaking country
- Daily life in a Spanish-speaking country: family, food, school, and pastimes

Conexiones

- ✔ Estrategias de estudio
- ✔ Geografía
- ✔ Tecnología

- Popular Spanish-speaking musicians and actors; film or music festivals
- Sporting events such as World Cup soccer
- Vacationing in the Caribbean
- Capital cities of Spanish-speaking countries

B. As a class, decide if all the groups will make games based on the same topics, different topics, or a mixture of the two. Then, in groups or as a class, select topics. Decide whether one topic or many would work best with your game and whether you want to have a special challenge section or some bonus questions. Remember that the cultural questions and answers you prepare on the Spanish-speaking countries will be in English.

¡Busquen los hechos interesantes!

Form pairs within your small group and divide the research according to your group's preferences. Using the sources listed in the **Herramientas útiles** box on page 61, make up a list of 5–10 possible questions for each topic. Include pictures of famous places and things, if you wish. Be sure to keep notes about the sources you use. You may have to go back later to find more information.

Make your game more challenging by creating some additional questions in Spanish. Base your questions on expressions you already know.

▶ *You already know*	*Variation*
¿Cuál es ___?	¿Cuál es la capital de Ecuador?
¿Cuándo es ___?	¿Cuándo es el día de la independencia de Bolivia?
¿Quién es/Cómo se ___?	¿Quién es/Cómo se llama el presidente de México?
¿De qué color ___?	¿De qué color es la bandera de España?

Seleccionen las preguntas

A. When you and your partner have finished your list, trade questions and answers with another pair. Check each other's lists to make the best possible questions and most accurate answers. In your small group, read all the questions and answers, and delete any duplicates.

B. Write your cultural questions and answers in English on 3" x 5" cards. Be sure to use cards of a different color from those used in Section A. Write the question on one side of the card and the answer on the other. If you wrote any cultural questions in Spanish (for the **Un poco más** activity), file that list in your folder for the moment.

¿Sabías que...?

In many countries, Spanish speakers still love to gather in town to play card games and board games. In Mexico, the card game canasta is very popular, especially among older ladies. In Cuba, dominoes is second only to baseball in popularity!

Las reglas del juego

Like all games, your board game needs a set of rules. Look at other games to help you decide what the objective, the rules, and the organization of your own game will be.

Herramientas útiles

- World map and maps of Spanish-speaking countries
- Several board games and their directions, particularly games that use information or questions on cards
- Rules Worksheet 4.C (2 per group)
- 3" x 5" cards in a third color
- Guidebooks for the Spanish-speaking countries
- Folder

1er Paso

Examinen las reglas de un juego de mesa

In your group, choose a particular game and spread out the board and playing pieces. Next, analyze the directions of that game by answering the questions on Rules Worksheet 4.C. Then discuss as a class what the rules of a game include and the order in which they should be explained.

2º Paso

Algunas decisiones preliminares

What will be the goal of your game? How will you use your question cards? Make some decisions about the basic procedures and moves of your game. As a group, answer the questions under Basic Decisions on a second copy of Rules Worksheet 4.C, but this time apply them to your game.

Conexiones

☑ Estrategias de estudio

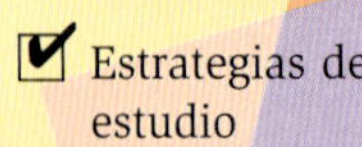

Un poco más

Decide what to do with the cultural questions in Spanish that you created in the **Un poco más** activity in Section B. Will they become a separate set of questions or will you combine them with one of the other sets? Write each one on a 3" x 5" card, the question on one side and the answer on the other. If you are using them in a different way from the other sets of cards, use a third color of cards; otherwise write them on cards of the same color as the set to which they belong.

3er Paso Las reglas del juego

Work with your group to develop some rules for your game. Study the questions under Rules of the Game on Rules Worksheet 4.C to help you make decisions. Write answers applicable to your game on your second copy of the worksheet. You'll probably want to revise some of your rules later as you perfect your game.

Lean las direcciones

In your group, check your directions against what you wrote on Worksheet 4.C. For example, should you add anything to what the players need to play the game? Have you changed your ideas about how to use the question cards? Record any additions or changes. Then write a first draft of your rules. Remember to be very careful about details.

¿Sabías que...?

Board games are not the only popular games in Spanish-speaking countries. **Los videojuegos** (*video/computer games*) have also become increasingly popular. Part of this popularity can be attributed to more and more homes having computers. As in the U.S., many of the computer games are on CD-ROMs.

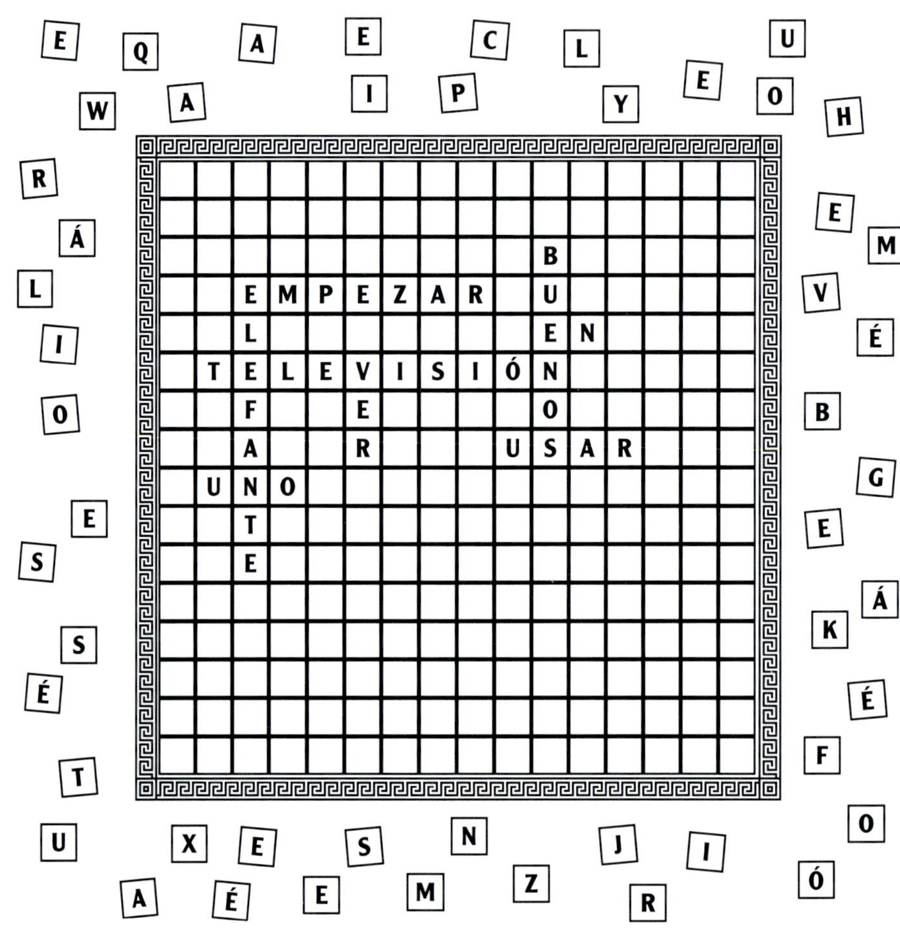

El tablero

The game is starting to come together. Now that you have an idea of what the rules are going to be, you need to design the game board. It has to work with the rules you've written, or else you'll have to change some of the rules.

Herramientas útiles

- Several board games and their directions, particularly ones that use information or questions on cards as part of playing the game
- Analyzing a Game Board Worksheet 4.D.1
- First draft of rules for your game
- Our Game Board Worksheet 4.D.2
- Materials for creating the game board: colored markers, cardboard, file folders, poster board, tape
- Folder

Examinen un juego de mesa

In Section C, you chose a board game and analyzed its directions. Now analyze the design of the same game's board. Spread out the board and playing pieces. Examine how the game board and the rules work together and identify features that had to be included on the game board because of its rules. For help, answer the questions under Features on Analyzing a Game Board Worksheet 4.D.1. Then complete the rest of the worksheet.

2° Paso

Los elementos necesarios

Since you've practiced looking for the features a game board might need, you're better prepared to design your own board. Keep Analyzing a Game Board Worksheet 4.D.1 nearby for reference. With your group, read through the basic game rules again. Look for features that *must* be included on the game board, such as directions that tell players:

- The starting place and the goal
- To go back or forward a number of spaces
- To take an extra turn or to skip a turn
- To choose a particular kind of card
- To go to a particular place on the board
- Where to put particular materials on the board

Record your decisions under Features on Our Game Board Worksheet 4.D.2.

3er Paso

El nombre del juego

The name of a game often relates to its goal or to how it's played. In your group, brainstorm some ideas for a Spanish name (you may have to do this in English). Record the suggestions, then take a vote. Record the group's choice under The Name of the Game on Worksheet 4.D.2.

La decoración del tablero

A. Keeping in mind the features you *must* have on the game board, discuss with your group how you want the board to look. There are some examples of game boards on the opposite page. Maybe you can adapt one of them to fit your game or come up with something unique. Jot down your decisions under Design on Our Game Board Worksheet 4.D.2 and draw a sketch if you'd like. Decide where to position the name of the game on the board and record that information too.

B. Now brainstorm ideas about how to illustrate some of the topics covered in your board game. What other kinds of decorations do you want to include? Write your decisions under Decorations on Our Game Board Worksheet 4.D.2. As you decide how to illustrate the game board, think about where you might find pictures that you can photocopy, cut and paste, or draw.

Un bosquejo

Make a first sketch of the game board in the same size as the final board. Be sure to draw in all the shapes and use the actual colors. If there are labels or directions on the board, write some samples to see if there is enough space. Check the sports and games vocabulary in the Almanac for the Spanish expressions you need. As a group, decide who will actually do the sketch. Will one person or a pair of students take full responsibility, or will each group member prepare a different part? Then make the sketch.

Los últimos toques

Before you can finalize your rules and make your game board, you need to do a test run. How well will your rules and game board work together?

Herramientas útiles

- Materials for playing pieces: stones, beans, marbles, dice, wooden/plastic pieces in various shapes
- Art materials, such as colored markers and glue
- Materials for the game board itself: cardboard, file folders, poster board, tape
- Container for the game: box or large envelope with a clasp
- Folder

Un ensayo

Use your rough draft of the rules and a sketch of the game board to try out the game. Choose one group member to record any needed changes to the rules or the board while the others play the game in order to find out what works and what doesn't.

Perfeccionen el juego

In your group, make any necessary changes to the directions or the game board, then play the game again. This time players speak Spanish during the game. Many of the needed expressions are in the sports and games section of the Almanac. Your group may choose to have non-playing members help players use Spanish expressions, so that they

Conexiones

- ☑ Arte
- ☑ Estrategias de estudio

can play the game at a reasonable speed. Once again, have one group member record any problems, including additional Spanish expressions that players will need to play the game. You don't need to think of everything that players might say, just expressions that they will have to use often.

Una prueba

If students who know nothing about your game can play it by reading the rules, it really works! Ask another group to play your game while a couple of students from your group look on. Your group members can help the other students play your game and record any problems. If there are difficulties, make the needed revisions.

La caja

Since you're making this game for yourselves and others to enjoy, it would be a good idea to keep it in some kind of sturdy container. You might consider using one file folder for the game board, another for the rules, and plastic bags, a large mailing envelope with a clasp, or a box as a container for the game pieces.

¡Ya estamos listos!

You're finally ready to put the game together. In your group, divide up the final tasks. Write a final description of the rules (make sure these are easy to read). Do you need additional Spanish expressions for playing the game? If so, make a list. Draw the final game board on the cardboard or poster board provided. Gather any materials necessary for playing the game. Prepare the containers that will hold the game and put in everything you've made and collected for the game. You've worked hard and your game is now ready to share with other groups. Take your show on the road!

PROJECT

5

¡Organicemos los Juegos Olímpicos!

Using your knowledge of sports and Spanish-speaking countries, you and your classmates will organize your own mini-Olympics for Spanish-speaking countries. In the process, you will:

- Decide which games to hold (Summer or Winter Olympics)
- Create and compete in 2–6 competitive events
- Prepare the opening ceremonies
- Design costumes or symbol cards and medals, and hold an awards ceremony
- Locate anthems and folk songs of the participating countries
- Hold your Olympic Games

You and your classmates will be grouped in committees and will work on many tasks at the same time to prepare for your mini-Olympics.

¡A jugar!

Conexiones

In the process of preparing and holding your Olympic Games, you will sharpen your skills in many areas.

- [x] Arte
- [ ] Ciencias
- [x] Estrategias de estudio
- [x] Geografía
- [x] Historia
- [x] Matemáticas
- [ ] Medios de comunicación
- [x] Música
- [ ] Salud y nutrición
- [x] Tecnología

Look for the **Conexiones** boxes throughout this project.

Warm-up: ¿Qué sabes de los Juegos Olímpicos?

Herramientas útiles

- Olympic Sports Worksheet 5.W
- Spanish-English dictionary
- Books about the Olympic Games
- Portfolio (a three-ring binder with pockets, file jacket, file folder) for each student
- The World Wide Web

A. Working with a small group, brainstorm in Spanish a list of sports and write them under Part 1 on Olympic Sports Worksheet 5.W. Write each sport under the season in which it is played. Some sports may be played in more than one season.

B. In your group, decide which of the sports on your list are Olympic sports. Put a question mark next to any sport that you are uncertain about. Then decide if each sport is part of the Summer Games (**los Juegos de verano**) or the Winter Games (**los Juegos de invierno**) and list it under the appropriate heading in Part 2 of the same worksheet.

¿Sabías que...?

A very popular sport in Spain, Mexico, and in parts of South America is jai-alai. It is a court game of Basque origin in which players toss a very hard ball back and forth using a basket strapped to their hands. Sometimes the games are so long and the players play so hard that they lose weight during the game! Jai-alai is promoted as the fastest ball game in the world, with a ball speed of 188 mph recorded at a game in 1979. In addition, a jai-alai court is so large that 102 Volkswagens could be parked on it!

C. Now work with your group to expand your list of Olympic sports. Use some of the resources listed in the **Herramientas útiles** box to find out what sports are played at either the Summer or the Winter Games. (Your teacher will tell your group which games it should investigate.) List at least five sports in Spanish on your Olympic Sports Worksheet 5.W.

D. Finally, exchange information with the rest of the class and add the new information to Olympic Sports Worksheet 5.W. Put your worksheet in your portfolio.

¡Investiguemos en el Web!

You can search the World Wide Web for information about where the Olympics have been held and what the geography and climate of the areas are like. This search is best conducted using a Web guide or catalog that will offer the option of performing the search in Spanish. Guides written specifically for Spanish speakers also exist. On the Web guide, look for Weather, Travel, and City sections or guides. Many city guides contain geographical and weather-related information. Remember to bookmark or note the Web address of any sites you may want to refer to later.

¿Verano o invierno?

Cities and regions around the world compete for the privilege of hosting the Olympic Games. In choosing a location for the games, one of the most basic considerations of the International Olympic Committee is the geography of a region. For example, are the mountains suitable for Winter Olympic skiing events and do they receive sufficient snowfall? Are there appropriate bodies of water for Summer Olympic rowing and yachting events? You'll begin to organize your games by deciding which games you'll hold—**los Juegos de verano** or **los Juegos de invierno.**

Herramientas útiles

- World atlas
- Guidebooks for Spanish-speaking countries
- Books about the Olympic Games
- Which Games? Worksheet 5.A.1
- Committees Worksheet 5.A.2
- Portfolio

1er Paso

El clima y la topografía

Working with your group, brainstorm in Spanish the kinds of climate and geography you think are needed to hold the Olympic Games. Continue with the same games—**los Juegos de verano** or **los Juegos de invierno**—that your group discussed in the Warm-up. Each of you should record the group's answers in Part 1 on Which Games? Worksheet 5.A.1. Share your information with the class.

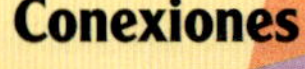

Conexiones

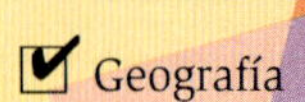

☑ Geografía

Los Juegos pasados

A. With your group, find out which Spanish-speaking cities have hosted the Olympics in the past using materials in the **Herramientas útiles** box. Record the places in Part 2 of Worksheet 5.A.1 under **Dónde**. List the games held in each location (**los Juegos de verano** or **los Juegos de invierno**) and the year.

B. As a group, choose one of the locations you listed. Find it on a map and then investigate and record its climate and geography. In Part 3 on the same worksheet, make a list in Spanish of the features that you think made it a good location for the Olympics.

Vocabulario útil

montañoso/montañosa	*mountainous*
plano/plana	*flat*

C. Report your group's findings to the class. Ask your teacher to list the results of these reports on the board: two combined lists of features—one for the Summer Games and one for the Winter Games.

¿Los Juegos de verano o los Juegos de invierno?

A. In your group, start your search for a Spanish-speaking city or town (and surrounding area) in which to hold *your* Olympic Games and research the climate and geography of your site. Would it be more suitable for the Winter or Summer Games? Perhaps your site is good for both games, only one, or neither **(ni el uno ni el otro)**. Investigate each location, and record your answers in Part 4. If you discover your first choice is not suitable for any Olympics, select other sites until you locate a good one. Report your findings to the class.

B. As a class, vote on which Olympic Games you will organize and hold and where they will occur. Remember your Olympics will take place during the current season and at your location, so make reasonable choices. Record the class's decision under **Nuestra selección** on the same worksheet.

¿Qué quieres hacer?

This is your chance to decide which part of organizing the Olympic Games you'd like to work on. Read through Committees Worksheet 5.A.2 for an overview of the project. Decide which committees you'd like to be part of and get together with the other interested students. You can be an athlete as well as work on one of the other committees, but you'll have to organize whatever else you do around the times when you're taking part in a game. Keep your worksheet(s) in your portfolio as you work through your part(s) of the games.

Los eventos

As part of Committee B, it's up to you to decide what sporting events will be included in your games. You're going to design your own unique set of competitive events in which you and your classmates can participate.

Herramientas útiles

- Competitive Events Worksheets 5.B.1 and 5.B.2
- Athlete Information Worksheet 5.E.1 (filled in)
- Symbol Information Worksheet 5.F (filled in)
- Poster board, strips of paper or cloth, glue or stapler, felt-tip marker
- Computer with word-processing software
- Portfolio

Inventen los eventos

A. Committee B needs to design the five or six games or contests that are appropriate for the Winter or Summer Games that your class is organizing. At least *one* of the contests must involve a result whose distance or height needs to be measured. At least *two* should require physical activity and *two* should not. Divide any additional games however you want.

Choose a partner and think about the kinds of games you like. You may use parts of different sports or board games that you know or invent totally new games. Perhaps you want a mixture of individual and team games, some with a lot of physical action and others with basically none. Some ideas follow:

- Can you set up your own **Tour de France**, **Vuelta de Colombia**, or other kind of bike race in the school parking lot or around the school track? How about a tricycle race?

Conexiones

- ☑ Estrategias de estudio
- ☑ Matemáticas
- ☑ Tecnología

- Did you enjoy those three-legged races from grade school?
- How about a salsa/merengue dance contest?
- Why not have an ice sculpture contest to create a culturally authentic replica of a monument such as **Chichén Itzá** or **Machu Picchu**?

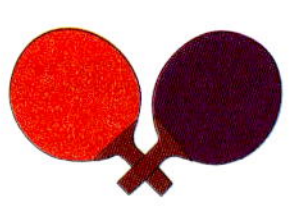

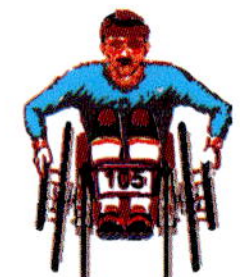

Remember to keep in mind the information under **Nuestra selección** on Which Games? Worksheet 5.A.1 as you develop your games. The events will occur in the place and at the season described there. Use the prompts under Description of a Game on Competitive Events Worksheet 5.B.1 to guide your designs. With your partner, record your answers in English on a separate sheet of paper for each game you make.

B. Now form a whole group again and discuss the games each pair has invented. As you choose the games, keep in mind the requirements laid out in Activity A.

After you choose the games, calculate the total number of winners so that Committee D knows how many medals to make. Remember that each contest will have first-, second-, and third-place winners and each player on a winning team will receive a medal. Then divide up the work of gathering the necessary materials for playing the games and keeping score. (See **2º Paso** for creating a measuring tape.)

C. Now members of Committee B may get together with the athletes (Committee E) and briefly describe the games. Be sure to state how many students are needed for each team in the team events. Next, write an explanation in English of how each one is played and scored.

To test whether the directions are clear, review them with the athletes. (Note: the word "athlete" refers to all competitors, whether they are participating in a game requiring physical activity or a board game.) You will know who the athletes in each game are because each one will give your committee a copy of Athlete Information Worksheet 5.E.1. Have the athletes practice each game and if the explanations are unclear, revise them. Write the final directions, a complete list of materials, and how the game is scored on Competitive Events Worksheet 5.B.2, which will be used at the games.

D. Give each game a name. At your Olympic Games, the names will be announced in Spanish and, for any non-Spanish speakers watching, in English. The name might indicate the action involved in the game (such as Snowman Building—**Hacer un muñeco de nieve,** Sandcastle Building**—Hacer un castillo de arena**) or the number of people and the equipment the game requires (Two-Person Board game—**Juego de mesa para dos personas**). Record two of the Spanish and English names on Competitive Events Worksheet 5.B.2. Finally, decide on the order in which the events will occur and write the numbers after Competition Number on the same worksheet.

To help the athletes practice, give them directions for the games in which they will compete. If a committee member wrote the directions on a computer, make multiple copies for your committee and the athletes.

E. Since the athletes at your games will all be speaking Spanish, review the sports and games vocabulary in the Almanac. Brainstorm and add any phrases you think they may need to use while playing the games.

F. Now that Committee B knows what your contests involve, talk with your teacher as a group about where to hold them. Can they be played in the classroom? Do they require gymnasium facilities or a track? When you know where each game will take place, add that information to Competitive Events Worksheet 5.B.2. Make and post signs to tell spectators when and where the various games are taking place.

2° Paso Las distancias

At international sporting competitions, distances are measured in meters rather than yards (1 meter = 1.094 yards). You can make your individual metric measuring tape by fastening together strips of paper or cloth and using a felt-tip pen to mark off 10-centimeter intervals (100 centimeters = 1 meter). A sample metric ruler is shown in the Almanac near the table of weights and measures. How many meters long does your tape need to be? Think about how far the athletes are likely to jump or how high they might build something.

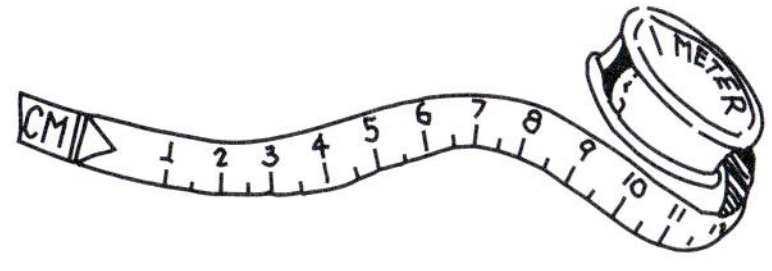

3er Paso Los papeles

As a committee, decide who will be the announcer and referee at the games. To allow as many students as possible on Committee B to participate at the games, change who plays these roles at each competitive event. Add this information to Competitive Events Worksheet 5.B.2.

- *Announcers:* The announcers tell the spectators in Spanish a little about the athletes before each competition and announce the results. (Ask the athletes for their Athlete Information Worksheet 5.E.1. Ask the athletes' uniform designers for their Symbol Information Worksheet 5.F. You will use the information on these worksheets to introduce the athletes before they compete.) If the events at the actual games are held in different locations, be sure to include an announcement for the spectators about where the next competitive event will be held.
- *Referees:* The referees explain to the spectators in Spanish how each game is played and scored. They supervise the game and take any necessary measurements. In addition, the referee keeps a record of each athlete's or team's score and gives that information to the announcer for Committee B. At the games, the referee will also tell the announcer for the Medal Committee the names of the first- (gold), second- (silver), and third-place (bronze) winners.

La ceremonia de inauguración

The Olympic Games begin and end with ceremonies. These entertaining ceremonies include the parade of athletes, speeches, and performances that reflect the culture of the host country. Committee C is going to design the opening ceremony for your mini-Olympics.

Herramientas útiles

- Guidebooks for Spanish-speaking countries
- Books on customs and traditions of the Spanish-speaking countries
- Recordings of Spanish music
- Competitive Events Worksheet 5.B.2 (filled in)
- Opening Ceremony Worksheets 5.C.1 and 5.C.2
- National Team Worksheet 5.E.2 (filled in)
- Portfolio

Describan una ceremonia

As Committee C, discuss Olympic Game opening and closing ceremonies you have watched. Use the **Vocabulario útil** box at the top of page 84 to help you speak Spanish as much as possible. What happens at the ceremonies? What props are used?

Conexiones

- ☑ Arte
- ☑ Historia
- ☑ Música

Vocabulario útil

los atletas desfilan	*the athletes march*
bailar	*to dance*
cantar una canción	*to sing a song*
el estadio	*stadium*
llevar una bandera	*to carry a flag*
pronunciar un discurso	*to give a speech*

2° Paso

Celebraciones, costumbres y leyendas

A. Individually, use some of the materials listed in the **Herramientas útiles** box to research celebrations, customs, or legends of the Spanish-speaking host site that can be performed or enacted at the opening of the Games. Record your findings in Part 1 of Worksheet 5.C.1.

B. Report your findings to Committee C, describing as much of the custom, celebration, or legend as you can in Spanish.

3er Paso

¿Qué talentos tienen?

Make a list in Spanish of all the talents you have in your committee. For example, who dances, sings, plays an instrument, draws, or speaks well in public? How can you combine the group's talents with a custom, celebration, or legend to make a special event that will be performed at the opening ceremony? Determine who will perform the special event. Record your decisions under The Performance at the Opening Ceremonies on Worksheet 5.C.1.

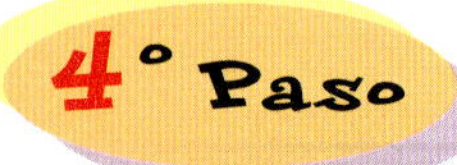

¿Dónde, cómo y quién?

As Committee C, decide how you want to organize the ceremony and where you will need to hold it. Will you require electrical outlets for plugging in a CD or cassette player? If a dance is part of the performance, can the dance be done outside on the school grounds? How long will the ceremony be? When will the athletes parade in? In what order? When will the performance take place? Discuss your decisions with your teacher so that he or she can arrange an appropriate space for the ceremony.

Now use Opening Ceremony Worksheet 5.C.2 to list Committee C's tasks in Spanish. Decide who will work on each one and record the names.

Record the order of the opening ceremony events in Spanish on Opening Ceremony Worksheet 5.C.2. Then, in Part 3, list the order in which the national teams will march in the parade.

¡A trabajar!

Now that your group has an idea of what the ceremonies will include and what your roles are, you need to work on the preparations, consulting with one another as you progress.

- *Speech writers*: Keep the opening speech brief and in Spanish. Announce the various parts of the ceremony, such as the parade of the athletes and the performance. To announce the parade, you need the names of the countries represented at the games from Committee E. Also prepare a brief description of the performance. Find out from Committee B where the competitive events will be held, the name of each game, and the order in which the games will be played. Include this information at the appropriate time in the remarks.
- *Announcers:* Practice your speech and the announcements.

- *Performers*: What music, costumes, or props do you need? Plan and practice your performance.
- *Organizers:* Help everyone get organized in the parade.
- *Ushers*: Be prepared to direct spectators and athletes to their seats. Find out from the athletes what countries they represent and prepare a name sign for each country. On the day of the games, display signs that show where the athletes should sit. Prepare signs for spectator seating.

Once all preparations are made, hold a rehearsal to make sure everyone knows what he or she is supposed to do and when. For rehearsal purposes, members of your group should role-play the parts of the athletes and spectators.

Un poco más

Write a theme song in Spanish for your games! Or choose a piece of classical, folk, or pop music, preferably from the host country. If necessary, the music could be from a different Spanish-speaking country.

La ceremonia de las medallas

A moving moment of every Olympic event is when the officials place the gold, silver, and bronze medals around the necks of the winners. The design for Olympic medals is determined by the country hosting the games and may reflect the history, geography, or culture of that country. You're going to design the medals and the awards ceremony for your Olympic Games.

Herramientas útiles

- Books about the history of the Spanish-speaking countries
- Books about the Olympic Games
- Colored markers, pencils, or paints; cardboard or poster board; scissors
- Competitive Events Worksheet 5.B.2 (filled in)
- Medals Worksheet 5.D.1
- Medals Ceremony Worksheet 5.D.2
- National Team Worksheet 5.E.2 (filled in)
- Computer with drawing software
- Portfolio

1er Paso

¿Cómo es una medalla olímpica?

Working with the other members of Committee D, locate at least one picture or description of an Olympic medal. Use some of the materials listed in the **Herramientas útiles** box. Note the games that the medal is from (the season, place, and year), its shape, and the words, images, and designs on it. Record the information in Part 1 of Medals Worksheet 5.D.1.

2° Paso Diseñen sus medallas

A. Now it's time to individually design your own set of three medals. Decide on the shape and size. Measurements should be metric. You can use the metric ruler near the table of weights and measures in the Almanac. What words, images, or designs will be on each medal? Perhaps you want to include a well-known geographic feature or a historic place, event, or person on the medal. Will you hang the medals from chains, ribbons, or strings? Record your decisions for each medal in Part 2 of Medals Worksheet 5.D.1.

B. Present your design to your group, describing it in Spanish. After all group members have presented their ideas, decide which design(s) will be used for your Games.

C. It's time to make the medals. Find out from Committee B how many winners you can expect. If any of the games are team events, find out how many people are on each team so you can prepare a medal for each team member. Record the information in Part 3 of Medals Worksheet 5.D.1.

3er Paso Preparen la ceremonia de las medallas

As a committee, determine who will award the medals at the games. You may want a different presenter **(anunciador/anunciadora)** for each game. The presenter(s) should be sure to get the winners' names and countries from the referees (see Committee B) at the games. Each presenter should prepare a short speech that he or she can use when awarding the medals and congratulating the winners. As a presenter, record your basic speech on Medals Ceremony Worksheet 5.D.2, leaving out the information about the athlete's (or team's) name and country until the actual games.

El ensayo

Once the medals and speeches are ready, rehearse the ceremony with members of your committee role-playing the winners. Check with students working on Committee F to be sure they have the national anthems ready. They will be responsible for playing them at the ceremonies. If possible, have them participate in your rehearsal.

Vocabulario útil

las medallas	*the medals*
la medalla olímpica	*Olympic medal*
conferir una medalla	*to award a medal*
Es redonda/ovalada.	*It's round/oval.*
Tiene forma de círculo/triángulo.	*It's shaped like a circle/triangle.*
la ceremonia	*the ceremony*
Señoras y Señores	*Ladies and Gentlemen*
La medalla de oro/plata/bronce se confiere a [*name of student*], ganador(a) de [*name of event*].	*The gold/silver/bronze medal is awarded to ___, winner of the ___.*
¡Felicitaciones!	*Congratulations!*

¿Sabías que...?

Although team sports such as soccer and baseball are favorites in Spanish-speaking countries, individual sports such as tennis, bicycling, and skiing are also extremely popular. In the Andes Mountains of South America as well as in the Sierra Nevada and the Pyrenees of Spain, there are excellent locations for **el esquí**. **El ciclismo** is a favorite sport in Spain, which sends representatives to the famous Tour de France every year. Spain's Miguel Indurain has won the Tour de France five consecutive times from 1991–1995. In addition, several famous **tenistas** are from Spanish-speaking countries, including Gabriela Sabatini of Argentina and Arantxa Sánchez Vicario and Carlos Moyá of Spain.

Los atletas

For athletes all over the world, competing in the Olympic Games is a great honor. On this committee, you are going to find out what the competitive events are, choose your contests, and practice for the games. You are also going to determine what Spanish-speaking town and country you will represent and will make a flag (alone or with teammates) to carry in the opening ceremony.

Herramientas útiles

- World atlas
- Competitive Events Worksheets 5.B.1/5.B.2 (filled in)
- Opening Ceremony Worksheet 5.C.2 (filled in)
- Athlete Information Worksheet 5.E.1
- National Team Worksheet 5.E.2
- Paper, colored pencils, pens, or paints; ruler
- Guidebooks about Spanish-speaking towns and countries
- A photo of yourself
- Portfolio
- The World Wide Web

1er Paso

¿En qué eventos vas a participar?

A. Ask classmates on Committee B to present to your group the Olympic sporting events they've designed. Choose the event(s) in which you personally want to compete. Then in Committee E, arrange for the athletes who are taking part in team events to get together and form teams. Each team will represent a specific Spanish-speaking country.

Conexiones

- ☑ Arte
- ☑ Geografía
- ☑ Tecnología

B. Committee B will ask you, as an individual and/or team member, to practice the games you are competing in to make sure the directions are clear. Once the committee has corrected any problems, you will get copies of the directions for the games. You can practice them on your own, with teammates, or with fellow competitors. Use the Spanish vocabulary and phrases in the sports and games section of the Almanac as you do so.

2° Paso ¿De dónde eres?

A. As an individual athlete or as a team, decide which Spanish-speaking country you represent. Next, group yourselves according to geographic areas. Using guidebooks and maps, individually select your hometown. Find out its population and one other interesting fact. If more than one athlete wants the same hometown, only one should include its population as part of the researched information. The other athlete(s) should look for two additional facts about it. Write your name and this information on your own Athlete Information Worksheet 5.E.1.

Next, meet as national teams and complete National Team Worksheet 5.E.2 in Spanish. Also have athletes who are participating as individuals record information about themselves in Part 3. Committee F needs this information in order to make your uniforms. You'll need to get your uniforms from them for the opening ceremonies and the games.

¡Investiguemos en el Web!

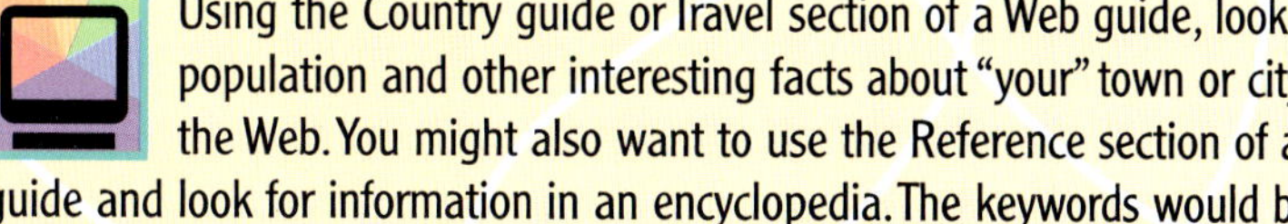

Using the Country guide or Travel section of a Web guide, look for the population and other interesting facts about "your" town or city on the Web. You might also want to use the Reference section of a Web guide and look for information in an encyclopedia. The keywords would be the name of the city or town.

B. During sporting events, information is often given about the contestants. Complete the rest of Athlete Information Worksheet 5.E.1 in Spanish so that the announcers will have information to pass along to the spectators.

Un poco más

Write a short paragraph in Spanish describing yourself for a press release. Include your age, where you're from, your hobbies, your favorite school subject, and your favorite food. Attach a photo to your description. With your group, display these paragraphs and photos in the classroom so that your fellow classmates can read up on the athletes who will be participating in the games.

¿Sabías que...?

El fútbol (*soccer*) is generally regarded as the most popular Hispanic sport. Many professional soccer players learned to play in poor regions of the cities and countryside and then went on to become famous sports heroes. However, in a number of Spanish-speaking countries baseball has surpassed soccer as the national sport. Most cities have a baseball stadium, and even the smallest towns have a playing field. Baseball is so popular in Venezuela that children in poor towns have invented a variation of the game called **pelota de goma** (*rubber ball*). In this game, players use their clenched fist in place of a bat and hit a small rubber ball. **Pelota de goma** is generally played in the street or on any flat ground.

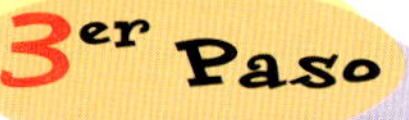

Las banderas

When Olympic athletes parade in the opening and closing ceremonies, one athlete from each country carries its flag. By obtaining a copy of Opening Ceremony Worksheet 5.C.2, you can learn where your country will march in the opening parade. Whether there is one person or several from the country that you're representing, find a picture of its flag. As a national team, decide who will make your flag and carry it in the opening ceremony. Then, using the picture you have found as a guide and some of the materials listed in the **Herramientas útiles** box, the selected athlete(s) will make the flag and attach it to a ruler. One very lucky athlete will carry it in the opening ceremony.

Los trajes y los himnos nacionales

In the opening and closing ceremonies, the Olympic athletes from a country wear similar clothing that often reflects their country or culture in some way. You're going to put together very simple costumes for the countries represented by the athletes at your games.

Herramientas útiles

- Books, magazines, and newspapers with information and pictures of the Spanish-speaking countries
- Materials for making costumes or symbol cards
- Recordings of national anthems of the Spanish-speaking countries and folk songs or popular music
- Competitive Events Worksheet 5.B.2 (filled in)
- National Team Worksheet 5.E.2 (filled in)
- Symbol Information Worksheet 5.F
- Portfolio
- Cassette player or CD player with speakers
- Computer with drawing software

1er Paso

¿Qué ropa usan los atletas?

A. In your group as Committee F, get a copy of National Team Worksheet 5.E.2 from Committee E. Decide which athlete(s) each of you will design a costume or symbol card for. On your own, list each athlete's name, hometown, country, and the games in which he or she will take part on Symbol Information Worksheet 5.F.

Conexiones

- ☑ Arte
- ☑ Estrategias de estudio
- ☑ Historia
- ☑ Música

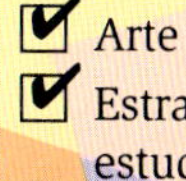

B. Continue on your own. Use the materials listed in the **Herramientas útiles** box or textbooks to research costumes or symbols that you think may reflect the area(s) from which your athlete(s) come. For example, if your athlete(s) are from Barcelona, you may feel that a bull is a typical symbol for the city. Record the information on Symbol Worksheet 5.F.

C. For each country that you chose, design a simple costume or hanging card that your athlete(s) can wear. It should reflect your research. At the games, be sure to give the card(s) to your athlete(s).

D. For each of your athletes, supply the information requested about your symbol in Spanish on Symbol Information Worksheet 5.F. Use the **Vocabulario útil** in Section D for help. Explain the meaning of the symbol in English and give the worksheet to the announcer on Committee B.

Un poco más

Explain the meaning of the symbol in Spanish. Have the announcer at the games use the Spanish instead of the English version.

2° Paso Los himnos nacionales

When the medals are awarded at the Olympics, the national anthem of the gold medalist is played.

A. With your committee, locate a copy of the national anthem of each Spanish-speaking country represented at your games. The Spanish Department, the school library, or the town library may have the music you need. If you cannot find a particular piece, e-mail or write to the cultural attaché of the country's embassy nearest you. Explain in English why you need the music and express your thanks for any help the person is able to give you.

B. If you're not able to find a recording of a country's national anthem, locate and use a piece of music by a composer or musician born in the country.

C. Consult with Committee D about when you'll play the national anthems at the awards ceremonies.

¡Los Juegos abren!

The big day is close at hand. To be sure everything is ready and that everyone knows how the games will proceed, you will have a dress rehearsal before holding the actual games.

Herramientas útiles

- All props, costumes, game equipment, music, and so on from Committees B–F
- Games Schedule Worksheet 5.G
- Computer with word-processing software
- Portfolio (three-ring binder with pockets, file jacket, or file folder)

1er Paso

¿Está todo listo?

A. With your class, brainstorm a checklist in Spanish of the preparations you have made for your Olympics. For example, the first items might be **Los eventos** and **Informar a los atletas**. They indicate first that Committee B has designed the competitive events and has collected all the equipment. Committee B has also let the athletes know what the events are and what language they will need to use while participating.

B. Now each committee needs to check that it has obtained any information, props, and so forth needed from other committees.

2° Paso

El programa

As a class, prepare a list in Spanish of what will happen and when it will happen at the games. To be sure that nothing is left out, use the list of preparations from **1er Paso** and the phrases at the top of Games Schedule Worksheet 5.G for help. Record the final list on the same worksheet.

Conexiones

- ☑ Historia
- ☑ Música

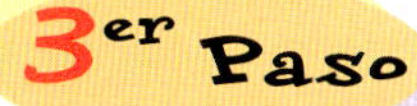

El ensayo

Run through a rehearsal of the games, using your Games Schedule Worksheet 5.G as a guide. Because it is just a rehearsal, you may not wish to play each of the competitive events to completion. Rework or adjust any part of the games that isn't running smoothly.

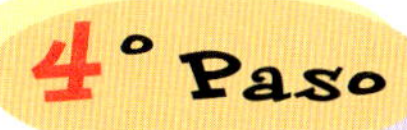

¡Que los Juegos comiencen!

The big day is finally here. Hold the games. Good luck and have fun!

Un poco más

The Olympic Games have something for everyone—from the sportsmanship of those competing, to the artistic talent of those designing medals, to the organizational ability of those overseeing the games as a whole. Now write and produce a short newsletter about your Olympics.

In your group, write a short article in Spanish about your part in the Olympics—for example, how the design of the athletes' clothing reflects their countries. If you have worked on more than one committee, choose your favorite to write about. Remember to give your article a headline. Ask your teacher to review your article. Then as a class, assemble your newspaper. Your teacher will distribute it to the other Spanish classes at your school.

PROJECT 6

¡Presenten su colegio!

For this project, you and your group are going to create a school guidebook (**una guía**), to be used by Spanish-speaking exchange students. In the process, you will:

- Create a map of your school and label rooms, important features, and classroom items in Spanish
- Prepare a profile of your school
- Present some of the extracurricular activities at your school
- Create a schedule of a typical day at your school
- Describe your school mascot (or create a new one) and invent a school cheer
- Design a school flag
- Videotape a guided tour of your school
- Create a title page and a table of contents for your school guidebook

¡Diviértanse!

Conexiones

In the process of creating your school guidebook, you'll sharpen your skills in many areas.

- [x] Arte
- [ ] Ciencias
- [x] Estrategias de estudio
- [x] Geografía
- [x] Historia
- [x] Matemáticas
- [x] Medios de comunicación
- [x] Música
- [ ] Salud y nutrición
- [x] Tecnología

Look for the **Conexiones** boxes throughout this project.

Warm-up: Antes de empezar ...

Before starting on your guidebook for Spanish-speaking students, you'll need to do some brainstorming about your own school experience.

Herramientas útiles

- One three-ring binder per group with one pocket insert (or a 3-hole punched 9" x 13" manila envelope)

A. Form small groups. In your group, you can then each write three words in Spanish that you associate with your school experience.

estudiar divertida clases

B. Exchange papers with a partner. Now write down one word that you associate with each word your partner wrote.

estudiar—mucho
divertida—cafetería
clases—difíciles

C. Exchange papers with your partner again. Using the six words you now have on your paper, write one or two brief sentences about your school experience.

▶ En mi colegio hay que estudiar mucho.
Mis clases son difíciles.
La cafetería es muy divertida.

D. Share your sentences with your group.

E. As you complete each part of this project with your group, you'll be creating material for your group's school guidebook. Place your sentences in your group's binder.

El colegio

For the first few days, it may be hard for new Spanish-speaking students to find their way around your school. Drawing a map is the perfect way to help them out!

Herramientas útiles

- Spanish-English dictionary
- Colored pencils or markers
- 3" x 5" (or 5" x 7") blank index cards

1er Paso

Un mapa del colegio

A. Working in a small group, draw a map of your school and the surrounding grounds. Your map needs to be large enough to accommodate small labels. If your school has more than one story, draw a floor plan for each story. If your own student handbook has a map, adapt it for this project.

B. Work together to see how many rooms, offices, and other features you can label in Spanish on your map. Then use your Spanish textbook or a Spanish-English dictionary to label any remaining features. Identify at least five classrooms by the names of the subjects taught in them.

C. Get together with another group and compare your maps. Have you forgotten anything important?

Conexiones

- ☑ Arte
- ☑ Estrategias de estudio

¿Sabías que...?

In most Spanish-speaking countries, the floors of buildings are numbered differently than in the U.S. What we would consider the first floor is called **la planta baja** (literally, *the ground floor*). Our second floor is **el primer piso** (*the first floor*) in Spanish-speaking countries. Our third floor is **el segundo piso**, and so on.

2° Paso

Las tarjetas bilingües

A. Create bilingual flashcards to help the new students learn the names of some rooms, offices, and other features of your school. In your group, make eight flashcards with the Spanish name on one side and the English on the other.

B. With your group, create eight bilingual flashcards for items in your Spanish classroom (desk, chair, bookcase, chalkboard, clock, and so forth).

3er Paso

Preparen la guía

Put your group's school map into the guidebook binder. Place your group's flashcards in the pocket insert of the binder.

Información general

A map provides a general picture of what your school looks like. A school profile, or an outline of different characteristics, can help new students see at a glance what life is like at your school.

Herramientas útiles

- Statistical information about your school
- Spanish-English dictionary
- School Profile Worksheet 6.B
- The World Wide Web

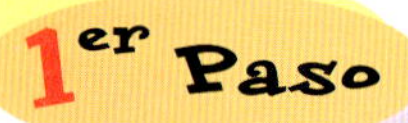

Las estadísticas

Gather some basic statistics about your school.

A. Answer the questions in Part 1 of School Profile Worksheet 6.B. Ask your school librarian, teachers, or administrators to help you find this information.

B. In your group, compare your answers to Part 1 of Worksheet 6.B. If your answers differ, find out why. What sources did you each use? Then compare your answers with those of other groups.

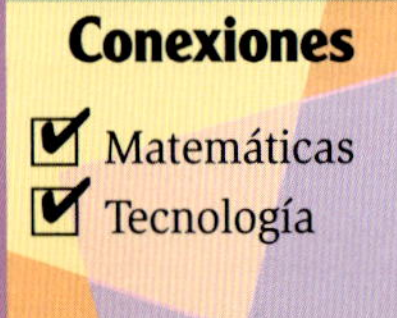

¡Investiguemos en el Web!

If your school has its own Web site, look for the information there. Ask your teacher for the school's Web address if you don't know it.

Las asignaturas

In addition to a general overview, the new students will appreciate a guide to the specific subjects offered at your school.

A. As homework, create a chart like the one below.

Asignatura	¿Es obligatoria?	Descripción
el español	*sí*	*divertido*
las ciencias	*sí*	*interesantes*
el arte	*no*	*fácil*

1. In the first column, list in Spanish ten subjects at your school that you have taken or will take. Turn to the Almanac for a list of courses and subjects.
2. In the second column, indicate whether or not you're required to take the subject this year (**sí** or **no**).
3. In the third column, write one adjective in Spanish that you think best describes each subject.

B. In Spanish, compare your chart with those of others in your group. Are all of your required subjects the same? How similar or different are your descriptions of the subjects? Are the descriptions positive?

Vocabulario útil

¿Qué clases tomas este año?	*What classes are you taking this year?*
¿Estudias ___?	*Are you taking ___?*
Tomo ___.	*I'm studying/taking ___.*
¿Es obligatoria la clase para ti?	*Is it a required class for you?*
¿Cómo es la clase?	*What's the class like?*

C. In your group, divide the subjects you have listed in your charts into three categories: academic (**las asignaturas académicas**), arts (**las asignaturas artísticas**), and other subjects (**otras asignaturas**). Then list at least three subjects under each category in Part 2 of School Profile Worksheet 6.B. Include descriptions as well. One member of your group should record an official list of the group's answers.

D. Add your group's School Profile Worksheet 6.B to your school guidebook.

¿Sabías que...?

In many Spanish-speaking countries, the grading system is based on a 10-point scale. Generally, a grade (**la nota**) between 0 and 5 is considered a failing grade (**suspendido**), 6 is satisfactory (**satisfactoria**), and 10 is excellent (**excelente**).

Las actividades extracurriculares

The Spanish-speaking students may want to get involved in extracurricular activities. Introduce them to some of the organizations and teams at your school.

Herramientas útiles

- Extracurricular Activities Worksheet 6.C

1er Paso — Los deportes

A. In your group, write a list in Spanish of at least six sports teams or intramural sports your school has. Organize your list according to season (fall, winter, spring, or summer) on Extracurricular Activities Worksheet 6.C. Refer to your textbook and the list of sports in the Almanac.

B. Now take your own survey of five classmates in other groups to find out what their favorite school sports are. Report your findings to your group. On Extracurricular Activities Worksheet 6.C, record which sport seems to be the most popular in your class. One member of the group should record the group's answers.

2° Paso — Los clubs y las organizaciones

A. As a group, find out what school clubs and organizations each of your group members belongs to. List them in Spanish on Extracurricular Activities Worksheet 6.C. Next to each club or organization, write a brief description of it in Spanish. Refer to the list of clubs and organizations in the Almanac.

Conexiones

☑ Estrategias de estudio

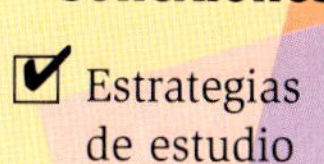

B. Now get together with another group and exchange information. Add any new information to Extracurricular Activities Worksheet 6.C.

Vocabulario útil

¿De qué club eres miembro?	*What club are you a member of?*
Soy miembro del club ___.	*I'm a member of the ___ club.*
¿Qué haces en el club de ___?	*What do you do in the ___ club?*
el periódico del colegio	*school newspaper*
Trabajo en el anuario.	*I work on the yearbook.*
preparar	*to prepare*
organizar	*to organize*
ayudar	*to help*
pensar en	*to think about*
practicar	*to practice*

C. Add Extracurricular Activities Worksheet 6.C to your group's binder.

¿Sabías que...?

In both Spain and Latin America, extracurricular school activities are not common. Since schools often don't have their own teams, most teenagers join independent teams to play the sports they enjoy.

Un día típico

Help the Spanish-speaking students experience a typical day of classes at your school. Assist them with schedules and directions.

Herramientas útiles

- School map from Section A

Tu horario

A. Create a chart with the days of the week in Spanish across the top and the times corresponding to your class periods down the left side.

B. Create a model schedule for new students at your school by filling in the chart in Spanish with your own school schedule. Add room numbers to indicate where the class meets.

¿Sabías que...?

Unlike teachers in the U.S., teachers in Spain and Latin America change classrooms throughout the day while students stay in the same classroom for all their classes. Thus, lockers are unnecessary. School supplies are brought to school every day in backpacks or bags.

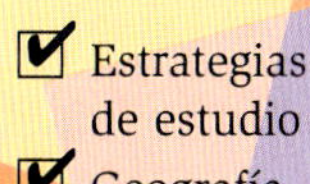

Conexiones

- ✔ Estrategias de estudio
- ✔ Geografía

2° Paso ¿Dónde está...?

A. Now help students find their way from one class to the next. Using your schedule and your group's school map, write directions in Spanish so that the new students can find their way from:

- the main entrance to your first class
- your first class to your second class
- the cafeteria to your first class after lunch
- one class to any other class on your schedule

▶ **Para llegar desde la cafetería hasta el aula de español:**

Dobla a la derecha.
Sigue recto hasta llegar al gimnasio.
Dobla a la izquierda.
Sube las escaleras.
El aula de español es la tercera al lado izquierdo.

B. Work in pairs. Give one set of your directions to your partner, who will trace the route you describe on a school map. Reverse roles. Are your partner's directions accurate? Are yours accurate?

Vocabulario útil

a la derecha	*to the right* or *on the right*
a la izquierda	*to the left* or *on the left*
camina	*walk*
el corredor/el pasillo	*hallway*
cruza	*cross*
derecho/recto	*straight ahead*
dobla	*turn*
las escaleras	*stairs*
hasta	*until*
sube/baja las escaleras	*go up/go down the stairs*

C. Put your schedule and directions into your group's binder as samples for the visitors.

¡Viva el colegio!

Students have many ways of expressing their school spirit. At a football game, for example, there may be a school mascot that represents the team. The cheerleaders try to inspire the crowd and support the athletes. Help the new Spanish-speaking students catch your school spirit!

Herramientas útiles

- Colored markers
- Spanish-English dictionary

Vocabulario útil

el aficionado	*fan*
el equipo	*team*
animar/alentar (al equipo)	*to cheer (the team on)*
la mascota	*mascot*
¡Viva!	*Go!*
¡Viva el colegio!	*Go [name] high school!*
¡Vivan los Tigres!	*Go Tigers!*

Conexiones

- ☑ Arte
- ☑ Música

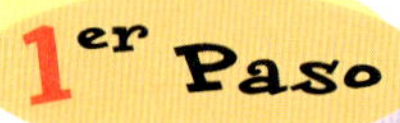

1er Paso La mascota

In your group, draw your school mascot and describe it in Spanish. Use your current school mascot or create one of your own. Then present your mascot to the class.

▶ Nuestra mascota es un tigre. El tigre es grande y feroz. Es anaranjado, con rayas negras ...

Un poco más

How does your mascot represent your school? With your group, write a sentence in Spanish that describes both your mascot and your school.

▶ El tigre y mi colegio son fuertes, grandes, inteligentes ...

¿Sabías que...?

In Spanish-speaking countries, there are usually several cheers that are familiar to almost everyone. Often these cheers contain nonsense syllables, much like the "shish-boom-bah" of cheers in the U.S. Here is a typical Mexican cheer:

¡A la vio, a la vao, a la bim bom ba
Tigres, Tigres, ra, ra, RA!

Try including some of these nonsense syllables in your cheers.

2º Paso ¡Tres hurras!

A. In your group, decide whether you're going to write a cheer for your whole school or for one team or organization at your school. Then brainstorm action verbs in Spanish related to your school, your team or organization, or your mascot. For example, if your mascot is a tiger, you might come up with verbs such as **correr** or **saltar**.

B. Now brainstorm some adjectives that describe your school, your team or organization, or your mascot. For example, **rápido**, **fuerte**, and **peligroso** are adjectives that might describe a tiger.

C. Finally, combine some of the verbs and adjectives you brainstormed into a simple but energetic school cheer, such as the one shown. Have your teacher review your group's cheer. Then teach it to the rest of the class.

D. Add your school cheer and the picture and information about your mascot to your school guidebook.

La bandera del colegio

Countries, states, schools, and organizations are often represented by a flag or banner. The colors and designs on these flags are usually carefully chosen to symbolize the ideals of the groups they represent.

Herramientas útiles

- An encyclopedia or almanac
- Colored markers
- Construction paper
- The World Wide Web

1er Paso

La bandera de los Estados Unidos

As a class, discuss the significance of the symbols and colors of the U.S. flag.

1. ¿Cuáles son los tres colores de la bandera de los Estados Unidos de América?
2. ¿Son importantes estos colores? ¿Qué representan?
3. ¿Cuántas estrellas (*stars*) hay en la bandera? ¿Por qué?

¿Sabías que...?

In most Hispanic countries, the national flag is never used as fabric for clothing as the U.S. flag is used here sometimes. To do so would be considered highly disrespectful. Also, people don't have flags at home, on their porches, in their windows, or at school.

Conexiones

- Arte
- Geografía
- Historia

- Tecnología

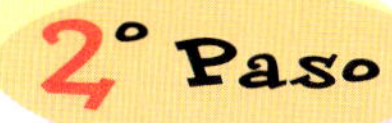

Las banderas del mundo hispano

Working with your group, look in an encyclopedia or your Spanish textbook and select the flag of one Spanish-speaking country. List in Spanish the colors and symbols on the flag. What values or history do you think the colors and symbols might represent? Discuss your ideas in English. Consult an encyclopedia to find more information about the flag you chose. How does this information compare with your own ideas about the flag? Present your findings to the class in English.

¡Investiguemos en el Web!

To find out more information about the flag you've chosen, search the World Wide Web using a Web guide.

Keywords

"flags of the world"

3er Paso

Diseñen su propia bandera

A. Create a flag for your school or town. With your group, make a list in Spanish of colors that you might want to include on your school flag. Next to each color, write what it could represent. You could include your school colors and perhaps add one or two more.

▶ el blanco = la verdad
el dorado = la excelencia

las rayas

el escudo — la luna — la serpiente

el árbol — la estrella — el ave — el sol

B. Now draw some symbols that you think would represent your school. Next to each symbol, write in Spanish what it stands for. You could include your school mascot or an important feature of your town or school. Use your imagination!

▶ el león = fuerza, fortaleza
las estrellas = la ambición

C. Using your lists of colors and symbols, draw your flag or make it out of construction paper.

Un poco más

Write a brief explanation in Spanish of the colors and symbols on your flag and how they represent your school or town.

▶ Nuestra bandera tiene dos colores. El blanco representa la verdad. El dorado representa la excelencia académica. En el centro de la bandera hay una estrella. La estrella representa la ambición, porque los estudiantes aquí trabajan mucho.

4° Paso Preparen la guía

Explain your flag to the class. Display your flag in the classroom. Create a small version of your flag and add it to your group's school guidebook, along with your description of its colors and symbols.

El videotur

Schools and towns attract students or residents by providing colorful informational brochures, videotapes, or even CD-ROMs about their schools and community facilities. Introduce the new Spanish-speaking students to your school by videotaping your own guided tour.

Herramientas útiles

- School map from Section A
- Spanish-English dictionary
- Video camera and blank videotape
- Construction paper, poster board, or colored paper
- Heavy-duty elastic band
- Computer with word-processing program

1er Paso

Las decisiones

A. With your group, review the map you made of your school and school grounds in Section A. Make a list of the rooms, offices, and features of the school that should be shown in your video tour.

B. Consulting your teacher, find two teachers willing to appear in your video. Teach them each a short greeting in Spanish (for example, **Buenos días** or **Bienvenidos a la clase de matemáticas**).

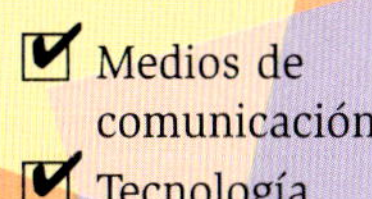

Conexiones

- ☑ Medios de comunicación
- ☑ Tecnología

2º Paso Los comentarios

Working with your group, write one or two sentences in Spanish to introduce and describe each of the teachers, rooms, and features you've chosen to highlight in your video. For each one, consider what significance it has for your school. Are there any relevant facts or statistics you can share? For example, how long has the biology teacher been at your school? When was the computer lab opened?

▶ **La señora ___ trabaja en el colegio hace diez años.**
El laboratorio de computadoras es nuevo.
Nuestro equipo de gimnasia es el mejor del estado.

Un poco más

Find someone in your school (other than your Spanish teacher!) who speaks Spanish. Videotape a brief interview in Spanish with him or her. You might ask for some advice for the new students.

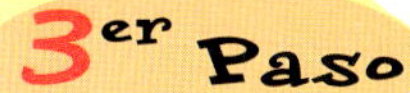

Los detalles de la producción

A. With your group, plot the route you will take in taping your video tour. Use the descriptions you wrote in the **2º Paso** to put together a short script for your video. Have the students in your group introduce themselves at the beginning of the tour.

B. Decide how you will divide up the roles of director, narrator, and camera operator. You may want to share a role or change with each new scene.

C. Create the title and credits of your video tour by using construction paper or poster board, or use attractive fonts from a word-processing program and print them out on colored paper.

4º Paso

¡Acción!

Finally, you're ready to tape the video tour of your school. It should be about three to five minutes long. All of the narration should be done in Spanish. Remember to speak clearly! Rehearse your tour at least once before you begin taping. When your video tour is complete, show it to your class; then include it in your completed school guidebook, along with your script. Use a heavy-duty elastic band to "attach" your video to your guidebook.

Los últimos detalles

To complete your school guidebook, make it easy to use by adding a title page, table of contents, and page numbers.

Herramientas útiles

- School guidebook binder
- Construction paper and colored markers
- Computer with word-processing program

1er Paso

El título

In your group, create a title page for your school guidebook using colored markers and construction paper or a computer word-processing program. Include the following useful information:

- Name, address, and phone number of your school
- Your group members' names and the date
- Other names, phone numbers, and office numbers that new students may need (the school nurse, principal, guidance counselor, and so on)

¿Sabías que...?

School uniforms are very common in Spanish-speaking countries from elementary school through high school. In many schools, boys are also required to keep their hair cut short and are not permitted to wear caps in class. These rules sometimes give Hispanic schools a more formal character than is typical of schools in the U.S.

Conexiones

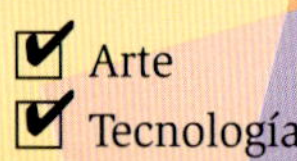

☑ Arte
☑ Tecnología

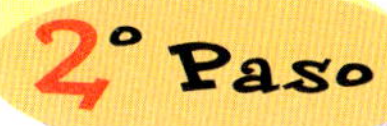

El índice

Make a table of contents. Assign each item in your guidebook a page number so that new students will be able to locate the information quickly and easily. On a separate sheet of paper, list each item in your school guidebook and add page numbers.

3er Paso

¡Ya está!

Insert your title page and contents page into the front of your school guidebook binder. Congratulations on a job well done!

PROJECT

7

¡Organicemos un desfile de modas!

Using your knowledge of clothing and Hispanic cultures, you and your group will produce a fashion show. In the process, you will:

- Find examples of what Hispanic teenagers are wearing and compare styles of American and Hispanic clothing
- Set up your own fashion design house
- Take on different roles for the preparation of the show
- Make a program and advertisement for the show
- Add decoration and music to the show
- Hold the fashion show

¡A las tijeras!

Conexiones

As you create your fashion show, you will sharpen your skills in many areas.

- [x] Arte
- [ ] Ciencias
- [x] Estrategias de estudio
- [ ] Geografía
- [ ] Historia
- [ ] Matemáticas
- [x] Medios de comunicación
- [x] Música
- [ ] Salud y nutrición
- [x] Tecnología

Look for the **Conexiones** boxes throughout this project.

Warm-up: ¡Hablemos de la moda!

Do you want to use your imagination and have some fun? You are going to be a fashion designer and present your unique creations at a show. Your clothing and accessories can show your interests, the kind of person you are, or just be for fun. Let's get started by talking about what you like to wear and where you like to shop.

Vocabulario útil

¿Te gusta/n ___?	*Do you like ___?*
A mí tampoco.	*Me neither.*
la ganga	*bargain*
la liquidación/la oferta	*sale*
la boutique	*boutique*
el catálogo	*catalog*
el centro comercial	*mall*
el escaparate	*display window*
el gran almacén	*department store (large store in a chain)*
ir a mirar escaparates	*to go window shopping*
llevar	*to wear*
la marca	*brand, name*
la revista de modas	*fashion magazine*
la tienda	*store, shop (small)*
la tienda de ropa	*clothing store*
la tienda de ropa de segunda mano	*second-hand clothing store*
la venta por correo	*mail-order shopping*

A. Do you prefer comfortable clothes? Do you like the latest fashions? In a small group, discuss in Spanish the kinds of clothes and accessories you prefer to wear. Here are a few sentences to get you started.

▶ ¿Qué tipo de ropa te gusta llevar?
Yo prefiero la ropa cómoda.
No me gustan los vestidos.
Me gusta estar a la moda.

¿Sabías que...?

In general, Spanish-speaking countries tend to have more small stores that specialize in the sale of a particular item such as shoes, or men's and women's clothing. Recently **los centros comerciales** (*malls*) have become more popular; however, each store within the mall continues to be independent. Large department stores such as Sears or J.C. Penney are found only in big cities.

B. Where do you usually shop for clothes? in department stores? discount stores? clothing stores? through catalogs? In a small group, talk in Spanish about your shopping habits.

▶ —¿Dónde compras la ropa?
—Yo compro la ropa en las boutiques. ¿Y tú?

C. Do you look at clothing ads? Where are you likely to look for the kind of clothes you like? In a newspaper, a special magazine, or elsewhere? In your small group, continue talking in Spanish about your shopping habits.

▶ —Yo busco la ropa en las revistas de modas como [*name of magazine*].
—Me gusta mirar los escaparates.

Los adolescentes y la moda

Traditionally clothing styles came from Europe and then became popular in the U.S. Like many other businesses, however, fashion is now more international. Since World War II, the U.S. has become more and more influential in fashion. You know what U.S. teenagers wear, but what about Hispanic teenagers? Investigate the fashions in Hispanic countries.

Herramientas útiles

- Clothing Comparison Worksheet 7.A
- Spanish-language magazines (Some, such as *Elle* and *Vogue,* are published in both Spanish and English.)
- Catalogs from Hispanic mail-order businesses
- Spanish-English dictionary
- The World Wide Web
- A folder to compile your worksheets and materials for this project

¿Qué ropa llevan los adolescentes hispanos?

Individually or in pairs, use some of the items listed in the **Herramientas útiles** box to determine what Hispanic teenagers are wearing. Remember to consider Spain and as many Latin American countries as you wish! Then complete the information in Part 1 of Clothing Comparison Worksheet 7.A.

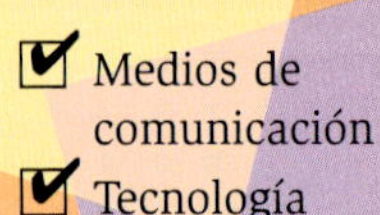

Conexiones

- ☑ Medios de comunicación
- ☑ Tecnología

¡Investiguemos en el Web!

Search the Web for Spanish teen fashions using both Spanish and English search engines. A Spanish search engine finds many documents that are available in both languages. For this search, a Web guide is particularly useful. Remember to use Spanish words, especially with Spanish search engines. It's also possible to find stores and boutiques by searching a particular region of the country. Some fashion magazines have Web sites, too. Remember to bookmark or record the addresses of the sites you like, so you can find them again later.

Keywords

"venta por correo"
moda
revistas
turismo

¿Sabías que...?

In many Spanish-speaking countries it is quite common for people to have their clothing tailor-made by **modistas** (*dressmakers*) and **sastres** (*tailors*). Men may have their shirts custom made by their favorite **camisero** (*shirtmaker*).

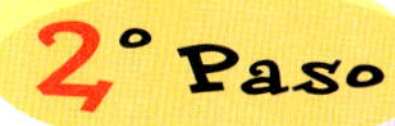

2° Paso ¿Qué descubriste?

In your group, discuss in Spanish what you have discovered, answering the questions in Part 2 on Clothing Comparison Worksheet 7.A. How are Hispanic and American clothes alike or different? What are the most popular colors and types of clothing? Refer to the Almanac for clothing and colors.

▶ Las adolescentes estadounidenses e hispanas llevan las faldas cortas.

El azul está de moda en México. El verde está de moda en los Estados Unidos.

Los primeros pasos

Before your fashions hit the runway, there are many decisions to make and many things to prepare. First, you'll need to decide the kind of clothing your group wants to create and present in the show. What about clothes of the future, or regional costumes, or simply casual clothes? You'll also have to decide how you want to present them.

Herramientas útiles

- Spanish-English dictionary
- Picture dictionary in Spanish or multiple languages
- Fashion Show Decision Worksheet 7.B
- The World Wide Web
- Worksheet folder

La casa de diseños

A. Fashion reflects a variety of styles and functions. In your group, think about and discuss in Spanish the overall idea of your fashion collection. Use the questions and suggestions under **Las ideas** on Fashion Show Decision Worksheet 7.B to come up with an outline of your collection. Be sure to record your decisions by checking the boxes or writing some additional ideas.

B. Fashion designers have to have a house name! What's yours going to be? Something unusual like **la casa de grunge** or something very impressive like **la casa de las mil estrellas?** Write the name of your fashion design house on Fashion Show Decision Worksheet 7.B.

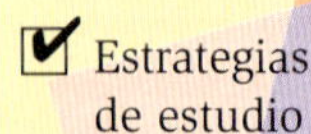

Conexiones

☑ Estrategias de estudio

La casa de las mil estrellas

2° Paso La organización del desfile

Keeping in mind the decisions your design house made in the **1er Paso**, discuss as a class—in Spanish—how to organize the show. Use the questions and suggestions under **La organización del desfile** on Fashion Show Decision Worksheet 7.B for help, and record your choices.

3er Paso El nombre del desfile

Next you need to choose a name for your fashion show. As a class, brainstorm names for the show. Vote for your favorite name and write your class's decision on Fashion Show Decision Worksheet 7.B. Put your worksheets in your folder.

¿Sabías que...?

Several famous high fashion designers are from Spanish-speaking countries. Oscar de la Renta, the famous women's clothing designer, is from the Dominican Republic. Paloma Picasso, daughter of the famous Spanish artist Pablo Picasso, is a well-known designer who specializes in jewelry. From Venezuela comes the world-renowned designer of women's clothes and perfume, Carolina Herrera.

¡A trabajar!

Being a fashion designer means you have a chance to do different things. Everyone will help design and assemble the fashions. Modeling, writing fashion descriptions, and so on, however, will be divided among group members to be sure that everything gets done. Keep the different choices in mind as you select what you want to do. You can't model and comment at the same time.

Herramientas útiles

- Materials such as cardboard, construction paper, feathers, cloth, rope, ribbon, plastic, glue, markers, tape, staplers, scissors
- Spanish-language newspapers, magazines, mail-order catalogs
- Spanish-English and picture dictionaries
- Fashion Show Decision Worksheet 7.C
- Worksheet folder

Los creadores y sus creaciones

Now comes the fun part, making those fashions! Everyone in your fashion design house will work together to create them.

A. Keep your fashion theme in mind as your fashion house brainstorms ideas for actual fashions in English. List the items you decide to create on Fashion Show Decision Worksheet 7.C. Then allow models to select what they will model. Write their names on Worksheet 7.C. You need to know who will wear each item, so that you can make the clothes "fit." Finally, decide on the order in which your house will show its fashions and record the information on the worksheet.

Conexiones

☑ Arte

B. You may use all kinds of materials to make your fashions—paper, foil, or leather, for example. You may make an entire piece of clothing or add to an existing one. In your group, make a list of who will bring in which materials to make your fashions. There are more suggestions in the **Herramientas útiles** box.

C. It's now time to actually create your collection. Don't forget to let the models try the outfits on before the show so you can make any necessary adjustments.

2° Paso Los modelos

At the same time you're creating your fashions, you need to decide who will be modeling them.

A. Step right up! Who's ready to be a model, or a **modelo**, as they say in Spanish? How can you resist the opportunity to wear some of these gorgeous new styles? On Fashion Show Decision Worksheet 7.C, write the model's name next to the item he or she will present.

B. Each model may wear one or more of the fashions during the show.

3er Paso Los comentaristas

When designers bring their fashions to the runway, they do more than show their designs—they describe and comment on them as well. A vivid description of each model's outfit will help capture your audience's attention.

A. In your fashion house group, divide the creations among pairs of students. On Worksheet 7.C, record who will comment on what item. In pairs and using the materials listed in the **Herramientas útiles** box, research how fashions are described. As you read, jot down expressions that you might want to use to talk about your own creations. Refer to the illustrations on the next page for ideas.

B. Then, work with your partner to answer these questions about each item you'll be describing.

1. ¿Qué tipo de ropa es?
2. ¿Cómo se llama el/la modelo que presenta la prenda (*item of clothing*)?
3. ¿De qué color es la prenda?
4. ¿De qué material es la prenda?
5. ¿En qué situaciones se lleva esta prenda?

de cuadros **de flores** **de lunares** **de rayas** **estampado**

C. In pairs, write an introduction for each of your fashion(s), using the information above. The example below shows one way the information collected might introduce a model and the fashion he or she is wearing.

▶ Aquí está Marcos.
A él le gusta jugar al fútbol.
Él lleva unos pantalones de rayas rojos y azules.

Un poco más

Expand the description by adding more details. The answers to these questions may help.

1. ¿Qué tiempo hace cuando una persona lleva esta prenda?
2. ¿En qué estación se lleva esta prenda?
3. ¿Por qué le gusta al modelo la prenda?

D. Practice reading or saying your part in the fashion show aloud.

El programa y la publicidad

Organizers of various kinds of shows often advertise their productions. A program will then help the audience follow what's happening. One half of the class will work on the Program Committee, the other half on the Publicity Committee.

Herramientas útiles

- Worksheets 7.B and 7.C
- Program and Publicity Worksheet 7.D
- Plain 8½" x 11" paper, poster board, and markers
- Newspapers and magazines that include clothing for teenagers
- Catalogs from Hispanic mail-order businesses
- Spanish-English and picture dictionaries
- Worksheet folder

1er Paso

¿Quiénes van a venir al desfile?

As a class, discuss in Spanish whom you want to invite to your fashion show. Do you want to present your creations to other Spanish classes, families, teachers, and so on?

2° Paso

El programa

Conexiones

- ✔ Arte
- ✔ Medios de comunicación
- ✔ Tecnología

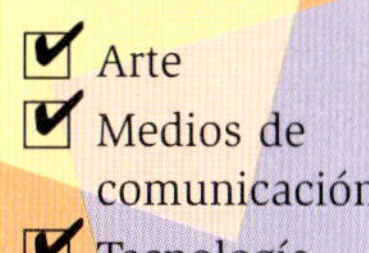

A. In your Program Committee, brainstorm a list of all the information that should be included in the program. Check with your teacher about your options for the place, date, and time of the fashion show before listing this information. Remember that Spanish speakers often state time according to a 24-hour clock for events such as this.

B. Now complete the information in Part 1 of Program and Publicity Worksheet 7.D. The information on Fashion Show Decision Worksheets 7.B and 7.C will also help you. As you make decisions about the program, remember to:

- Plan what the cover will look like
- Determine who is responsible for keyboarding and duplicating the program
- Coordinate your information with the Publicity Committee

Vocabulario útil

tener lugar	*to take place*
fascinante	*fascinating*
emocionante	*exciting*
el acontecimiento	*event*
el espectáculo	*show*

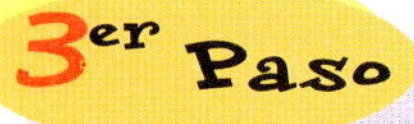

La publicidad

An important fashion show needs a good advertising campaign. It's time to get the word out! Decide how you want to advertise the fashion show—with flyers, through posters, or by some other means. If you want to use your school public address system or your school Intranet, read the suggestions in B and C on the next page.

A. In your Publicity Committee, using materials listed in the **Herramientas útiles** box on page 133, look for ads for various kinds of events—plays, concerts, and so forth. List the kinds of information these ads contain. Then discuss in Spanish the information needed to advertise your show. Complete the information on Part 2 of Program and Publicity Worksheet 7.D. Jot down any English or Spanish expressions that might help you write an ad. Make sure you coordinate your information with the Program Committee.

B. How about making a radio ad? If you have Spanish-language radio stations in your area, listen to some of their ads. Otherwise, try ads on English-language radio stations. Decide how you're going to present the information in your ad—through the voice of one announcer? in the form of a conversation? Write, practice, and record your ad. Don't forget to use background sound effects!

C. If your school has an Intranet, use it as a quick way to get the word out about your fashion show. Since not everyone can read Spanish, be sure to post your ad in English, too. Using the information you've gathered, write the details in both languages. Use descriptive words and/or art to make the ad more interesting. Before you send off the final copy, be sure to proofread it. Everyone in the whole school will read it!

¿Sabías que...?

Clothing sizes in many Hispanic countries differ from those in the U.S. Men's and women's shirts and sweaters are often marked 1, 2, or 3 for small, medium, and large. Although there are size conversion charts for items such as dresses, suits, slacks, and skirts, the sizes are only approximately the same. Shoes provide another challenge. Half-sizes and large sizes are hard to find. Shoes ordinarily do not come in different widths except orthopedic shoes and shoes for children. Refer to the size conversion chart in the Almanac.

Los últimos detalles

You're about to invest time and effort into the finishing touches that can make the difference between a good show and a great one—the music, the decorations, and a dress rehearsal to make sure everyone knows what to do.

Herramientas útiles

- Poster board or plain butcher paper
- Art supplies such as markers and construction paper
- Musical instruments, music tapes, or CDs
- Spanish-English dictionary
- Video camera or tape recorder and blank tapes

El maestro de ceremonias

Next up is finding a master of ceremonies to open and close the show and to introduce each fashion design house. Select one of your classmates for this role. Then as a class, brainstorm what should be included in his or her speeches. The master of ceremonies will then finalize the text on his or her own.

La música

Now form a Music Committee to select and list the music that you are going to play. Choose a committee member to tell the Program Committee what the music program will be. Arrange when and where you are going to rehearse. Be prepared to play the music during the dress rehearsal of the show.

Conexiones

- ✔ Arte
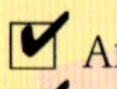
- ✔ Medios de comunicación
- ✔ Música
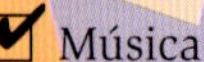

3er Paso

Las decoraciones

You will also need to form a Decorating Committee. Use your imagination and have fun! Try to coordinate the decorations with the fashions being presented. If it is necessary to change decorations during the show, be ready to practice this during the dress rehearsal.

4° Paso

El ensayo

It's almost time for the real thing, but first a rehearsal. There are many things to check out. Can the models present their fashions with the decorations in place? Are the fashions wearable? Is the music ready? Here's an opportunity to hear and improve your performance. Videotape or tape-record the rehearsal so that the master of ceremonies, models, and announcers hear their Spanish. There's nothing like hearing and seeing yourself to know what you've got down pat and what needs a little more practice.

El día del desfile

When you're preparing for a show, it seems as if the show will never happen. There are only more and more things to do, but **¡el día ha llegado!**

Herramientas útiles

- Spanish-English dictionary
- All the materials you made and gathered for the fashion show
- Worksheet folder

1er Paso

¿Está todo listo?

As a class, make the final preparations for your show. Arrange the decorations and the furniture. Set out the programs. Make sure the music is ready and get into your designer clothes. Have copies of your speeches handy in case you need them. If you have more than one task, make sure everything is laid out so you can easily move from one to the other.

2° Paso

¡Abran las puertas!

If you have guests, seat them and hand out the programs. Ready, set, music! Enjoy the show!

Vocabulario útil

¡Qué suéter más bonito!	*What a beautiful sweater!*
¡Qué fantástico!	*How great/terrific!*
... pasado de moda	*. . . old-fashioned*
... feo [hermoso]	*. . . ugly [beautiful]*
quedar bien (*used with clothing*)	*to look good on*
Este abrigo le queda bien.	*This coat fits him/her well./ This coat looks good on him/her.*

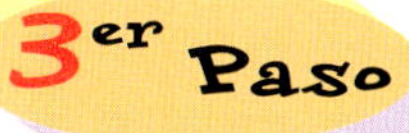

Las reacciones del público

During a fashion show, the audience often comments on what they like and dislike. If you're part of the audience, you need to be able to express and exchange your opinions. Use some of the following questions to help you discuss the clothing at the fashion show.

- ¿Te gusta [ese suéter]?
- ¿Qué falda prefieres? ¿La azul? ¿La negra?
- ¿Te gustaría comprar unos pantalones como aquéllos?

Un poco más

Take notes at the fashion show to expand into a newspaper review. Use what you have gathered throughout the project to help you. Pay attention to items such as these:

1. ¿Cuál es tu ropa favorita del desfile? ¿Por qué?
2. ¿Qué ropa del desfile no te gusta? ¿Por qué?
3. ¿Qué piensas de las colecciones?
4. Para ti, ¿cuál es la mejor parte del desfile?
5. ¿Hay algo del desfile que te interesa especialmente?

PROJECT

8

Pasemos a la meteorología ...

Have you ever wanted to control the weather? Well, here's your chance! Using your knowledge of weather and Spanish, you and your group will create a local cable news weather report for Spanish-speaking visitors to the U.S. You can present it live or on videotape. In the process, you will:

- Collect ideas from weather reports that you watch and read
- Write a local weather forecast covering several days and give temperatures in Celsius
- Create a weather map and other illustrations to accompany your forecast
- Stage a live, on-the-scene weather report
- Rehearse and present your weather forecast

¡Pasemos ahora a la meteorología!

Conexiones

In the process of making a weather report, you'll sharpen your skills in many areas.

- [x] Arte
- [x] Ciencias
- [x] Estrategias de estudio
- [x] Geografía
- [ ] Historia
- [x] Matemáticas
- [x] Medios de comunicación
- [ ] Música
- [ ] Salud y nutrición
- [x] Tecnología

Look for the **Conexiones** boxes throughout this project.

Warm-up: ¡Hablemos de la lluvia y del buen tiempo!

Herramientas útiles

- Climate and Weather Expressions Worksheet 8.W
- Map of the U.S.
- Portfolio (binder with pockets, a file jacket, or a file folder) for each student
- The World Wide Web

A. Are you a person who is fascinated by the weather and follows forecasts closely? Or do you prefer to be surprised by the weather? As a class, brainstorm in English the times when the weather is important to you. List your ideas on the board.

B. You know what your local climate is like, and you already know some weather expressions in Spanish. As a class, brainstorm the Spanish expressions you know. Record them on your Climate and Weather Expressions Worksheet 8.W under Expressions I Know. Then think of other words and expressions in English that you could use to describe your local weather. List them under Expressions I May Need.

C. As a class, discuss any special or unusual facts or characteristics of your local climate and weather in English. Record them on Climate and Weather Expressions Worksheet 8.W. File your worksheet in your portfolio for later use.

D. Now think about the ways in which weather affects your daily life. In a small group, brainstorm in Spanish the kinds of clothing you wear and the activities you do in different types of weather. Share your ideas with the class, and add to your list any new information you get from your classmates.

¿Sabías que...?

Because the majority of countries in South America are in the Southern Hemisphere, their seasons are the exact opposite of seasons north of the equator. When it is summer in the U.S., for example, it is winter in Argentina. South American weather varies from ours in other ways, too. High in the Andes Mountains, it's cold most of the year, despite being located close to the equator. In lower altitudes near the equator, there is no winter, just a hot wet season and a hot dry season.

E. Collect a few weather forecasts from your local newspaper and store them in your portfolio for later use.

¡Investiguemos en el Web!

You can find information about the weather in the U.S. and the world via the World Wide Web. A great variety of information is available on-line—maps showing entire countries and regions, satellite photos, three- to five-day forecasts, and details that are only a few hours old and are updated as often as every three to six hours. Using your preferred search engine, locate several forecasts of your local area on the Web.

Keywords

news
weather
"weather [+ name of area researching]"

Examinemos el estado del tiempo

Weather reports can range from simple statements of the temperature and local conditions to elaborate forecasts that give the long-term outlook and show weather patterns around the country or even around the world. As you prepare to give your weather broadcast, gather some ideas from weather reports you watch on TV and read in the newspaper.

Herramientas útiles

- Televised weather report
- VCR
- What's in a Weather Report? Worksheet 8.A.1
- Weather maps from newspapers or the World Wide Web
- Weather Symbols Worksheet 8.A.2

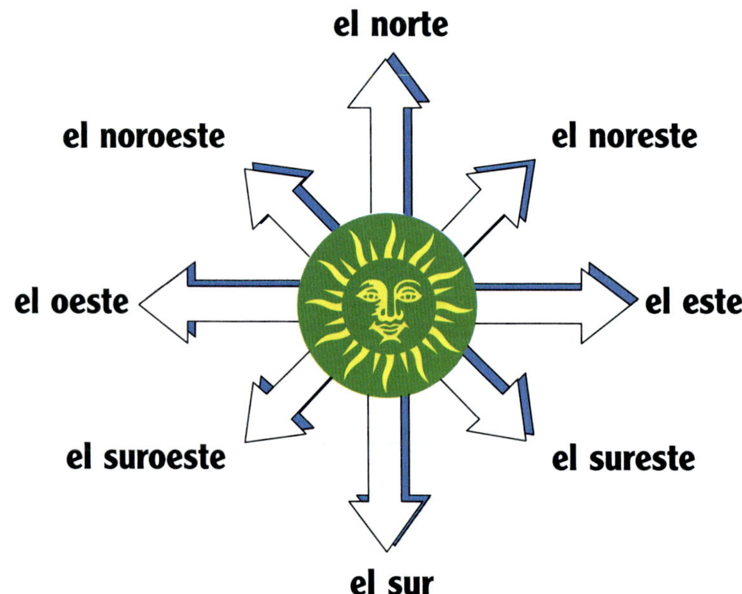

Conexiones

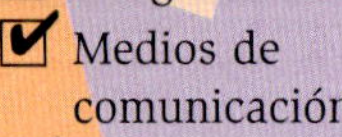

- ✔ Arte
- ✔ Ciencias
- ✔ Geografía
- ✔ Medios de comunicación
- ✔ Tecnología

Los pronósticos de su región

A. What kinds of information are given in a weather report? Watch one or two on television. If possible, record one so you can look at it a few times as you collect ideas. Fill out Part 1 of What's in a Weather Report? Worksheet 8.A.1.

B. In your small group, compare in English what you recorded on your worksheets. Then talk about which features of the weather reports you might like to include in your own broadcast. Fill out Part 2 of the worksheet together. Don't worry about details at this point; just gather some ideas that you can develop in the next part of the project.

2° Paso

El tiempo en español

A. In your small group, choose two or three different weather maps that members have collected. As you look at each one, see how much you can say about the weather in Spanish. Use the vocabulary and expressions you've gathered on Worksheet 8.A.1 for help. If you use any Spanish expressions that aren't already listed, jot them down. If there's an expression you don't know but want to use, look it up in the list of weather expressions in the Almanac or in a dictionary, and add it to your list.

B. As a class, discuss which expressions are proving most helpful. Be sure to add any new information on Worksheet 8.A.1.

¿Sabías que...?

In Spanish, there are many expressions used to try to predict the weather. Just as English has *Red sky at night, sailors delight*, Spanish has **"Horizonte claro con cielo nublado, buen tiempo declarado"** (literally, *a clear horizon with a cloudy sky means good weather*). To predict the length of the winter, people in the U.S. look for the groundhog's shadow. In Spain, they follow the saying **"La nieve de octubre, siete meses cubre"** (literally, *if there is snow in October, it will cover the ground for seven months*).

3er Paso Los símbolos meteorológicos

Weather reports in newspapers and on television generally use symbols to provide a quick visual overview of the weather. In your small group, look again at the weather maps you've collected, and gather some ideas for weather symbols you might want to use in your weather report. Add them in Column 1 on Weather Symbols Worksheet 8.A.2. Do you have other ideas for weather symbols? Draw them as well. In Column 2, write in Spanish what each symbol stands for. Consult your dictionary or the weather expressions in the Almanac for help. When you're done, add your worksheets to your portfolio.

¡Investiguemos en el Web!

The Web site of the National Weather Service provides a good deal of information about U.S. weather in the past, present, or future. It also provides definitions of weather symbols. Follow the path: "national weather service," weather maps, chart reference guide.

¡Formen sus pronósticos!

Now that you've gathered some general ideas and information for your weather report, it's time for the details.

Herramientas útiles

- Weather Report Decision Worksheet 8.B
- Newspaper weather reports from different times of the year
- Almanacs with information about average annual temperatures

1er Paso

¿Cómo quieren empezar?

How do you want to begin your weather report in Spanish? With your small group, look at the ideas you recorded on What's in a Weather Report? Worksheet 8.A.1 as well as the possibilities given below. Write a short introduction to your weather report on Weather Report Decision Worksheet 8.B. Have the news anchor introduce the forecaster. Then have the forecaster say "hello" and state the place, the day, and the date.

▶ Ahora nuestra pronosticadora, Graciela Gómez.
Buenos días, señoras y señores.
Éstos son los pronósticos para El Paso, Texas, para lunes, el 25 de mayo.

2o Paso

¿Qué tiempo hace hoy?

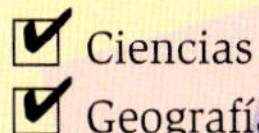

Conexiones

- ☑ Ciencias
- ☑ Geografía
- ☑ Matemáticas
- ☑ Tecnología

With your small group, choose the day of the year when your weather report will be broadcast. What's the local weather usually like at that time of year? If possible, check a newspaper weather report for the

time of year you've chosen, or use an almanac to find information about average temperatures. Then decide what the weather will be like on the day of your broadcast. On Worksheet 8.B, write in Spanish: the date you've chosen, the high and low temperatures in degrees Fahrenheit, and at least five weather expressions in Spanish to describe the local weather for the day you've chosen.

3er Paso

¿Cómo se mide la temperatura?

As you may know, most U.S. weather maps use the Fahrenheit scale to report temperatures. Your Spanish-speaking viewers will understand your weather report better if you give the temperatures in degrees Celsius (C). Use the Fahrenheit and Celsius Conversion Chart in the weather section of the Almanac to learn how to change temperatures from one scale to another. Convert the temperatures you provided in the **2° Paso** from Fahrenheit to Celsius. Check your results with your group and record them on Weather Report Decision Worksheet 8.B. From now on, give all your temperatures in Celsius!

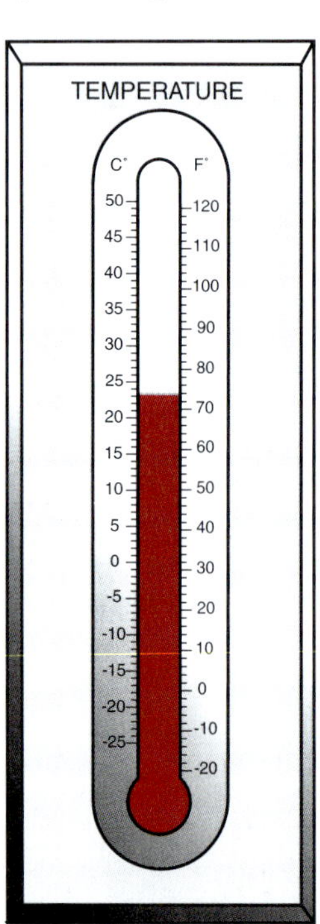

El tiempo del próximo día

A. What's the weather outlook for the next day? Your group's forecast should include some change in the weather. Write your ideas on Weather Report Decision Worksheet 8.B, and include at least five weather expressions.

B. An extended weather forecast (**los pronósticos meteorológicos**) usually outlines the weather and temperatures for the next three to seven days. On Weather Report Decision Worksheet 8.B, write a short statement in Spanish describing the general weather trends for the next three days.

Un poco más

Find out the times of the sunrise and sunset for the time of year you're covering in your weather report. If you live near a coast, include the times of the high and low tides as well.

Vocabulario útil

Está [nublado].	*It's [cloudy].*
Hay una posibilidad de [nieve en los Andes].	*There's a chance of [snow in the Andes].*
La temperatura mínima/ máxima va a ser [20° C].	*The low/high temperature will be [20° C].*
La temperatura mínima/ máxima fue [20° C].	*The low/high temperature was [20° C].*
La salida del sol va a ser a las [7.20].	*Sunrise is at [7:20 A.M.].*
La puesta del sol va a ser a las [19.37].	*Sunset is at [7:37 P.M.].*
La marea alta/baja va a ser a las [6.24].	*High/low tide is at [6:24 A.M.].*

¿Sabías que...?

The geographical variety in Latin America includes natural phenomena such as **el Lago de Nicaragua** (*Lake Nicaragua*), a huge fresh water lake that has sharks, and **el Lago Titicaca** (*Lake Titicaca*), located between Bolivia and Peru, the highest navigable lake in the world (3,812 m/12,507 feet above sea level). **El Aconcagua**, located in the Andes Mountains, is the highest mountain in the hemisphere. In addition, because of the fault line that extends from Central America to Chile, volcanic eruptions and earthquakes are not uncommon. Two major disasters occurred in 1985: the first was an earthquake in central/southeastern Mexico, which claimed more than 25,000 lives, and the second was a volcanic eruption in Colombia, which killed over 20,000 inhabitants.

Ilustremos el tiempo

From simple illustrations to advanced radar maps and satellite pictures, visual aids are an important part of a television weather report. They can help us to understand weather patterns or give us a quick overview of the most important weather information. A weather forecaster (**el pronosticador/la pronosticadora**) can also use maps and pictures for guidance during the weather report.

Herramientas útiles

- What's in a Weather Report? Worksheet 8.A.1
- Weather Symbols Worksheet 8.A.2
- Weather Report Decision Worksheet 8.B
- Poster board or foam core
- Colored markers, removable tape, index cards

1er Paso

Sus ideas

How can you illustrate the weather in your televised weather report? Before you look at the ideas in the following steps, review the ones you collected on What's in a Weather Report? Worksheet 8.A.1. In your small group, choose an idea you think would work well and discuss what you need to do to carry it out. Make a list of any materials you need, and divide the work among the members of your group.

2° Paso

Un mapa del tiempo

Conexiones

- ✔ Arte
- ✔ Ciencias
- ✔ Estrategias de estudio
- ✔ Geografía

A weather map (**un mapa del tiempo**) is a basic part of most televised weather reports. Your group is going to create one with removable weather symbols, so you can show changes in the weather over a period of time. If you're giving your weather report live, you'll need to create a map large enough to be seen easily by your audience. If you're videotaping your broadcast, you can feature close-ups of a smaller map.

A. With your small group, locate a map of your state or region to use as a model for your weather map. On poster board, foam core, or another sturdy material, draw the basic outline of your forecast area. Add your town and a few other important towns and landmarks.

B. Now make some symbols to illustrate the weather you've described on Worksheet 8.B. Look at Worksheet 8.A.2 for ideas about how to represent the weather. On poster board, draw, color, and cut out the symbols you need. To attach them to your map during the forecast, you can use removable tape.

C. Finally, create removable labels that you can attach to the map to show each temperature and day of the week you're illustrating. On blank index cards or pieces of poster board, write each temperature in degrees Celsius and each day of the forecast in Spanish. Attach them to your map with removable tape.

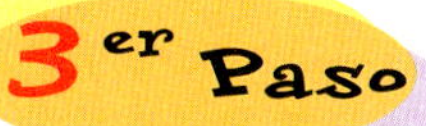

¡A ilustrar el pronóstico meteorológico!

Now give an illustrated long-term forecast. On a piece of poster board, draw a row of pictures illustrating the general weather conditions for each day of the long-term forecast you outlined on Weather Report Decision Worksheet 8.B. Include the high and low temperatures as well.

¿Sabías que...?

Even though Guatemala is small (only about the size of Ohio), it has a tremendously varied climate. This is due to the great change in altitude as you travel from the coast toward the center of the country. The climate is so varied, in fact, that nearly every crop grown in the Western Hemisphere can be cultivated somewhere in Guatemala.

El boletín especial

Weather reports sometimes go beyond merely describing the local and regional weather. When there are important weather-related events, on-the-scene reports help viewers understand the true impact of the weather. Visitors to your area will appreciate hearing about local events and activities affected by the weather.

Herramientas útiles

- What's in a Weather Report? Worksheet 8.A.1
- Props for staging a live report

1er Paso

¿Qué tiempo va a hacer?

With your small group, decide what kind of weather you want to show in your on-the-scene report: a snowstorm? a very cold or windy day? a heat wave? a thunderstorm or hurricane? Brainstorm ideas for staging your weather scene. For example, a fan can be used to create the effect of a strong wind; a shivering reporter dressed in a heavy parka can show how cold it is; or lights turned on and off can depict lightning. Use your imagination!

2º Paso

Un reportaje de la escena

Write a short script in Spanish for your on-the-scene reporter. Describe the weather and what it feels like to be there. Include some interviews with passersby as well. What do they think about the weather—rain for five straight days or three feet of snow? How do they feel? How do they stay warm or keep cool? How are they dressed? What are they planning to do in this weather?

Vocabulario útil

¿Qué piensa Ud. del tiempo hoy?	*What do you think of the weather today?*
¡Es un día muy bonito!	*It's a beautiful day!*
¡Me encanta!	*I love it!*
¡No me gusta para nada!	*I don't like it at all!*
¡Es insoportable!	*It's unbearable!*

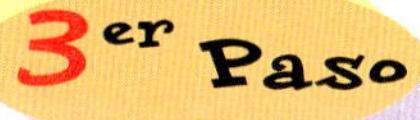

¿Algo más?

Look at the features you listed in Part 1 of Worksheet 8.A.1. Think of other features you'd like to add to your weather report. With your group, draw up a plan and divide the work.

Create a commercial for a weather-related product (umbrellas, ski resorts, air conditioners, and so on) to be broadcast during your weather report.

¿Sabías que...?

The Caribbean has the world's third highest number of hurricanes per year. This affects many Spanish-speaking countries, including Puerto Rico, Cuba, Mexico, the Dominican Republic, and all of Central America. Hurricanes are such a part of people's lives that legends and superstitions have developed around them. For example, there is a superstition in Puerto Rico that a good avocado harvest means no hurricanes will come to the island that year.

Y ahora las presentaciones

It's almost airtime. How are all the parts of your weather broadcast going to fit together? It's time to put the final touches on your work.

Herramientas útiles

- All materials created for the weather report
- Equipment to videotape the weather report

1er Paso

¡Organícense!

With your group, make the following decisions. Be sure to record them.

1. In what order are you going to present the different parts of your weather report? Make an outline, leaving a couple of lines free between items for additional notes.
2. Which group member will present each part of the weather report and special features? Record this information on your outline, and make sure that each person has a script for his or her part.
3. Are you going to give your weather report live or record it on videotape? If you videotape it, decide who will record each part. Add this information to your outline.
4. How are you going to change scenes and set up and use maps and other props? Videotaping will give you more flexibility in your performance, since you can record your report in parts and stop the camera at any point to set up a new scene. If you're performing live, make sure you know who's responsible for setting up materials and helping the presenters in each part of your report. Add this information to your outline.

Conexiones

- ✔ Estrategias de estudio
- ✔ Medios de comunicación

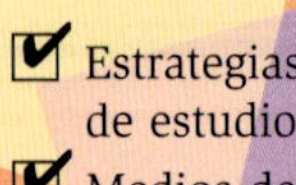

2° Paso Preparen sus comentarios

The key to a good performance is practice. Rehearse individually and as a group, using your maps, pictures, and other props. Have someone in your group coach you as you practice. Remember that your visual aids can help guide you through your weather report. Simply pointing to different symbols can remind you of what you want to say.

3er Paso ¡Ustedes son meteorólogos!

Now it's time for the evening news and the weather report! Flip the channels and compare weather forecasts!

4° Paso ¿Quién tiene razón?

So which forecast is accurate? You decide! You'll find out tomorrow!

¿Sabías que...?

Rain forests cover a vast portion of South America and parts of Central America, but did you know that there are also cloud forests? Cloud forests are mountain rain forests at high elevations drenched with permanent moisture provided by the clouds that pass through them. They exist on the eastern slopes of the Andes Mountains in Peru, Ecuador, and Colombia as well as Central America. Cloud forests may receive up to two meters of rainfall each year, or about 79 inches!

PROJECT

9

La buena salud

In this project your class will set up and run a health center. Its purpose will be to help educate Spanish-speaking clients about the benefits of a healthy lifestyle and how to maintain their health through nutrition, exercise, and so on. Working with a group of your classmates, you'll accomplish the following tasks along the way:

- Complete and label a drawing of the human body
- Research good nutrition and make a food pyramid
- Create a chart illustrating the health benefits of physical activity
- Design forms to be used by clients and health counselors
- Create a brochure to advertise your health center
- Set up and run your health center

¡A su salud!

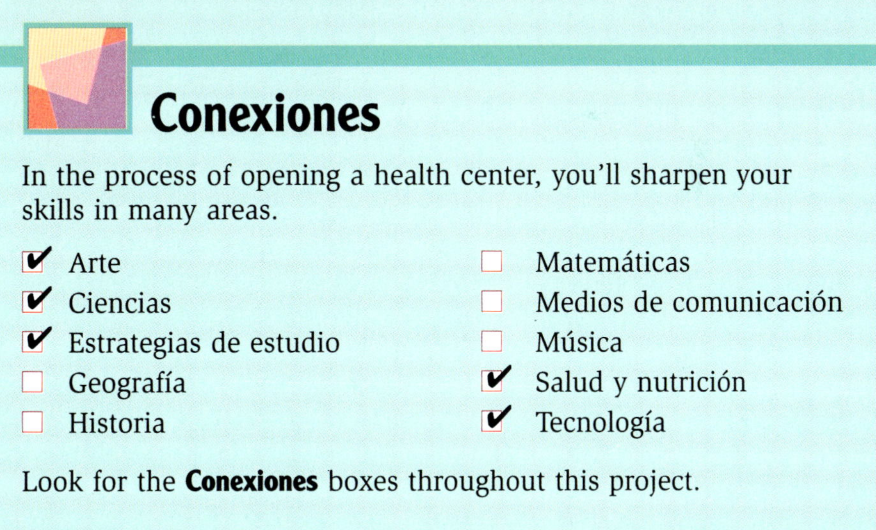

Conexiones

In the process of opening a health center, you'll sharpen your skills in many areas.

- [x] Arte
- [x] Ciencias
- [x] Estrategias de estudio
- [ ] Geografía
- [ ] Historia
- [ ] Matemáticas
- [ ] Medios de comunicación
- [ ] Música
- [x] Salud y nutrición
- [x] Tecnología

Look for the **Conexiones** boxes throughout this project.

Warm-up: Pensemos en la salud

Herramientas útiles

- Newspapers and magazines
- Cardboard, poster board, or construction paper
- Tape, string, or stapler

1er Paso Las fotos

Working in your group, search magazines and newspapers to find pictures that you associate with good health. They might include pictures of athletes, people exercising, or healthy foods, to give you just a few ideas. Gather a variety of images.

2° Paso Un collage de la salud

A. With your group, arrange the pictures you've found into a colorful collage showing many different images of health. Label as many of the pictures as possible with words and descriptive captions in Spanish.

B. Look at some of the other collages in your class to see how many different ideas, activities, and topics are associated with the word *health*. Then, have a short class discussion about what you've discovered.

3er Paso Los recursos de la salud

At the end of each section in this unit, you'll need to save what you've made and learned for later use in your health center. To organize this material, your group needs to make a large portfolio. (It should be about 2 feet x 3 feet when closed.) You can do this by tying, taping, or stapling together two large pieces of cardboard, poster board, or construction paper. Attaching a handle will make your portfolio easier to carry. Label your folder **Los recursos de la salud** (*health resources*).

¿Sabías que...?

In Spanish, there are many figures of speech that refer to parts of the body. For example, **hablar con el corazón en la mano** (literally, *to speak with one's heart in one's hand*) means to speak honestly about love or emotion. **Costar un ojo de la cara** means *to cost an arm and a leg,* but if you want to *pull someone's leg,* in Spanish you'd **tomarle el pelo** (literally, *to pull someone's hair*)! If you're up to your ears in work, you'd say **tengo trabajo hasta los ojos** (literally, *up to the eyes*). Finally, be careful not to **meter la pata** when you're speaking Spanish, or *to put your foot in your mouth!*

El cuerpo humano

An important resource in a health facility is an illustration of the human body. It's used to illustrate the bones, muscles, and systems of the body, such as how blood flows through the body or how food is digested.

Herramientas útiles

- Spanish-English dictionary
- Encyclopedia or anatomy book
- Colored markers
- Human Body Worksheet 9.A
- Health resources folder

1er Paso El exterior

On Human Body Worksheet 9.A, give Spanish names for the parts of the body that can be seen by looking at a person, such as nose, ears, arms, and toes. Before you consult your textbook or a dictionary, see how many you can come up with on your own!

2° Paso El interior

A. With your group, find an illustration of the human body's internal organs, such as the heart, lungs, and stomach in an encyclopedia or anatomy book. Make a list of eight major internal organs to add to the illustration on Human Body Worksheet 9.A. Then find their Spanish names and write them down as well.

B. Draw the basic forms of eight internal organs on the illustration on Human Body Worksheet 9.A. Refer to the illustration in the encyclopedia or anatomy book to be sure you locate them properly in the body. Finally, use colored markers to label the organs.

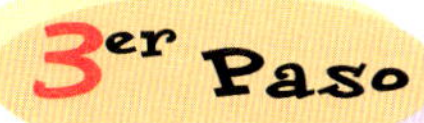

Los recursos de la salud

Add completed Human Body Worksheet 9.A to your health resources folder for later use.

¿Sabías que...?

Many sayings or proverbs enrich the Spanish language. Some of these relate to the features of the face. For example, a common way to urge someone to keep something quiet is to say, "**En boca cerrada no entran moscas,**" (literally, *no flies can enter a closed mouth*). A common saying that is the equivalent of "*two heads are better than one*" is "**Más ven cuatro ojos que dos,**" (literally, *four eyes see more than two*).

La nutrición

Proper eating habits are necessary for a healthy lifestyle. One function of a health center is educating clients about good nutrition. You may be surprised by how much you already know about eating sensibly!

Herramientas útiles

- Encyclopedia, health or science textbooks, and books about health and nutrition
- Spanish-English dictionary
- Colored markers or computer-drawing software, poster board, paper
- Nutrition Worksheet 9.B
- Health resources folder

1er Paso

La alimentación

In your group, brainstorm in Spanish a list of as many different foods as you can without using a dictionary. Refer to the food vocabulary in the Almanac to get started. You may be surprised at how much you know! When your list is ready, share it with another group in your class, and expand your list with ideas from the other group.

La pirámide

A. Nutritionists, people who study how the body uses different foods, have developed the food pyramid as a guide for sensible eating. It shows what people should eat to get the right amount of each food group. Look at the food pyramid in the Warm-up section. Write the different types of foods in Spanish on the pyramid in Part 1 of Nutrition Worksheet 9.B. Now record the foods you listed in the **1er Paso** in the correct section of the food pyramid. Where would you list **las judías verdes,** for example? Or what about **el yogur?**

Conexiones

- [x] Arte
- [x] Ciencias
- [x] Salud y nutrición
- [x] Tecnología

B. What is good nutrition? In your group, discuss in English what you know about the food pyramid and good nutrition. Then use colored markers or a computer with drawing software to draw a large food pyramid on poster board or a large piece of paper. Label each part of the pyramid with the Spanish name for the type of food that belongs there. Using the list your group created in the **1er Paso**, draw foods in each category on your pyramid and label them in Spanish. Display your food pyramid in the health center.

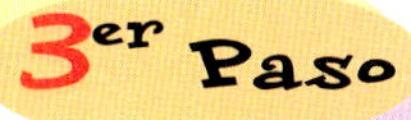

Las reglas

The bottom level of the food pyramid is the largest, showing that such foods should be eaten the most. The foods on the top level should be eaten in the smallest quantities. Using your food pyramid, create a list of four rules for healthy eating. Record your rules for proper nutrition in Part 2 of Nutrition Worksheet 9.B. Add your food pyramid and Nutrition Worksheet 9.B to your health resources folder.

Vocabulario útil

Se debe [+ *infinitive*].	*You should ___.*
Hay que [+ *infinitive*].	*It is necessary to ___.*
Tiene que comer/beber ___.	*You have to eat/drink ___.*
Es importante [+ *infinitive*] ___.	*It's important to ___.*

¿Sabías que...?

Dietary guidelines vary slightly from one country to another because of the different types of foods available in each country and the particular needs of the population. In Mexico, for example, a diet has been proposed to combat the effects of the heavy air and water pollution in Mexico City. It's called **la dieta anti-ozono** (*the anti-ozone diet*), and it includes especially large quantities of fresh fruits and vegetables.

El ejercicio

Physical activity and exercise are necessary for overall well-being. Your health center will give visitors information about how proper exercise can improve their health.

Herramientas útiles

- Encyclopedia and books about health
- Exercise Worksheet 9.C
- Nutrition Worksheet 9.B
- Health resources folder

1er Paso

Las actividades

A. There are many different ways to get exercise. On your own, list in Spanish five of your favorite free-time activities **(actividades para el tiempo libre)** that use physical energy. Write them in Part 1, column 1, on Exercise Worksheet 9.C.

▶ montar en bicicleta (*to go bike riding*)

B. Continue on your own on the same worksheet. In Part 2, column 1, under the **Actividades diarias** (*Daily activities*), write the names of three daily activities or chores that you think take enough energy to offer health benefits.

▶ cortar el césped (*mowing the lawn*)

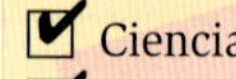

Conexiones

- ☑ Ciencias
- ☑ Estrategias de estudio
- ☑ Salud y nutrición

2° Paso Los beneficios del ejercicio

A. What are the health benefits of all eight activities you've listed? Decide which parts of the body are exercised during each activity. Record them on Exercise Worksheet 9.C in column 2 under **Las partes del cuerpo**.

▶ aeróbicos — el corazón
cortar el césped — las piernas

B. In your group, use the phrases below to compare your lists of exercises, activities, and health benefits. Come up with a list of four suggestions for getting exercise, and write them in Part 3 of Exercise Worksheet 9.C for use in your health center.

Vocabulario útil

Me gusta [+ *infinitive*].	*I like to ___.*
Es bueno para [la parte del cuerpo].	*It's good for ___.*

Un poco más

Use some of the resources listed in the **Herramientas útiles** box to find out how many calories are burned during each activity you've listed. Remember to include how long you must perform the activity to use that number of calories. Add this information to Exercise Worksheet 9.C. in column 3, under **Número de calorías/tiempo transcurrido**. Add the worksheet to your health resources folder.

Los formularios

Your health center will communicate with clients in various ways. You'll talk on the phone with them, interview them in person, and educate them with the charts and pictures you've made. But first you'll need to get some basic information from your clients by using a standard form that they will fill out when they visit the center. Such information will be used by doctors, nurses, counselors, the billing department, and so on.

Herramientas útiles

- Computer with a word-processing program
- Spanish-English dictionary
- Health resources folder

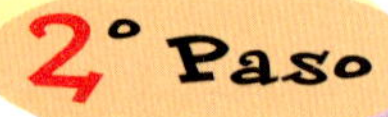

La información general

As a class, brainstorm a list of questions in Spanish that a receptionist at a health center might ask. Come up with at least five useful questions. Go over the questions to make sure you haven't forgotten anything important. Write the questions on the board.

2° Paso

Hacer los formularios

In your group, organize the information you brainstormed into a Spanish-language form. You might want to design it on the computer. Be sure to include blanks for the visitors to fill out and a space for the health counselor's comments. Since group members will take turns playing different roles, be sure to make multiple copies. Add the forms to your health resources folder for use in Section F.

Conexiones

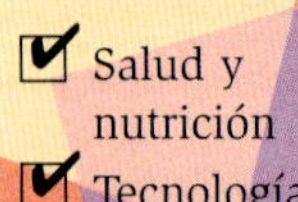

El folleto

In order to attract clients, it's important to advertise the services available at your health center. One of the best ways to do this is by making a brochure to distribute to the public.

Herramientas útiles

- Computer with a word-processing program
- Health resources folder
- The local telephone book with yellow pages

1er Paso

Los detalles del centro

A. Working in your group, come up with a creative idea for a Spanish name for your health center. It may be helpful to review the information in your health resources folder. Consider practical names (**El centro de la salud**) and clever ones (**Una manzana cada día**). Present your ideas to your class, and together choose one to be the name of your center. All of the groups will be working together in the center, so you need only one name.

B. As a class, decide on the schedule of your center. Will it be open only on weekdays? Will it operate any evenings in order to accommodate clients' school and work schedules? Come up with a list of hours **(Horario)** to include in your brochure. Remember to start with **lunes** as the first day of the week. Since you're making a schedule, use a 24-hour clock—1:00 P.M. is 13:00, 2:00 P.M. is 14:00, and so forth.

C. Next, decide what general information about your health center will need to be included in your brochure. Brainstorm this information in English, while your teacher lists it on the board. Remember to include the basic details about your clinic (name, address, and so on) as well as a description of its function, services, and so forth. Will you include any drawings or photos?

Conexiones

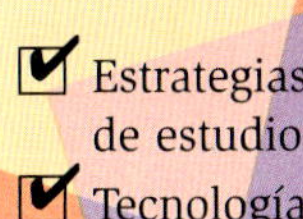

- ☑ Estrategias de estudio
- ☑ Tecnología

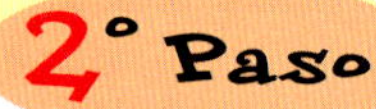

La organización

Divide the information you listed on the board among the groups in your class. Each group will be responsible for creating one section of the informative brochure about your clinic (for example, A. Our Mission, B. Nutrition Courses). Remember that you may need to invent some of the information, such as the Spanish-language address, phone number, and so on. A word processor may make the brochure look more professional. Use the resources in the **Herramientas útiles** box to help you, and be creative!

Hacer su folleto

When all the groups are finished, put your brochure together. Make multiple copies or ask your teacher to photocopy them for you. Put your brochures in your health resources folder.

Un poco más

Design business cards for your health center.

¡El centro abre!

Your health center is nearly ready to open. There are just a few final preparations to be made. When everything is ready, open the center.

Herramientas útiles

- Completed health resources folder, including worksheets 9.B and 9.C, food pyramids, brochures
- Poster board and colored markers
- Spanish-English dictionary

1er Paso

Los últimos detalles

A. Choose one group to make a sign in Spanish for the outside of your center. Post the name of the center and the days and hours it's open to the public.

B. Another group in your class should make smaller signs for the different departments of the center such as the reception area, waiting room, and counselors. Make your signs in Spanish, of course!

LA SALA DE ESPERA
(waiting room)

Los consejeros
(counselors)

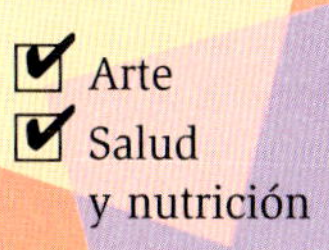

Conexiones
- ☑ Arte
- ☑ Salud y nutrición

c. Meanwhile, the remaining groups should set up the classroom for use as a health center. Chairs need to be placed in the waiting room, desks arranged for the receptionists and health counselors, and so on. Hang the collages and drawings of the human body and food pyramids in appropriate places in the classroom for use in the center. Finally, post the signs that the other groups have created and put the brochures on display.

2° Paso

¿Listos?

Within each group, divide up the roles of receptionists, health counselors, and clients visiting the center.

Receptionists (**los recepcionistas**) need pens and the forms you created. Health counselors (**los consejeros**) should take the remaining health resources from the health resources folder and sit at the desks placed in the counseling area to wait for clients. Clients (**los clientes**) should decide on at least two questions to ask the health counselors, along with the reason for their visit to the clinic. Is it to learn about health in general? to learn new exercises? to get nutritional information? Jot this information down in Spanish.

3er Paso

¡A su salud!

Your health center is open. Clients enter, talk with receptionists, and fill out forms. A few clients call the center to inquire about hours and receptionists answer.

▶ Buenos días/buenas tardes. [*name of clinic*].

Some receptionists can sit near the door of the classroom, handing out forms. Others answer phones. Still others receive completed forms and direct clients to the health counselors.

Health counselors ask clients how they feel and what they want to learn at the center. Using information from the food pyramid and from Nutrition Worksheet 9.B and Exercise Worksheet 9.C, counselors should suggest nutrition and exercise options to clients. After talking with a counselor, clients may then become receptionists or counselors, so that everyone gets to play more than one role. Be creative!

Vocabulario útil

los recepcionistas:	*receptionists:*
¿Cómo puedo ayudarle?	*How may I help you?*
Por favor, llene este formulario.	*Please fill out this form.*
los clientes:	*clients:*
¿Qué información desean aquí en el formulario?	*What information do you want here on the form?*
¿Cuánto tengo que esperar para ver a un consejero?	*How long do I have to wait to see a counselor?*
¿Hay que hacer una cita para ver a un consejero?	*Do I have to make an appointment to see a counselor?*
Me siento [cansado/a, mal, tenso/a, etc.].	*I feel [tired, bad, stressed, etc.].*
¿Qué ejercicios son buenos para [la parte del cuerpo]?	*Which exercises are good for [part of body]?*
¿Qué comidas son saludables?	*Which foods are healthy?*
Quiero aprender sobre ___.	*I want to learn about ___.*
los consejeros:	*counselors:*
¿Qué quiere saber?	*What do you want to know?*
[Las frutas] son buenas para la salud.	*[Fruit] is good for your health.*
[La natación] es excelente para los músculos.	*[Swimming] is great for the muscles.*

PROJECT

10

¡Vamos a abrir un restaurante!

Using your knowledge of the foods and cultures of Spanish-speaking countries, you and your group will open your own restaurant. In the process you will:

- Choose a type of restaurant and a name
- Decide on a location
- Decide on your restaurant's specialties
- Devise a decorating scheme and select background music
- Hire staff
- Design your menu
- Advertise your restaurant
- Prepare a shopping list of the foods you need to make your menu items

On opening day you will set up your restaurant in the classroom, greet customers, seat them, take their orders, and enjoy your food.

¡Buen provecho!

Conexiones

In the process of opening a restaurant, you will sharpen your skills in many areas.

- [x] Arte
- [ ] Ciencias
- [x] Estrategias de estudio
- [x] Geografía
- [x] Historia
- [x] Matemáticas
- [x] Medios de comunicación
- [x] Música
- [x] Salud y nutrición
- [x] Tecnología

Look for the **Conexiones** boxes throughout this project.

Warm-up: ¡Hablemos de la comida!

Herramientas útiles

- Cookbooks and magazines with recipes from Spanish-speaking countries
- Guidebooks for Spanish-speaking countries
- The World Wide Web
- Folder or portfolio to store your research

A. With a small group of your classmates, discuss in Spanish some of your favorite foods. Refer to the food vocabulary in the Almanac.

Vocabulario útil

¿Qué te gusta comer?	*What do you like to eat?*
Mi plato favorito...	*My favorite dish . . .*

B. Now think about any experiences you may have had with Hispanic restaurants in the U.S. Mention foods from Spanish-speaking countries that you have tasted or have heard about. Have you tried them? Would you like to? Are they different from your own favorite foods? Discuss your ideas with your group.

C. Using some of the resources listed in the **Herramientas útiles** box, find some information about foods or meals in a Spanish-speaking country. Write down in Spanish at least two interesting facts to share with your group. Then put them in your folder.

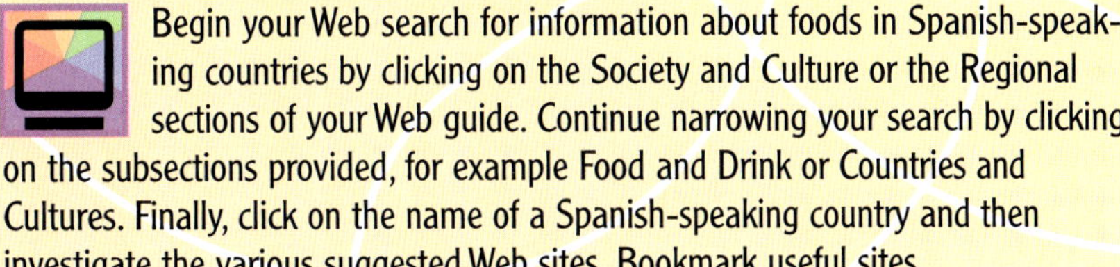

¡Investiguemos en el Web!

Begin your Web search for information about foods in Spanish-speaking countries by clicking on the Society and Culture or the Regional sections of your Web guide. Continue narrowing your search by clicking on the subsections provided, for example Food and Drink or Countries and Cultures. Finally, click on the name of a Spanish-speaking country and then investigate the various suggested Web sites. Bookmark useful sites.

D. In your group, discuss what you have learned about foods and meals in the countries you chose. Did anything surprise you? As a class, discuss any differences and similarities you have discovered between foods and mealtimes in the U.S. and in Spanish-speaking countries.

Un poco más

As homework or in your group, make a chart showing the usual mealtimes and the typical foods eaten at each meal in the U.S. and in one or more of the Spanish-speaking countries. The U.S. section should be in English, and the Spanish section in Spanish. Use the following table as a guide.

Meal/Comida	U.S.	[Spanish-speaking country]
breakfast/**desayuno**	time: typical foods:	la hora: la comida típica:
lunch/**almuerzo**	time: typical foods:	la hora: la comida típica:
dinner/**cena**	time: typical foods:	la hora: la comida típica:

¡Tantas decisiones!

When opening a restaurant, or any business, you must make many decisions—some big, some small. You are going to begin by choosing the type of restaurant you will open and deciding on a name for it.

Herramientas útiles

- Spanish–English dictionary
- Business Decisions Worksheet 10.A
- Portfolio or folder for storing worksheets

1er Paso

¿Qué tipo de restaurante?

Keeping in mind what you have learned about foods and mealtimes in Spanish-speaking countries, decide with your group what type of restaurant you would like to open. Are you interested in a café-style restaurant with outdoor seating or a fastfood restaurant for business people? a carry-out place at the beach? an after-ski coffee shop? Will your restaurant be casual or elegant? large or small?

2° Paso

El nombre del restaurante

A. Working with your group, brainstorm a list of adjectives in Spanish that could describe your restaurant. Use your dictionary or textbook for further inspiration.

B. Using your list of adjectives and your creativity, work with your group to invent a clever Spanish name for your restaurant.

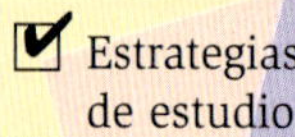

Conexiones

☑ Estrategias de estudio

3er Paso ¿Qué otras decisiones?

Now that you have made two key decisions about your restaurant, ask your teacher for a copy of Business Decisions Worksheet 10.A and record these and future decisions. Put the worksheet in your portfolio (or folder) for future reference.

¿Sabías que...?

Meals in Spanish-speaking countries generally have three courses: soup, the main course, and dessert. The main course may or may not be spicy, depending on the country. Dessert is often fruit. In some countries, people drink wine or bottled water with meals. Coffee is usually drunk after the meal and is much stronger than in the U.S.

El lugar perfecto

In opening a business, location is everything. Restaurants are often placed in or near well-populated areas to attract as much business as possible. Restaurants need to be easy for their customers to find and there needs to be a demand for them in the chosen location. It may be better, for example, to open a bakery-café near a movie theater rather than near a health club. Locating your restaurant near a busy intersection or a tourist attraction would also help bring in customers. Or perhaps you are a risk-taker and want to locate it in a lesser-known area.

Herramientas útiles

- Travel guides; maps of Spanish-speaking countries, regions, and cities
- Encyclopedias, travel magazines, guidebooks
- Business Decisions Worksheet 10.A
- The World Wide Web

Conexiones

- ☑ Arte
- ☑ Geografía
- ☑ Tecnología

Las posibilidades

A. Keeping in mind the type of restaurant you have chosen to establish, discuss the following questions in your group:

1. ¿Es importante la geografía para su restaurante?

   ¿Prefieren abrir el restaurante en el campo o en la ciudad? ¿En la playa? ¿Cerca de un río? ¿En las montañas? ¿En una calle del centro?

   ¿Cómo va a llegar la gente a su restaurante? ¿En carro, o hay transporte público cerca del restaurante?

2. ¿Quiénes van a ser los clientes del restaurante? ¿Los turistas? ¿Familias? ¿Gente de negocios?

B. Using the resources listed in the **Herramientas útiles** box, look for locations that fit the criteria you have established.

¡Investiguemos en el Web!

Use the Recreation or Travel section of a Web guide to link to listings of restaurants or Web sites of restaurants in cities in Spanish-speaking countries.

La decisión final

A. In your group, discuss the possible locations for your restaurant and decide on an ideal location together.

B. On Business Decisions Worksheet 10.A, write a brief description in Spanish of your restaurant's location, including important geographical markers. Explain why you chose the location. Put the worksheet in your portfolio (or folder) for future reference.

C. As homework or in your group, draw a map of the location, labeling landmarks, geographical features, and streets (in Spanish, of course!). Mark the exact location of your restaurant.

Las recetas

Many restaurants have one or two menu items that are their customers' favorites. In locations near the ocean, for example, lobster may be the specialty. In Argentina, where there is a great deal of cattle ranching, beef dishes are often the featured items.

Herramientas útiles

- Cookbooks and food magazines
- The World Wide Web

1er Paso

Las especialidades de la casa

Look through cookbooks or food magazines to find recipes for menu items you might want to feature in your restaurant. Put together a recipe book of dishes you want to serve.

¡Investiguemos en el Web!

You can find recipes on the Web! Use a search engine and the keywords to the right or click on the Lifestyles, Travel, or Culture sections of a Web guide. Then continue narrowing your search by clicking in appropriate sections such as Food and Drink, Recipes, or Restaurants, until you reach a list of Web sites.

Keywords

"comida de [name of country]"
"[name of menu item or type of food] + receta"

Conexiones

- ✔ Estrategias de estudio
- ✔ Matemáticas
- ✔ Salud y nutrición
- ✔ Tecnología

2° Paso La receta secreta

Work with your group to choose one item from your recipe book that you would like to feature as your house specialty. Remember to take into account the location of your restaurant.

¿Sabías que...?

Measurements for ingredients in recipes from Spanish-speaking countries may vary from those of a typical recipe in the U.S. For example, flour is usually measured by weight (in grams) rather than by volume (in cups), and liquids are measured in liters.

Un poco más

Imagine that your group has chosen the recipe that follows as your restaurant's specialty. Adapt it to the quantity needed to feed your customers!

Limonada

- *12 limones*
- *1.5 litros de agua*
- *300 gramos de azúcar*

Se cortan los limones. Se exprime el jugo de los limones en un jarro grande. Se añade el azúcar y se mezcla con un poquito de agua caliente. Se llena el jarro con agua fría y se mezcla todo. Se enfría por un mínimo de 2 horas antes de servir. Sirve a 6 personas.

A. Keeping in mind the size and the clientele of your restaurant, estimate the number of people per day who will be ordering your house specialty. If your recipe serves more than one person, divide the number of servings into the number of customers per day who will order the item. The result is the number of batches of the recipe you will need to make in one day. For example, the lemonade recipe above serves six. If sixty people per day will order lemonade, then the number of pitchers of lemonade needed is ten.

B. You now need to increase the ingredient amounts in your recipe. To do this, multiply the quantity of each ingredient in your recipe by the number of batches needed. Here are the calculations for the lemonade recipe.

Limonada

10 x 12 limones = 120 limones

10 x 1.5 litros de agua = 15 litros de agua

10 x 300 gramos de azúcar = 3000 gramos de azúcar

Vocabulario útil

multiplicado por — *multiplied by*
dividido por — *divided by*
igual a — *equals*

El ambiente

The ambiance, or atmosphere, of a restaurant is established subtly through the décor of the dining room, the lighting, and the background music.

Herramientas útiles

- Cookbooks and food magazines
- Magazines showing decorating ideas
- Guidebooks for Spanish-speaking countries
- Art books or pictures of artwork from Spanish-speaking countries
- Recordings of popular, traditional, and classical music from Spanish-speaking countries
- Business Decisions Worksheet 10.A
- The World Wide Web and encyclopedias

Vocabulario útil

la alfombra	*rug*
la candela/la vela	*candle*
empapelar	*to paper*
la losa, loseta	*floor tile*
la luz tenue	*soft lighting*
el papel pintado	*wallpaper*
pintar	*to paint*
la pintura	*paint (for walls)*
el piso/el suelo	*floor*
el piso de madera	*hardwood floor*

Conexiones

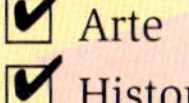

- ✔ Arte
- ✔ Historia
- ✔ Medios de comunicación
- ✔ Música
- ✔ Tecnología

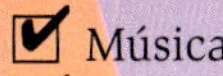

1er Paso Ideas generales

A. Keeping in mind the type of restaurant you have chosen, discuss the following questions:

1. ¿Qué colores quieren Uds. usar en el restaurante?
2. ¿Qué tipo de suelo quieren? (una alfombra, piso de madera, etc.)
3. ¿Cómo van a ser las luces? ¿Quieren poner velas en las mesas?

B. Draw a picture of your interior decorating scheme or cut out and compile magazine photos that reflect your ideas. Label the various elements in Spanish, using the preceding **Vocabulario útil** section as a guide.

2° Paso El arte

A. As homework or in your group, consult textbooks, art books, and encyclopedias to identify four pieces of art to decorate your restaurant.

B. Present one piece of art to your group and explain in Spanish or in English why you have chosen it.

¡Investiguemos en el Web!

You can also locate information about artists and pictures of their works on the Web. If you already have an artist in mind, use his or her entire name in your Web search. You can enclose the entire name in quotes or try first the last name and then refine your search with the other names. You may, however, want to browse at a museum's Web site for artwork from the country where your restaurant is located. If you find the work of an artist whom you like, try a search of that artist's name to find more works.

Keywords

name of artist
name of museum
museo
name of an artistic genre (e.g., cubism)

Un poco más

Write a brief description in Spanish of each piece of art you have chosen. Include the artist's name, the date of the work, and a brief description of the work.

3er Paso Poner la mesa

Using plastic or paper plates, create the china pattern your restaurant will use. Does your china pattern reflect the cultural heritage of the region where your restaurant is located? For instance, did you use Mayan or Aztec designs? Or is your design for a restaurant in Spain influenced by the historical presence of the Moors? Also choose the color and design of your napkins and place mats or tablecloths.

Un poco más

Make some sample napkins and place mats.

¿Sabías que...?

In the Caribbean, there are many popular and delicious foods. Rice, beans, chicken, and fried plantains are popular at meals. In addition, tropical fruits such as mangos, pineapples, bananas, and guava are common and often made into delicious fruit drinks.

La música

Now choose some background music to set the right mood.

A. What do you know about the music of the country you have chosen? Discuss your ideas with your group.

B. There are several ways you can find out more about music from the country you have chosen. Your library may have books and recordings. Using these or other resources, find one or two musicians, music groups, or composers who interest you and share information about them with your group.

C. With your music research in hand, consider the type of restaurant you are going to open. Include its clientele, location, and menu. For instance, an Argentine restaurant in downtown Buenos Aires might choose to play traditional tango music rather than the latest Top 40 rock hits, unless it caters to students. With your group, choose some background music for your restaurant.

¡A escribir!

Record your decisions about décor and music on Business Decisions Worksheet 10.A, and place it in your portfolio (or folder).

El personal

No matter how big or small your restaurant is, you need to hire a staff to help you run it.

Herramientas útiles

- Help Wanted ads from Spanish-language newspapers
- Interview Worksheet 10.E

Vocabulario útil

el cajero/la cajera	*cashier*
el/la chef	*chef*
el cocinero/la cocinera	*cook*
el camarero/la camarera	*waiter/waitress*
el director/la directora	*manager*
el/la recepcionista	*host/hostess*

Conexiones

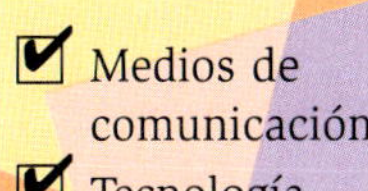

- ✔ Medios de comunicación
- ✔ Tecnología

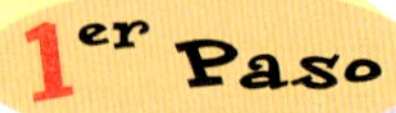

Los puestos

In your group, discuss the types of positions you need to fill (cooks or chefs, waitstaff, and so forth) in order to run your restaurant. Make a list in Spanish of the help you will need and what their duties will be.

Look at some Help Wanted ads in Spanish-language newspapers, in your textbook, or the ad shown below. Then write an ad for one of the positions open at your new restaurant. Be creative!

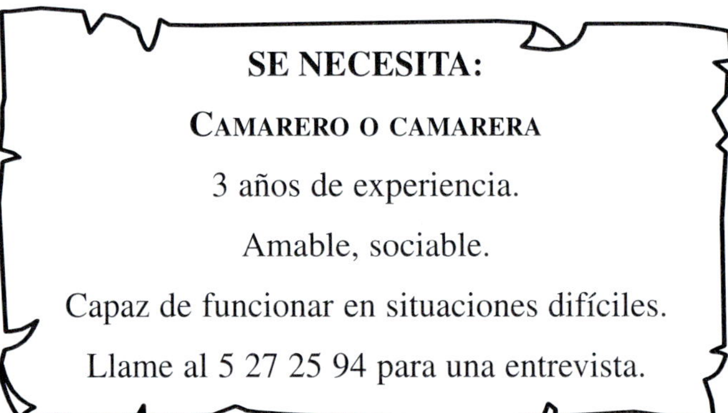

SE NECESITA:

CAMARERO O CAMARERA

3 años de experiencia.

Amable, sociable.

Capaz de funcionar en situaciones difíciles.

Llame al 5 27 25 94 para una entrevista.

Prepárense para las entrevistas

Prepare to interview potential employees. Find out each applicant's name, address, phone number, where he or she currently works, and for what position he or she is interviewing. With your group, make a list in Spanish of the questions you can ask to get this information.

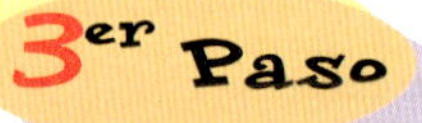

Las entrevistas

Take turns interviewing applicants from another group in your class. Record your interview notes on Interview Worksheet 10.E. Put the worksheet in your portfolio (or folder) for future reference.

El menú

Choosing dishes and creating the menu is an exciting and challenging aspect of opening a restaurant. Let your taste buds and sense of design run wild!

Herramientas útiles

- Cookbooks, food magazines
- Restaurant menus
- Currency exchange rate table from newspaper, bank, or the World Wide Web (see Almanac)
- Computer with drawing tool software
- Colored markers or pencils, paper

Vocabulario útil

asado/a	*roasted*
bien sazonado/a	*well seasoned*
cocido al vapor	*steamed*
fresco/a	*fresh*
frito/a	*fried*
jugoso/a	*juicy*
horneado/a	*baked*
picante	*spicy*
rico/a	*rich, delicious*
sabroso/a	*delicious, tasty*
salteado/a	*sautéed*
suave	*mild*
tostado, crujiente	*toasted, crisp*

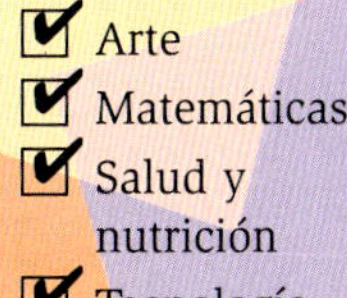

Conexiones

- ☑ Arte
- ☑ Matemáticas
- ☑ Salud y nutrición
- ☑ Tecnología

1er Paso

¿Qué van a servir?

In your group, use some of the resources listed in the **Herramientas útiles** box on page 189 and your recipe book from Section C for help in selecting at least two dishes for each category on your menu. Refer to the categories on the following menu as guides, and keep in mind the type of restaurant and location you have chosen.

Los precios

To appeal to tourists or business people from the U.S., you may want to give prices in both U.S. dollars and in the local currency (for example, **pesos** in Mexico or **pesetas** in Spain).

A. Consider how much you want to charge for your food and beverages, and assign prices in dollars to your menu items.

B. Now determine the currency of the country where your restaurant is located by consulting the monetary unit chart in the Almanac section of this book. Look up the current rate of exchange for this currency in a local or national newspaper, or use the Web search guidelines supplied in the Almanac below the monetary unit chart.

C. Finally, multiply the dollar price of each of your menu items by the current exchange rate, and list your menu prices in the local currency. For example, if a dollar is worth 136 pesetas, a $2.00 glass of juice would cost 272 pesetas.

3er Paso

Hacer el menú

A. How do you want your menu to look? Before you design your own menu, look at some sample menus for layout and design ideas. Bring in a menu to discuss with your group and compare it to the ones brought in by your classmates. Describe what you like and don't like about the menus.

B. Make a menu using paper, pencils, and markers or design it on the computer, possibly with the aid of drawing tool software. Remember to include the various categories (first course, main course, and so on), the items within those categories, and prices both in the appropriate local currency and in U.S. dollars.

Un poco más

Expand the menu by including a brief description of each item on it.

¿Qué les puedo traer?

Make a form that the waitstaff can use to take customers' orders. You may wish to use a simplified version of your menu, leaving space next to each item to check off customer orders. Be sure to leave some room at the bottom for the servers to total the bill.

¿Sabías que...?

Going out for **tapas** is a common Spanish custom. **Tapas** are appetizers, such as fish, cheese, meat, olives, and so on, that are eaten between meals. Spaniards often go out for **tapas** with family or friends in the evenings and enjoy discussing politics, work, and life in general.

Los anuncios públicos

One of the ways to get customers to come to your restaurant is through advertising. Printed advertisements range from flyers distributed on car windshields to newspaper and magazine ads. Radio and television ads are generally more expensive and complicated than print ads.

Herramientas útiles

- Local newspaper, radio, and television advertisements
- Advertisements in Spanish from newspapers or magazines
- Cassette recorder and/or video camera

Vocabulario útil

el folleto	*flyer*
la inauguración	*grand opening*
el lema	*motto*
la oferta	*special offer*
ubicado	*located*
¡Luz! ¡Cámara! ¡Acción!	*Lights! Camera! Action!*
el actor/la actriz	*actor/actress*
el anuncio	*ad, advertisement*
la banda sonora	*soundtrack*
cortar	*cut*
el director	*director*
los efectos sonoros	*sound effects*
grabar	*to audiotape*
grabar en videocinta	*to videotape*
rodar, filmar	*to shoot*

Conexiones

- Arte
- Medios de comunicación
- Música
- Tecnología

¡Abre el 3 de septiembre!

Café del Norte
97 Domicilio del Norte
Paraje Nuevo, Veracruz

Un café veracruzano que sirve pescado, pollo y carne, además de una variedad de especialidades vegetarianas regionales.

En la esquina de la Calle Norte y la Avenida de Santo Tomás.

1er Paso

Un anuncio breve

Create a flyer in Spanish announcing the opening of your restaurant. Include the name, location, and type of food served. Add directions to the restaurant, including a simple map.

2° Paso

El anuncio para el periódico

A. Read some restaurant ads from your local newspaper or Yellow Pages and from one of the Spanish-language sources listed in the **Herramientas útiles** box. Choose one ad to discuss with your group, answering the following questions:

1. ¿Qué información hay en los anuncios?
2. ¿Cómo es el tono de los anuncios?
3. ¿Qué palabras descriptivas hay en los anuncios?
4. ¿Hay arte en los anuncios?

B. Now write a brief, catchy newspaper advertisement in Spanish for your restaurant, using the ads you have analyzed as guides.

Un poco más

¡Ser director/a! Live announcements need to be simple and concise, but also lively and, in the case of television, visually interesting.

A. Choose a favorite radio or television advertisement and describe it in Spanish for your group, answering the following questions:

1. ¿Qué información hay en los anuncios?
2. ¿Cómo es el tono de los anuncios? ¿tranquilo? ¿animado? ¿romántico?
3. ¿Hay música en los anuncios? ¿Qué otros sonidos (*sounds*) oyes?
4. ¿Qué ves en los anuncios?
5. ¿Cuántas personas oyes o ves?

B. Write a script in Spanish for your own radio or television ad publicizing your restaurant. Add background sounds and music. Consider interviewing restaurant patrons or staff members. Write! Produce! Direct! Star! If you can, record your radio ad on audiotape, or videotape your television spot.

Al mercado

Before your restaurant's grand opening, you will need to order the food required to prepare your dishes.

Herramientas útiles

- The menu for your restaurant

1er Paso

¡Organízate!

Looking carefully at the menu for your restaurant, list in Spanish the categories of foods you need to buy to prepare each menu item (fruits, vegetables, meats, and so on).

2° Paso

La lista

What fresh food items will you purchase? List each item under the appropriate category, such as fruits, vegetables, and meats.

Frutas	Verduras	Carne
los mangos	las habichuelas	el bistec
las papayas	los tomates	el lomo de cerdo

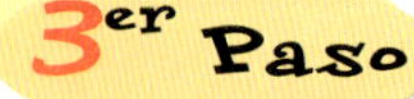

Las tiendas

Finally, next to or above each category on your list, write the type of store in which you will purchase the items. The food stores vocabulary in the Almanac will help you. In many Spanish-speaking countries, people shop at smaller specialty shops, which often have fresher food or a better selection than supermarkets.

Conexiones

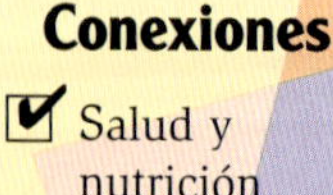

¿Sabías que...?

In many Spanish-speaking countries, people go grocery shopping daily. That way the food is fresher, and people have a chance to chat with neighbors and acquaintances. However, this is now changing as more and more people go to **el supermercado** (*supermarket*) to buy all their food in one place. Some countries even have **hipermercados** (*superstores*) that sell a vast selection of food and non-food items.

Un poco más

¡Qué servicio! Sometimes restaurant owners order their groceries to be delivered, instead of going to the stores themselves.

A. From your shopping list, choose two stores you need to visit.

B. Working with a partner, take turns calling the shops you chose and ordering in Spanish the groceries you need. Remember to be specific about what you are ordering and to include quantities. (Consult the Almanac section of this book for information on weights and measures.) Give your name, business address, and phone number, and discuss prices. Be prepared to present your conversation to the class.

Un poco más

As homework on the day before the grand opening of your restaurant, get together with your group and prepare the house specialty you will serve to your class the next day. Be ready to explain how the dish is prepared and served.

¡El primer día!

After all your preparations, the big day is here. You are ready to open your restaurant. **¡Felicitaciones!**

Herramientas útiles

- Your folder of materials created or gathered so far
- Tableware

Vocabulario útil

bienvenidos	*welcome*
la sección de (no) fumar	*(non)smoking section*
pedir	*to order*
las especialidades de la casa	*specialties of the house*
¿Qué hay en la carta?	*What's on the menu?*
¿Qué quiere comer?	*What would you like to eat?*
¿Y para tomar?	*And to drink?*
Yo le(s) recomiendo ___.	*I recommend the ___.*
La cuenta, por favor.	*Check, please!*
la propina	*tip*

1er Paso

Los actores

Working with your group and the group you interviewed for restaurant positions, choose roles to play in your restaurant. Remember to have some people play the role of customers!

2° Paso

Preparen las mesas

Set up a dining table for your group (push desks together if your classroom does not have tables). Decorate your part of the classroom with any materials you have created or collected. When it is time to open for business, turn on the background music.

3er Paso

¡Abran las puertas!

Finally, the dining room is ready. The hosts and hostesses greet the customers, who come in chatting in Spanish. The customers are seated and begin to discuss the menu. Servers come to the table to take orders and answer questions. The rest is up to you!

¿Sabías que...?

Tipping customs vary among the Spanish-speaking countries. In Ecuador, for example, a 10% service charge is automatically included in the bill. In other countries, service is included in the price of each item. Customers may round up to the nearest peso, dollar, and so on if the service is good, but no tip is required.

Spanish

Almanac

Table of Contents

Web Search Guide

Searching the World Wide Web

The World Wide Web[1] contains vast resources that would be hard to locate without **search tools** such as **search engines** and **Web guides.** These two tools allow you to search the Web for useful information by using **keywords** and phrases. You may have already done such searches in English. However, you will find that doing a search in Spanish is most productive if you use Spanish search engines, Web guides, and keywords.

Some of these words and phrases are provided in **¡Investiguemos en el Web!** boxes in individual projects, but you may need to find others more closely related to your specific topic. Brainstorm helpful Spanish keywords and phrases with other students before you begin your search. When you don't know a word or phrase in Spanish, look in a dictionary or ask your teacher.

Begin your search by **clicking** on the **search button** in your **browser's toolbar.** This will open a **Web site** that offers you a variety of search tools. One of these will probably be automatically chosen for you, but you can change the choice by clicking on the names of other search engines or Web guides. Usually, if you scroll to the bottom of the page, you'll find a pop-up box or **links** that bring you to browsers in other languages. Choose Spanish and click on the link or the **go button**. If the search tool you are using doesn't seem to have an option for Spanish, scroll back up the page and try clicking on a different search tool.

Once you have found a Spanish search tool, it's time to begin your search in earnest. There are two ways that you can do this. The first is to use a Web guide. Web guides select sites for you and list information in general categories with more specific subcategories. Using a Web guide is often the quickest and easiest way to conduct a search. Let's say you want to find descriptions of schools in several Spanish-speaking countries. Try clicking on "travel," then "destinations," then a continent where Spanish is spoken, then a country, then a city. If you are sent to a city's Web site, you will probably find a listing of schools or a way to search for them. Since each Web guide organizes its data differently, **paths** to the same information may vary.

The second way of searching the Web, using either a Web guide or a search engine, is to enter a **search term** in a **text field** and then click on a word like "go," "begin," or "search." This kind of search is useful only when your search term is very specific. If you search for the keyword "school," for example, your

[1] Terms in bold are defined in the glossary on the next page.

search engine will retrieve all pages that have the term "school" in them. Some of these pages will certainly describe specific schools, but others may include a description of someone's education or even schools of fish! If your search term is more than one word, you must put quotation marks around the entire term so that the search tool treats it as a single search item. If you don't enclose it in quotation marks, the search engine will look for each of those words separately and you'll end up with a lot of useless information. For instance, typing *Job Lane School* without quotation marks in an English text field would retrieve *all* pages relating to jobs, lanes, or schools.

No matter which search tool you use, you will eventually end up with a results page that has links to different Web sites that might or might not contain the information you are looking for. Often there is a short summary of the contents of the site. Scan these summaries, and choose the sites that you think will be most useful. If the results don't fit on one page, click on the link "next" at the bottom of the page.

You can also do more sophisticated searches than those described here. Although each search tool works slightly differently, the basic techniques for using them are fairly consistent. You can learn how each search tool can help you do more effective searches by clicking on terms like "help" or "advanced search."

Make sure you evaluate any sites you find to determine whether they are factual and complete. One way is to check several sites on the same topic or to check the information in a reputable print source, such as an encyclopedia.

Glossary of Web Search Terms

ADDRESS See **URL.**

BEGIN or **GO BUTTON** Appears next to a **pulldown menu** or **search term** box on a page. Clicking on it initiates the next action.

BOOKMARK Used to save a **Web site** address you want to return to. Click and hold on the bookmark menu and then choose "add bookmark." The names of other addresses you have saved will also appear in this menu.

BROWSE The act of moving through the **WWW** by means of **links**.

BROWSER A software application that allows you to access the resources of the **WWW**. Netscape Navigator and Internet Explorer are examples of browsers.

CLICK The action of depressing a mouse button while the **pointer** is pointing at a specific object.

GO BUTTON See **begin button.**

HOMEPAGE A page that a user or organization has designated as the first page of its **Web site**.

HOT SPOTS Graphics or areas of graphics that allow you to **click** on a **link** that corresponds to the graphic.

INTERNET A vast, worldwide network of computers and related networks that are able to communicate with each other by means of common standards.

KEYWORD See **search term.**

LINK Words or graphics that allow you to move within a document or to another document on the **Internet**. Text links are often indicated by words that are highlighted in a different color and/or underlined. Graphic links are sometimes outlined in a contrasting color. Links can always be identified by the way your **pointer** changes as you pass over them. Also known as "hyperlink."

LOCATION BOX Contains the **URL** of the page that you are looking at. This is the information that you will need to note to locate a page again quickly, or you can **bookmark** it.

NAVIGATION Similar to **browsing,** but is usually more focused.

NET Short for **Internet.**

NET SEARCH BUTTON A button on the **toolbar** that accesses a variety of **search tools.**

PAGE Document on the **WWW**; also referred to as **Web page**.

PATH The route one follows to arrive at a list of **Web sites** when using a **Web guide**.

POINTER Associated with movement of your mouse. It changes shape for different functions that are defined by the software program you are using. Common functions are an arrow to indicate where you are on a screen, a hand to indicate a **link,** and an I-bar to indicate that you can enter text.

PULLDOWN MENU Shows the options associated with that menu. **Scrolling** to the desired option and releasing the mouse selects the option. The resulting action may occur automatically or you may need to click on a **go, begin,** or **start button.**

SCROLL The act of moving through an electronic document.

SCROLL BARS Bars at the edges of a document that allow you to move through the document.

SEARCH BUTTON Similar to the **begin button,** a button that initiates a search.

SEARCH ENGINE A program that works with your **browser** to find information on the **Web**.

SEARCH TERM The word or phrase you use to find specific content in a **search engine** or **Web catalog.**

SEARCH TOOL A **search engine** (such as Alta Vista) or **Web guide** (such as Yahoo!).

START BUTTON See **begin button.**

SURF See **browse.**

TOOLBAR Graphics and/or text at the top of a **browser** that allow you to initiate certain functions by clicking on the graphics or text.

TEXT FIELD The area in which you type in text on-screen. For example, the place you type in your **search term** in a **search engine**.

URL Short for Uniform Resource Locator, and sometimes known as an **address.** URLs are used for identifying all content on the **WWW**.

WEB Short for **World Wide Web.**

WEB CATALOG See **Web guide.**

WEB GUIDE A database of **Web pages** and other materials on the **Web.** These pages and materials are reviewed regularly for their usefulness and appropriateness to the subject heading used in the catalog.

WEB PAGE A document on the **WWW**, often containing text and graphics.

WEB SITE A collection of related **Web pages** in a single location connected by **links.**

WORLD WIDE WEB A part of the **Internet** that allows users to exchange information using text, graphics, sound, animation, and video.

WWW Short for **World Wide Web.**

Spanish-Speaking Countries and Monetary Unit Chart

Country or Region	Capital	Monetary Unit
Argentina	Buenos Aires	Argentine peso
Bolivia	*Administrative:* La Paz *Historical/Judicial*: Sucre	boliviano
Chile	Santiago	Chilean peso
Colombia	Santa Fe de Bogotá	Colombian peso
Costa Rica	San José	colón
Cuba	la Habana	Cuban peso
Ecuador	Quito	sucre
El Salvador	San Salvador	colón
España	Madrid	peseta
los Estados Unidos[2]	Washington, D.C.	dollar
Guatemala	Guatemala	quetzal
Guinea Ecuatorial	Malabo	CFA franc
Honduras	Tegucigalpa	lempira
México	México, D.F.	Mexican peso
Nicaragua	Managua	gold córdoba
Panamá	Panamá	balboa
Paraguay	Asunción	guaraní
Perú	Lima	new sol
Puerto Rico	San Juan	dollar (U.S.)

[2] The states with the highest percentage of Spanish speakers are: California, New Mexico, Texas, Nevada, Arizona, Colorado, Florida, and New York.

la República Dominicana	Santo Domingo	Dominican peso
la Unión europea	_____	euro
Uruguay	Montevideo	Uruguayan peso
Venezuela	Caracas	bolívar

To calculate the amount of foreign currency in dollars, simply multiply the dollar amount by the current exchange rate. For example, if $1 = 100 pesos, then $20 = 2000 pesos (20 x 100).

¡Investiguemos en el Web!

From a Web guide, type "exchange rates" in quotation marks in the Search Keyword box and click on Search to locate Web sites that provide daily rates of exchange of currencies throughout the world. Once the list of selected sites comes up, review the descriptions and investigate sites that you think will have the exchange rate you require.

Clothing and Accessories

el abrigo *coat*
los accesorios *accessories*
la blusa *blouse*
el bolso, la cartera *handbag, purse*
las botas *boots*
los calcetines *socks*
la camisa *shirt*
la camiseta *T-shirt*
el chaleco *vest*
la chaqueta, el saco *jacket, men's jacket*
la chaqueta de plumón *down jacket*
el cinturón *belt*
la corbata *tie*
el cuello clásico *spread collar*
el cuello con botones *button-down collar*
la falda *skirt*
las gafas de sol *sunglasses*
la gorra *cap*
los jeans amplios *baggy jeans*
los jeans anchos *wide-legged jeans*
el overol, el mono *overalls*
los pantalones *pants*
los pantalones acampanados *bell-bottoms*
la playera *tank top*
el polo *polo shirt*
la ropa deportiva *sportswear, casual clothing*
las sandalias *sandals*
el sombrero *hat*
la sudadera *sweatshirt*
el suéter, el jersey *sweater*
el suéter de cuello de tortuga *turtleneck sweater*
el traje de baño *bathing suit*
el traje de entrenamiento *jogging suit*
el traje pantalón *jumpsuit*
el vestido de verano *sundress*
los zapatos *shoes*
los zapatos de tenis *sneakers*

Clothing Descriptions

el algodón *cotton*
bonito(a) *pretty*
de colores vivos *colorful*
de cuadros *checked*
el cuero *leather*
el estampado *print*
de flores *flowered*
la lana *wool*
de lunares *polka-dot*
de manga corta *short-sleeved*
de manga larga *long-sleeved*
la pana *corduroy*
la seda *silk*
el vellón *fleece*

Expressions

¿Cómo te queda? *How does it fit you?*
Me queda perfecto. *It fits me perfectly.*
¿Cuánto cuesta ___? *How much does ___ cost?*
Está muy de moda. ¡Es lo último! *It's the latest style.*

Size Conversion Chart[3]

Men's Suits

U.S	36	38	40	42	44	46
Europe	46	48	51	54	56	58

Men's Shirts

U.S.	14	14.5	15	15.5	16	16.5
Europe	36	37	38	39	40	41

[3] These are approximate conversions. There are variations among countries; U.S. sizes are also common in many Latin American countries.

Women's Dresses, Coats, Blouses

U.S.	6	8	10	12	14	16
Europe	36	38	40	42	44	46

Women's Shoes

U.S.	6	6.5	7	7.5	8	8.5	9	9.5	10
Europe	37	38	38	39	39	40	40	41	41

Men's Shoes

U.S.	7.5	8	8.5	9	9.5	10	10.5	11	11.5	12
Europe	41	41	42	43	43	44	44	45	45	46

Clubs and Organizations

el boletín *newsletter*
el club de ajedrez *chess club*
el club de alemán *German club*
el club de ciencias *science club*
el club de debate *debate club*
el club de español *Spanish club*
el club de esquí *ski club*
el club de fotografía *photography club*
el club de francés *French club*
el club de letras *literary club*
el club de matemáticas *math club*
el club de teatro *drama club*
el gobierno estudiantil *student government*
la organización voluntaria *volunteer organization*
el periódico *newspaper*
la sociedad de honor *honor society*

Colors

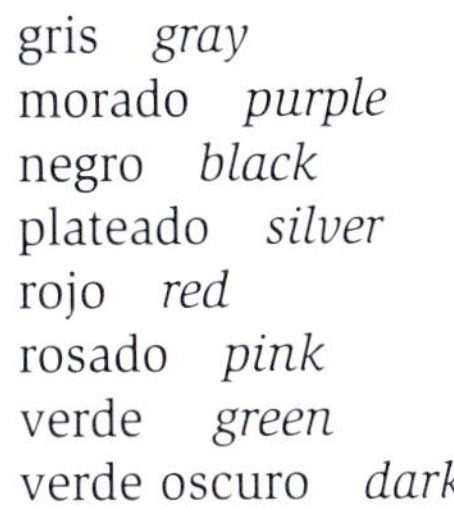

amarillo *yellow*
anaranjado *orange*
azul *blue*
azul claro, celeste *light blue*
azul marino *navy blue*
blanco *white*
café, marrón *brown*
dorado *golden*
gris *gray*
morado *purple*
negro *black*
plateado *silver*
rojo *red*
rosado *pink*
verde *green*
verde oscuro *dark green*

Food and Nutrition

el aceite *oil [for cooking]*
los alimentos congelados *frozen foods*
el arroz (frito) *(fried) rice*
el azúcar *sugar*
la banana *banana*
el batido *shake*
el café (con leche) *coffee (with hot milk)*
los carbohidratos *carbohydrates*
la carne *meat*
el cereal *cereal*
la cereza *cherry*
la comida *meal*
la crema de maní y mermelada *peanut butter and jelly*
los dulces *sweets*
la ensalada *salad*
la ensalada de atún *tuna salad*
los espaguetis *spaghetti*

la fresa *strawberry*
la fruta *fruit*
la grasa *fat [on meat]*
los guisantes *peas*
la hamburguesa *hamburger*
el helado *ice cream*
el huevo *egg*
la jalea *jelly, marmalade*
el jamón *ham*
las judías verdes *green beans*
el jugo, el zumo *juice*
la lasaña *lasagna*
la leche *milk*
la manzana *apple*
el melocotón, el durazno *peach*
el mineral/los minerales *mineral/minerals*
la naranja *orange*
las palomitas (de maíz) *popcorn*
el pan *bread*
el pan dulce *pastries*
las papas *potatoes*
las papas fritas *French fries*
las papitas *potato chips*
el pastel, el bizcocho *cake*
el pavo *turkey*
el perro caliente *hot dog*
el pescado *fish*
la piña *pineapple*
la pizza *pizza*
el pollo *chicken*
una porción *serving [of food]*
los productos lácteos *dairy products*
los productos perecederos *perishable foods*
la proteína *protein*
el queso *cheese*
la salsa *sauce, gravy*
la sopa *soup*
la tarta *pie*
el té helado *iced tea*
el tocino *bacon*
la toronja *grapefruit*
la uva *grape*
la (uva) pasa *raisin*
vegetariano(a) *vegetarian*
la vitamina *vitamin*
la verdura, la legumbre *vegetable*
la zanahoria *carrot*

Expressions

bien cocido *well done*
muy poquito, frugalmente *very little, sparingly*
poco hecho *rare*
término medio *medium*
¿Qué nos recomienda? *What would you suggest?*
Trate de comer menos grasa. *Try to eat less fat.*
Trate de comer más verduras. *Try to eat more vegetables.*

Food Stores

la carnicería *butcher*
ir de compras *to go shopping*
la lechería *dairy store*
el mercado *open-air market*
la panadería *bakery*

la pastelería *pastry shop*
la pescadería *fish market*
la tienda de comestibles *grocery store*
el vendedor/la vendedora *vendor [at market, and so on]*

Expressions

Quisiera un kilo de ___ por favor. *I'd like a kilo(gram) of ___ please.*
Una libra de ___. *A pound of ___.*
¿Cuánto cuesta? *How much does it cost?*
Cuesta ___. *That costs ___.*
Necesito hacer unos mandados, recados. *I need to run errands.*

Furniture and Furnishings

Los muebles *(furniture)*

la cama doble, matrimonial *double bed*
la cama individual *(twin) bed*
la cama (tipo) litera *bunk beds*
la cómoda *chest of drawers*
el escritorio *desk*
el librero *bookcase*
la mecedora *rocking chair*
la mesa *table*
la mesita *nightstand*
la silla plegable *(folding) chair*
el sillón *armchair*
el sofá *sofa*
el taburete *footstool*

El mobiliario *(furnishings)*

la alfombra *rug, carpet*
alfombrar *to carpet*
la almohada *pillow*
las baldosas, las losas *tiles [for floor]*
los carteles *posters*
la colcha, el cubrecama *bedspread*
las cortinas *curtains*
los cuadros *paintings*
el edredón *comforter*
empapelar *to wallpaper*
el espejo *mirror*
el estéreo *stereo system*
las fotos *photos*
la grabadora *tape recorder*
la iluminación *lighting*
la lámpara (de mesa) *(desk) lamp*
el papel pintado, el papel de empapelar *wallpaper*
las persianas *blinds*
pintado(a) *painted [of wall, furniture, room]*
pintar *to paint*
el radio *radio*
el teléfono *telephone*
el televisor *television set*
el tocadisco CD *CD player*

Las partes de un cuarto *(parts of a room)*

el armario, el ropero, el clóset *wardrobe, closet*
la pared *wall*
el piso *floor*
la puerta *door*
el techo *ceiling*
la ventana *window*

Expressions

¡Diviértanse como decoradores! *Have fun as interior decorators!*
Vamos a pintar ___ de color ___. *We're going to paint [object] in [color].*
Vamos a empapelar las paredes. *We're going to wallpaper the walls.*

Holidays

la bandera *flag*
la canción *song*
la celebración *celebration*
la ceremonia *ceremony*
civil *civil*
conmemorar *to commemorate*
la costumbre *tradition/custom*
el desfile *parade*
el día feriado *legal holiday*
la fiesta nacional *national holiday*
las festividades *festivities*
las flores *flowers*
los fuegos artificiales *fireworks*
el himno nacional *national anthem*
histórico(a) *historic*
militar *military*
la música *music*
el país *country*
el plato *dish*
político(a) *political*
religioso(a) *religious*
una reunión de familia *family reunion*
simbolizar *to symbolize*
el símbolo *symbol*
la tradición *tradition*

Some Holidays

el Año Nuevo *New Year's Day*
el Carnaval *Mardi Gras*
el Día del Trabajador (*May 1*) *Labor Day*
Jánuca *Hannukah*
la Navidad *Christmas*
la Pascua (de los Judíos) *Passover*
la Pascua Florida *Easter*
el Ramadán *Ramadan*

Musical Instruments

la armónica *harmonica*
el bajo *bass*
el clarinete *clarinet*
el fagot, el bajón *bassoon*
la flauta *flute*
la guitarra *guitar*
el oboe *oboe*
el piano *piano*
el saxofón *saxophone*

el tambor, la batería *drum, drum set*
el teclado *keyboard*
la trompa *(French) horn*
el trombón *trombone*
la trompeta *trumpet*
la tuba *tuba*
la viola *viola*
el violín *violin*
el violoncelo *cello*

Sports and Games

General Terms

el atleta/la atleta *athlete*
la cinta métrica *measuring tape*
el equipo *team*

ganar *to win*
el ganador/la ganadora *winner*
hacer trampa *to cheat*

la línea de salida *starting line*
mal, buen perdedor *bad, good loser*
medir *to measure*
la meta *finish line, goal*
perder *to lose*
el perdedor/la perdedora *loser*
¡Preparados! *On your mark!*
¡Listos! *Get set!*
¡Fuera! *Go!*
¿Quién gana? *Who's winning?*

Games

el dado/los dados *die/dice*
la baraja; el juego de cartas *deck of cards; card game*
el cronómetro, el reloj de arena *timer, hourglass*
la ficha *man (playing piece for game)*
el juego de mesa *board game*
el jugador/la jugadora *player*
el tablero *game board*

Sports

los (ejercicios) aeróbicos *aerobics*
las artes marciales *martial arts*
el básquetbol, el baloncesto *basketball*
el béisbol *baseball*
escalar *rock climbing*
la esgrima *fencing*
el esquí *skiing*
el esquí acuático *water-skiing*
el fútbol *soccer*
el fútbol americano *football*
la gimnasia *gymnastics*
el golf *golf*
el hockey sobre hielo *ice hockey*
el hockey sobre hierba *field hockey*
el levantamiento de pesas *weightlifting*
la lucha grecorromana *wrestling*
montar a caballo *to go horseback riding*
la natación *swimming*
pista y campo *track and field*
el remo *rowing, crew*

Expressions

¿A cuánto está el juego/el partido?/¿Cómo está la anotación? *What's the score?*
¿A quién le toca? *Whose turn is it?*
Me toca a mí. *It's mine.*
Le toca a [Anne]. *It's [Anne]'s.*
Te toca a ti. *It's your turn (to play).*
apuntar los tantos *to keep score*
¿Cuántas cartas necesitas? *How many cards do you need?*
(Yo) necesito [tres cartas]. *I need [three cards].*
contar los puntos *to count the points*
Muévete hacia adelante (atrás) ___ espacio(s). *Move ahead (Go back) ___ space(s).*
Pon tu ficha en el primer espacio. *Put your piece on the start space.*
el punto, el tanto *point*
la puntuación *score*
¿Quieres jugar un juego? *Do you want to play a game?*
Roba una carta. Toma una carta. *Pick/draw a card.*
Si paras en ___, muévete a ___. *If you land on ___, go to ___.*
Tira el dado/los dados. *Roll the die/dice.*
Ve a ___. *Go to ___.*

Subjects and Courses

la administración de empresas *business*
el alemán *German*
el álgebra *algebra*
el arte *art*
las artes industriales *industrial arts*
el baile *dance*
la banda (militar) *(marching) band*
la biología *biology*
el cálculo *calculus*
la cerámica *ceramics*
las ciencias naturales *natural sciences*
la clase de laboratorio *lab class*
la contabilidad *accounting*
el coro *singing/chorus*
la costura *sewing*
el deporte *sport*
el diseño *drawing*
el diseño técnico *technical drawing*
la economía *economics*
la economía doméstica *home economics*
la educación física *physical education*
el español *Spanish*
la filosofía *philosophy*
la física *physics*
el francés *French*
la geometría *geometry*
la historia de los Estados Unidos *American history*
la historia mundial *world history*
la informática, las computadoras *computer science, computers*
el inglés *English*
el latín *Latin*
las matemáticas *math*
la mecanografía *typing*
la música *music*
la orquesta *orchestra*
la pintura *painting*
la química *chemistry*
el ruso *Russian*
la sicología *psychology*
la reparación de autos *car repair*
la sociología *sociology*
el teatro, el drama *theater, acting*

Weather

¿Qué tiempo hace? *What's the weather like?*

Buen tiempo *(nice weather)*

despejado *a clear sky*
Hace buen tiempo. *It's nice weather.*
Hace calor. *It's hot.*
Hace fresco. *It's cool.*
Hace sol. *It's sunny.*
parcialmente soleado *partly sunny*
soleado *sunny*

Las nubes *(clouds)*

Está nublado. *It's cloudy. It's overcast.*
la neblina *fog*
la nube de lluvia *rain cloud*
nublado *cloudy, overcast*
parcialmente nublado *partly cloudy*

La lluvia *(rain)*

el aguacero, la tempestad *heavy shower, downpour*
el chubasco *shower (of rain)*
chubascos intermitentes *scattered showers*
Está lloviendo a cántaros. *It's pouring.*
la inundación *flood*
la llovizna *(fine) drizzle*
Llovizna. Está lloviznando. *It is drizzling.*
Llueve. Está lloviendo. *It's raining.*

Mal tiempo *(bad weather)*

la tormenta, la tempestad *storm, thunderstorm*
advertencia/aviso de huracán, tornado *hurricane, tornado warning*
la brisa (ligera) *breeze, light breeze*
la brisa fuerte *strong breeze*
Está cayendo granizo. *It's hailing.*
Está muy húmedo. El clima está sofocante. *It's muggy, sultry.*
Hace mal tiempo. *It's bad weather.*
Hace (mucho) viento. *It's (very) windy.*
el huracán *hurricane*
el relámpago *lightning*
la sequía *drought*
el tornado *tornado*
el trueno *thunder*
el viento *wind*
el viento fuerte *strong wind*

El frío *(cold weather)*

el aguanieve *(f.)* *sleet*
la escarcha, la helada *frost*
Hace (mucho) frío. *It's (very) cold.*
helado(a) *icy*
nevoso(a) *snowy*
Nieva. Está nevando. *It's snowing.*
la nieve *snow*
la ventisca *blizzard*

Temperature: Fahrenheit and Celsius Conversion

As you change temperatures from one system to another, notice that you are using opposite math operations.

To convert Fahrenheit to **Celsius**, subtract 32 from the Fahrenheit temperature and divide by 1.8.

To convert Celsius to **Fahrenheit**, multiply the Celsius temperature by 1.8 and add 32.

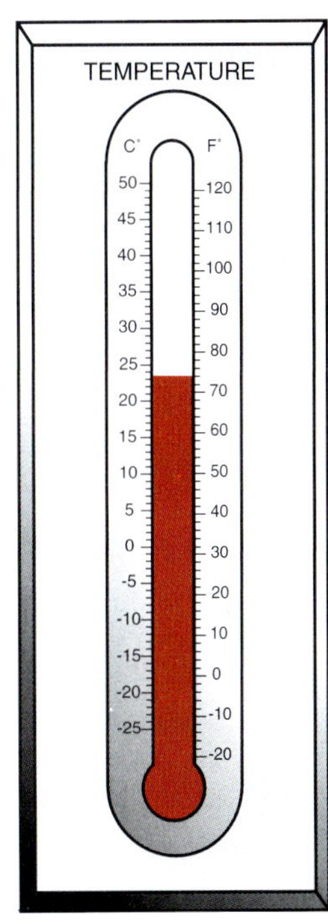

Weights and Measures

Weight

Metric	American/Standard
1 gram	0.03 ounce
1 kilogram (kilo)	2.2 pounds
28 grams	1 ounce
0.45 kilogram	1 pound
900 kilograms	2,000 pounds (1 ton)

Liquid Measure

Metric	American/Standard
1 liter	1.06 quarts
0.47 liter	1 pint
0.95 liter	1 quart
3.8 liters	1 gallon

Distance

Metric	American/Standard
1 meter	39.5 inches (1.1 yards)
1 kilometer	0.62 mile
2.5 centimeters	1 inch
0.3 meter	1 foot
0.9 meter	1 yard
1.6 kilometers	1 mile

Conversion

Multiply **miles** by 1.61 to get **kilometers**
Multiply **kilometers** by 0.62 to get **miles**

Multiply **inches** by 2.54 to get **centimeters**
Multiply **centimeters** by 0.39 to get **inches**

Multiply **feet** by 0.30 to get **meters**
Multiply **meters** by 3.28 to get **feet**

Multiply **yards** by 0.91 to get **meters**
Multiply **meters** by 1.09 to get **yards**

Spanish Equivalents:

el centímetro *centimeter*
el cuarto de galón *quart*
el gramo *gram*
el kilogramo *kilogram*
el kilómetro *kilometer*
la libra *pound*
el litro *liter*
el metro *meter*
la milla *mile*
la onza *ounce*
el pie *foot*
la pinta *pint*
la pulgada *inch*
la tonelada *ton*
la yarda *yard*

Writing Letters

Spanish speakers usually include the city from where they are writing in front of the date, even in a personal letter.

For the date, use **el** + cardinal number + month (lower case). Exception: For the first of the month, use **1ro** (**primero**), not **1** (**uno**).

In writing to another young person or a very good friend, **¡Hola!** (*Hi!*) is a fine greeting. The most common salutation is **Querido/a/os/as** (*Dear*). Don't forget to make it agree.

After greetings, Spanish speakers use a colon instead of a comma, even in informal letters.

Chicago, el 21 de septiembre

Querido amigo:

Hola. Me llamo Tom. Tengo 14 años. Soy de Chicago, Illinois. Tengo dos hermanos y un perro (estamos en la foto). Me gusta jugar al tenis, leer y nadar. ¡Hasta pronto!

Tu nuevo amigo,

Tom

As a sign-off for this letter, **Tu nuevo amigo** (*Your new friend*) is a good choice. You can use **Atentamente** (*Yours truly*) for slightly more formal letters, or **¡Saludos!** (*Regards*) in most personal letters.

XXX XXXXX
XXXX XXXXXXX XXXX
XXXX, XX
U.S.A.

Sr. Pablo Gómez-Lovo
Calle 26 No. 30-28
Calle, Colombia

In an international letter, be sure to include your country (U.S.A., Canada) below the city and state or province.

The abbreviation for *Mr.* is **Sr.**; for *Mrs.* it's **Sra.**; and for *Miss* it's **Srta**. The abbreviation for *Ms.* (**Sa.**) isn't very commonly used in Spanish.

Notes

Notes

Made in the USA
Middletown, DE
03 May 2020

fruitful and it brings him a lot of joy, the winds subside at the yellow house because of his newfound confidence. V's mom read "dream-catalyst," and was inspired by her daughter's story. She ended up opening up her own interior design company, it started off for local customers but the company expanded. She ended up getting her own interior design television show where she designs dream homes for the dreamers.

Caprice didn't have a daughter, she had a son, and she named him H. See she wanted to name him after his father, but after meeting V, she grew attached to the idea of H searching for his name someday, just like V did. H got good use out of the sky-fort as a child, in his teens he would sneak up with his boyfriend and they would stargaze together, this was before he was out, they would paint the starry sky just as Caprice wanted. The fairy shop never thrived financially, but it did get to a point where it could support itself and Caprice's family consistently. Caprice learned how to be selfish. She dated several suitors and left them when they started making her unhappy, she finally settled on a peddler who took her on his journeys. They traveled the world together.

Sunny signed on with the same agency as V and she became a success on her own. When Sunny made it big, she donated a large sum of money to the bookstore under Yippie's name. Mitty and Cheery lived in comfort for the rest of their days in the Artistic Alcove. No matter how busy the three would get, they always made time to read together on Sunday's in the shop. Thanks to Sunny's generous donation, Frivy was always well fed.

The barista and Elfin went on a trip together after Elfin came to her senses and broke it off with Heathen. They traveled to Europe to climb Mount Teide, it wasn't exactly a mountain, it was a volcano, but they did see the overdue view. Elfin went back to school as she planned and the barista decided to do set design for local theatre productions, not exactly Broadway, but she was just as happy with the local theatre company as she would have

'I guess I'm on my own now,' I thought to myself, 'I guess I only ever was.'

****

V did as she said she would and she got a kitten and puppy for her New York City apartment. V still had to tie up a few loose ends before she launched into her career, she decided to take the next few months to work on her music, and a very special personal project.

But to launch into the future, V had to look back into her past one last time. She mailed Yippie's lover, the cashier at the dress shop, their completed sketchbook. V felt the cashier deserved to see it most, and she thinks that is what Yippie would have wanted.

The sketchbook made the cashier cry, she ended up putting it on her bedside table beside the copy of "Wuthering Heights," she saw in the change rooms one night as she was closing up shop. It had stardust inside the front cover, the cashier knew who it was from.

It was something she needed to do. Something she was proud of. There was just one more place she needed to visit before she could truly move forward in her life. That involved confronting her past head on, so that she could see how far she has come.

****

I walked to the dead-end neighborhood with the yellow house in the cul-de-sac. I walked to the door and knocked on it. Out stepped my mother, she looked surprised to see me standing there.

"V, you're back!"

"I promised I would be back," I said, "but I'm not staying. I wanted to come back to the city one last time, I'm about to become a success mom! As I've told you over the phone, I got signed on with that agent. She says she thinks she can launch my career! But anyways, I have something for you," I handed feel."

We started setting up for the event. People began to trickle in over the half hour before our set. We noticed a few well-established agents come in and sit front row. We took note of them. Two of them, the woman and the non-binary person sitting beside her, were the agents of widely recognized vocalists. These agents didn't mess around, they found artists who would make hits. It was that simple. When the time came, the technicians dimmed the house lights and they focused a spotlight downstage onto the MC of the night. She introduced me to the room.

"I would like to welcome V to the stage, an up and coming vocalist who once sang songs by a ravine at midnight. V came a long way to perform for you here today, let's give her a round of applause," I couldn't think of a more accurate and genuine introduction. I had come a long way.

"Hello everyone," I said over the mic, probably not the most creative way to start an introduction, but I was here to sing, not to be charismatic, "I'm going to start tonight's set with a song about a cat, as ridiculous as it may seem. Most people sing about love or sometimes even politics," I turned back to wink at Wonder-Lust, "but I sing about defying archetypes and categories. I sing about personality types and characteristics; I am interested in human nature. Leery was the name of my cat. She was not a human being obviously, so I guess this song isn't about human nature per se," the audience chuckled, "but in a strange way, it is. Something about her seemed very human, she had trouble trusting others, as many do, but this anxious rebellion against trusting humanity caused her a lot of grief. When I had to leave her with someone else, it hurt me. It broke me actually, so, I dedicate this song to people, and cats, like Leery. I hope they can someday learn to trust, both others and most importantly, themselves, just as she did."

If one could record the energy circulating around a death

"Yes Wonder-Lust," I laughed, "For this one you can."

"I think that another person's brains defined the function of a brain so maybe yes, it is possible."

"Okay so, can an individual, such as myself, define myself? Or am I somehow not able to define my own characteristics as well as another person might be able to define me? I am biased to my own tendencies and I have preconceptions, assumptions I make about myself, assuming how I come across, and they may not be accurate."

"Okay, so here is my idea," started Wonder-Lust, "I think we can define ourselves by doing what we define ourselves as. Like if we define ourselves as empathetic, we should try and be helpful and understanding of others."

"That's true," I started, "Oh—I tripped on a rock sorry, okay, so we can call ourselves empathetic, but we'll only be accurate if we make a conscious effort to be empathetic."

"Yes, exactly," Wonder-Lust replied, "Okay, I can see where the 'yes, and' philosophy part is kicking in."

"Yeah, no kidding. Anyways I think, a lot of the time, we define ourselves. Even if we don't fit that description 100%, people start to define us by it too. For instance, if someone goes around and brags about their accomplishments and tells everyone how intelligent they are, everyone considers them to be 'the smart one.' Maybe they are, but maybe someone else, who has a lot more accomplishments, and a lot more reason to brag, does not brag as the one we call 'the smart one.' So, the humble counterpart is not regarded as 'the smart one,' rather 'the kind one' or 'the sporty one' because that's how they define themselves."

"Yeah, kind of," Wonder-Lust said, I was stumbling over my own feet, he had to pull me back to the left because I was leaning to the right. I felt as though we were going up a steep incline. I wasn't going to question it though, I wanted the destination to be a surprise, I was curious now. Wonder-Lust

"Alright V," I hated the sound of my name on his tongue, "You see that car over there? Red one? It still runs, it's in good condition too, but it's starting to get old and sometimes it breaks down. I can't imagine the car is worth more than a couple hundred dollars. I see you ride a bicycle, sounds like the car might be an upgrade. It has got a full tank of gas, and if you ain't got money, the very least you can do is ride it to the next city over and find yourself a proper job, or just a daytime thing. You strike me as the creative type, like an actress or a dancer."

"I'm a singer," I corrected.

"Yeah, a singer, whatever. Point is, I like trade better than sales and I've noticed you've got a couple of jewelry pieces on you there, now I take it you're a religious girl. Believes in God and keeps herself pure. Probably Catholic or something. Well if that be the case, then that around your neck is a baptism necklace, and those suckers usually go for a couple hundred dollars. Then on your wrist, I see a silver watch, probably a communion gift. Those can usually sell for a hundred dollars give or take. I was never the best with math in school, but it looks to me like you got yourself several hundred something dollars on your person. Plus, the bike. That could be a good trade for you. Imagine the miles you could cover by car. Don't get me wrong, she still runs fine, but she's gonna cost you sweetheart, and I think that exchange pays the price."

"You want to trade my watch and necklace for the car?" I questioned.

"Yes, ma'am, and the bike too," stated Sullen with a sly grin plastered onto his face.

I looked at the car and noticed the hood was propped open. "May I ask why the hood is propped open if it's in such good condition?" I asked impatiently.

"Just filling up the windshield wiper fluids. Forgot to close it from this morning. It's in pretty good condition. Could take

you wherever you want to go as long as you put some gas in her."

The offer seemed disingenuous, and I was hesitant to accept. Something about this exchange seemed dishonest. Sullen did not appear to be very trustworthy, and I couldn't say that I all that much liked him. But being a peddler was a lot of work, and it was draining to peddle from one location to the next. I wanted to travel vast distances, but I was struggling to do so by bike. I decided to do business with Sullen. I needed a car, I needed mobility. I was not getting anywhere in my current predicament.

"Okay Sullen," I said, "You have yourself a deal."

"Excellent," said the devious fellow. He extended his hand, not to shake mine to confirm the deal, but rather he outstretched his fingers demanding the necklace. I mirrored his informal method of conducting business with the same incivility.

"First the keys," I demanded.

"Clever girl," said the man, "but I'm not stupid. If I give you the keys, you'll make a break for it. You have the car leaving me with the bike and no jewelry, and I lose. Give me the necklace, and I give you the keys. That's the way it'll go."

"Oh no," I retorted, "If I give you the necklace, you will go inside and never come back out. I'll start banging on your door, and you'll call the police and have me arrested for harassment and deny the deal occurred."

"Then you start crying that I stole your little baptism necklace and they search my house and find it. Then who gets screwed, young lady?"

"Here," I said, handing him my watch, "Go get the keys, and I'll give you the necklace. I'm an honest woman. I always keep my word."

"Keys were in the ignition the whole time," said Sullen slyly, I felt embarrassed not to have noticed. "I knew you were

call yourself Spontaneous again if you really wanted to. It will just take a little more honey in your morning coffee." I nodded at him as he stared back at me perplexed. I hoped he would consider my notion. I rode off.

****

Sullen is not a nice man, nor is he particularly apt. His harshened demeanor fostered by years of dealing by unfair trade led by cruel incentives had left him quite experienced in the discipline of scheming. When a person is swindled by another, they have one of two options; they may pity the scammer or learn how to scheme. Sullen selected the latter. Yes, the car was not in the best of shape, but he knew it was still kicking. The vehicle would take V a long distance before completely buckling. The tires were inflated, the oil was newly changed. In fact, he might have been able to sell the vehicle in its current state for more than what he accepted from V. You may ask then dear reader, why would Sullen trade the car off so willingly? Is Sullen truly an honorable person after all? Is he simply misunderstood or significantly underestimated? Or, did he have another unknown motive in trading the vehicle? To answer your question, dear reader, Sullen believes the deal was still in his favor, but why? Why did he feel so compelled to trade off a car in fair condition? A vehicle of some value?

As he watched V travel off in the little red car down the dusty country road, Sullen smirked to himself.

"Stupid girl," he grinned, "In a couple hours, that car will smell like decay and rot. Won't be worth a damn thing."

Before we proceed onward, and before we learn what Sullen meant by this statement, let us give this shrinker a little redemption. It very well may be the first time anyone has attempted to give him any. Sullen is a shrinker, and a schemer, but he was not always this way. In fact, some might have regarded him as a reasonably honest man. Now mind you, he is not above lying by omission, but the little minded man holds true

to his belief that if a person is smart enough to ask the right question, he should respond with a truthful answer. Though he did not confess all of the statements a truthful person might, the statements he did make were all—for the most part—true. Sullen really was once Spontaneous. He was one of those 'creative types' himself. He was a man of the stage. An actor. To be more specific, he was a comic actor. Some might consider this ironic when considering his now stoic demeanor. Believe it or not, it is true, he was once quite the comedian.

Sullen once liked to make others laugh. He would amuse crowds of hundreds, in fact, he was regarded as quite talented. Though just as an artist has their fans, Sullen also had his fair share of critics to offset their support. Oh, dear reader, and did he have his critics. His most influential critic was his father. His father wanted him to go into construction. The boy wanted nothing more than to be a comedian, maybe do some animation voice-overs, perhaps land a role in a comedy series on a television network. He was good at his craft, but the boy was bullied into practicality. He is not big on reading, neither is Yippie, though Sullen cannot think critically the way Yippie can. He does not read, not because he prefers to learn through shared life experience, but instead because he puts very little value into learning and lessons.

Sullen rejected his father's wish that he pursue a fruitless career in construction. This isolated him from his family, but he did not view this isolation as freeing, nor did he take it as an opportunity to rise above; instead, he regarded the rejection as a punishment. An ill-humored omen from the gods. He instead decided to live off of the land. So, he bought some chickens and a few cows. He bought a shotgun for hunting and a pair of riding boots, and he built himself a little house off of a small patch of farmland with money he loaned out from the bank. When the farm didn't yield enough to pay its land tax, he decided to convert the little house into a pawn shop. Sullen bartered and

sold off others prized possessions; he scammed people out of their valuables. He got by off of others miseries. He quickly forgot his dream of becoming a comedian; instead, he made his clients the fools, and he assigned himself as the remorseless crowd.

Let us not hate Sullen, instead, let us pity him. While he laughs in the hours of the day, he lies awake in the hours of the night. He has no one but his pillow for company, no one but his alarm to wake him.

****

The car ran smoothly. Sullen was even kind enough to trade it off with a full tank of gas. It had been twenty minutes now since I had last spoken to Sullen. The country road had no speed limit. I could only imagine how long it would have taken to travel as far as I did if I was still a peddler. Though at present I didn't miss my bike, I knew that eventually I would. Being a peddler was a challenge, but one of its significant perks was that it provided the opportunity to see the world up close. In this car, the land I whizzed past became blurred and nonspecific. The faster I went, the less I saw of the world.

When I walked, I saw the ladybugs and heard the squirrels climbing up tree trunks. As a peddler, I scared away the birds before I could get a good glimpse of them, but I saw other pedestrians and waved to them. I saw the cars whizzing by, I saw the details of Sullen's porch and the pebbles on the gravel sideroads. Though in the car, I saw nothing but the vast country road ahead and blurred green fields to my left and right. I saw other vehicles in limited detail and I vaguely noticed the light from the lamp posts above me. I counted the headlights of other cars as they zoomed past. I saw the electrical wires that outlined my view of the sky, but I did not see the robins that perched themselves on them. The car had heat and air conditioning; I was relieved to find that both still worked. The radio was also in good condition, but only static

played on the channels on these country roads.

I thought for a moment about Sullen. Perhaps he truly was a good person, after all, trading a car of this condition for a necklace and a watch was a deal I benefited greatly from.

'It's almost too good to be true,' I thought to myself, but soon I realized I was right. The deal was too good to be true; I began to notice a squeaking I supposed was sounding from the engine.

'Great,' I thought to myself, 'Something is wrong with the car after all.'

I was unsure of what the noise was precisely, but I knew better than to assume it was something to be ignored. It appeared to be coming from the front of the car.

'There's probably something wrong with the engine, but I can't do anything about it now,' I thought to myself. I kept driving, but the squeaking persisted. I contemplated pulling over. Up ahead I noticed a parking lot belonging to a tiny grocery store, I decided to pull into it so I could check the engine. The squeaking kept getting louder.

'What is that?' I thought again. I looked to the grocery store and saw that I was the only one present in the lot, well, with the exception of the occasional pedestrian that would walk past the shop. It seemed like this was a popular path for the locals.

I was sure that there must be a convenience store or something of the kind up ahead, though that was not my main concern. I wanted to figure out what the source of the sound was. I propped open the hood and peered inside. I did not know a lot about cars, so the act of checking the engine was sort of pointless. I suppose I was just checking to see if anything was overtly wrong, like if the engine was smoking or if there was clearly something missing. I saw nothing noticeably wrong to my untrained eye, and yet the squeaking persisted. I was not sure what I should do. I was puzzled that

the squeaking would continue even after the car was turned off. I was not a car expert by any means, though I figured it was safe to assume that the squeaking would cease if the vehicle were not running especially if the problem was with the engine. I scratched my head, I hadn't the slightest idea of what that sound could be. What had I done? I traded my baptism necklace for a car like this. How could I be so foolish? Just then, the squeaking stopped.

'How peculiar,' I thought to myself. I decided that my best course of action was to sit idle and wait until I began to hear the squeaking start up again. I sat in the car and I decided I would read a little. I had grown quite tired, and I figured I could use this predicament to my advantage and take a break from driving. I realized then that I no longer had a book to read. I chuckled to myself recalling the events of the evening proceeding this, down in the Artistic Alcove back in the city of conformity.

Just then I realized I had forgotten to look at the book Yippie traded me for my copy of "Wuthering Heights." Curiosity struck me, I realized then that I traded books with a person who did not know how to read, nor did they agree with the concept of reading. I laughed at the thought. I decided to examine the book to ease my curiosity. I reached into my backpack and pulled out the little black book Yippie presented me in the City Center. The book did not have a decorative cover, it was just a hardcover black book. No title on the front page, no title on the spine, no summary of the book at the back, nothing. I started to laugh to myself, Yippie was so critical of the cover of my copy of "Wuthering Heights," because it had a haunted house on a hill illustrated onto it, while Yippie's book had no cover at all. It was the most modest book cover that I had ever seen. There was nothing wrong with that per se, but why were they so critical of my cover while theirs had no design? I opened the book, and I was amazed.

It was the cashier from Bills Boutique; it was the dress; it was Sunny and Cheery and Mitty. This was a sketchbook, and Yippie drew everything they saw. I was even there on the very last page, Yippie drew me sitting on the bench in the City Center reading my book. How long had they been there before we officially met? Frivy was also in the book, she was eating from a little pottery bowl. Yippie was an artist too. This was shocking because they made such a fuss about artists only being heard in their art. What was Yippie trying to tell me? Yippie was a very secretive person. I did not learn much about them in the one day that I got to know them, but I had a feeling that if I had known them for several years, I would still not know much about Yippie. Though by looking through Yippie's sketchbook, I was able to learn a great deal about them. I saw the charcoal sketches of the woman in the dress boutique. I saw her many times, in many different poses, holding a variety of dresses. I saw a sketch of what Yippie envisioned what the cashier might look like in the dress Yippie tried to purchase.

Some of the earlier sketches even had the cashier drawn with long hair. In one of the very first sketches, she was reading a book while sitting next to Yippie on the subway. There were sketches of the two talking and holding hands. Why would Yippie trade this for a book they couldn't read? "Wuthering Heights," would be useless to them. This little sketchbook had so many memories tied to it, and the act of trading it required that they show their art to someone else, someone that they barely knew. This seemed out of character for Yippie. They seemed the type to want to hold onto their secret sketches as if they were holding onto a part of their soul. Why would Yippie risk vulnerability for a novel they couldn't read? Then I found my answer. I suppose not all of life's questions are left to the abyss.

In one of the earlier sketches of Yippie's love interest, before she had cut her hair into a bob, she was reading a book,

"I think so," said the woman, "Usually they do just fine in there, I heard them meowing up a storm, it's hard to hear inside the car though so I don't blame you for missing it. Plus, cats get shy when you go too close to the engine."

I pulled the lever beside my seat and popped the hood open, I stepped out and propped the hood up for the woman to look inside. The squeaking had started up again, though now I recognized the sound as meowing.

"Do you mind shining your cell phone's flashlight over the engine so I can get a closer look?" asked the woman.

"I actually don't have a cell phone," I admitted. The woman looked so surprised.

"You do not have a cellphone?" exclaimed the woman, "Well that's a surprise for someone your age. I usually see millennials glued to them at work," the woman passed me her cellphone and I held it above her.

"Yup, I see it alright," said the woman. "and it isn't a cat," I was scared now, if it was not a cat, what could it be?

"Is it a raccoon?" I asked a little nervous.

"No, no," laughed the woman, "Looks like a kitten!"

A kitten! How adorable. Wait a minute, maybe this is why Sullen sold me the car. He must have known the kitten was in there, that was why the hood had been propped open, he was trying to get the kitten out. Why did Sullen omit this crucial information from me? Then I realized what had happened. Sullen thought the kitten was dead. He was expecting that in an hour or two, the car would begin to reek of rot and he did not want to pay to have the kitten's body removed. That bastard! I started to doubt whether he ever really did go by the name Spontaneous. I highly doubt anyone willing to kill a kitten in their car and then pawn off that very car to the next person could ever be considered spontaneous. What a jerk!

The woman reached into the engine, "Hold on!" she exclaimed, "I think I got them," it looked as though the

woman's entire arm was being consumed by the engine. She pulled an adorable little silver tabby kitten out from the hood.

"Meow," it exclaimed innocently. It was probably the cutest kitten I had ever seen in my entire life. Its paws looked like it was wearing tiny mittens and her eyes looked like green marbles. The woman scooped up the kitten and started to stroke her fur.

"Well, here we are!" exclaimed the woman, "looks like you've got yourself a female kitten here, young lady. Look out, though! These things can make you one hell of a cat lady. Keeping kittens can get addictive," the woman handed me the kitten. She was quite adorable.

"I wish I could keep her," I sighed looking into her emerald eyes, "but I'm not sure I would make the best owner right now, my living situation is a little, um, inconsistent. Would you like to keep her?"

"I would love to keep her," explained the woman, "but my husband wouldn't be too happy about it, we already have three," she winked at her daughter, "I'll let you hold onto her."

"Wait," I exclaimed, "I don't know..." As I held the kitten in my arms, I realized that she was shaking. She was scared.

"Well keep her or not, regardless you'll have to bring her to the animal shelter," explained the woman, "It's just up the street from here. But before you're quick to give her away, I'll tell you something, I'm a religious woman, and I believe in faith," she explained, "God is trying to tell you something, but if it's the right love at the wrong time, it will be a tragedy worse than Shakespeare. That said, even if you can't keep her, I'm sure the shelter will find her a loving home."

"Thank you for your help," I was grateful for the woman's time. The silver tabby looked quite frightened, and I imagine she would not have lasted much longer if I had left her to her own devices. It looked like the kitten had found her way into the car with ease, but it did not look as if she would have been

able to get herself back out without assistance. I checked the back of the vehicle to see what Sullen had left behind that might be useful in this situation. There was not much, but I was able to find a tiny blue basket in the backseat. I pulled a shirt from my backpack and bundled the kitten in it. I heard kittens like to jump out of their boxes if they were not properly contained in them. I once read an article about a woman who had lost her pet kitten in her car. Apparently, it jumped out of its box while she was driving and climbed up into the dashboard of her car. She had to call six organizations to get her out; the police, two humane societies, animal control, and two mechanics. The second mechanic was able to rescue the kitten, thankfully.

The animal shelter was just up the block like the woman had mentioned. Once I pulled up to the humane society, I took the blue basket inside. I noticed a black woman sitting behind the front desk. There was a name tag in front of them that read as Dr. Amicable K. they must have been the vet. When I looked closer at the sign, I noticed in brackets that their pronouns were 'they/them.'

"Hello, Dr. Amicable," I waited for them to finish their paperwork.

"Hello," they said, "Call me Ami please, how can I help?"

"Well actually Ami, this is kind of a funny story, but I, um, I found a kitten in my car engine." Ami began to laugh.

"Did you now?" Ami asked, "and, how are they?"

"I think she's fine," I said, passing her the silver tabby bundled in the blue basket. Ami looked at her, then looked back up at me. They had a strange look on their face, but I didn't recognize it.

"Right," Ami began, "and so you're looking to return her?"

"I just wasn't sure what I should do," I said.

"Let me take her to the back and make sure she has all her shots," Ami took the cat into the back room and asked me to

take a seat in the waiting area. I sat down and waited a moment.

I kept flipping through Yippie's sketchbook in the meanwhile. There were so many pictures of Yippie's love interest, I wondered to myself whether or not she would appreciate the book. Was it worth it for Yippie to exchange such a valuable sketchbook for a 'silly book about a haunted house,' as they referred to it, further still, a book that they could not read? It looked as though Yippie had kept this sketchbook for years. Why would they give it away so quickly for someone who did not love them in return? Sure, Yippie did not come from money, but they were above that. Everyone loved Yippie, I don't think anyone who couldn't look past their social class was worth any of Yippie's energy. That cashier must have been someone special before that bob cut.

"Well!" exclaimed Ami, I sat up in my chair, "Kitten has all her needles and she has been sterilized by its previous owner," I was not sure how Ami could have known all of that after only a couple of minutes with the cat, but then again, they were the vet, not me.

I walked up to the counter and thanked them for taking the kitten. I turned to walk out, but before I did, Ami asked me a question that I was hoping they wouldn't. A question I knew I would not be able to answer yes, or no to.

"Would you like to keep her?" God did I regret buying that car. Part of me wanted to keep her. The problem was, I was not sure if my lifestyle would accommodate her needs.

"I don't know," I said, I started thinking back to the car, I knew I did not have a home for the kitten, the car was so tiny she would not be pleased in there. I thought back to the money I had saved up, it wasn't much. I had $20.00 in my back pocket and that was all, well $18.00 now that I bought a coffee at Cheery's. I could barely feed and house myself, let alone a kitten.

Before I could answer, I heard the door of the shop chime. Ami and I turned our attention to the newcomer. Sure enough, it was Sullen! How did he get here? I looked outside and noticed my red bike on the curb. I thought about it logically, Sullen knew about the kitten, he must have been traveling down this path to travel to the convenience store. He must have noticed my red car in the parking lot. How horrible! Perhaps he was just here to check up on the situation. He must have figured I was able to save the kitten after all and was too nosy to keep on riding past without stopping in.

"Good evening, ladies," said Sullen slyly. Ami didn't correct him, but I was confident it bothered them. Why did Sullen have to be so insensitive? "I noticed your car outside, how is it going B?"

"It's V," I corrected.

"Hello, Sullen," Ami knew him, "What seems to be the matter?"

"Nothing is the matter, I was just looking for my lost kitten," he nudged my shoulder, I brushed him off.

'The devil!' I thought, first he sells the car with the kitten lost under the hood, and now he wants to steal her back! What a jerk.

"You'll have to be more specific," Ami said flatly, it was apparent that they too were familiar with Sullen's mischievous nature.

"Sure thing," Sullen said slyly, "It's a grey tabby, tiny white paws," he exclaimed, "Do you have one today in stalk?"

Ami rolled their eyes, "We might, do you have any ownership papers?" asked Ami.

"Ownership papers?" inquired Sullen, "No ownership papers, but it's my cat. I knew what it looked like, it's not as if I could just suppose you had a grey tabby kitten in the shop. I pawned it off from an old man, God rest his soul, the old man was financially struggling so I pawned the kitten off him, told

him I'd keep it safe. Return it to him when he had the money. Passed on a couple weeks later, supposedly from loneliness. Now I promised that old man I'd watch his cat, you wouldn't stand in the way of a dead man's will, would you?"

"I know full well what you're talking about," said Ami growing impatient, "His grandchildren told me they tried to repurchase her from you, but you wouldn't sell her back to them. The old man died heartbroken. They came here and begged me to help their case, but the law was on your side. Unfortunately for you, today, it is not. Unless you can provide me with papers proving the kitten is yours."

"Fine," said Sullen sourly, "I'll just adopt it." My heart sank. She couldn't go back with him, it was so unfair, she was just a baby and Sullen was such a bitter, horrible man. I looked toward Ami in a panic.

"Well," said Ami, "The cat is vaccinated and is technically ready to be put on the adoption list. It will be $200.00. Do you have the money?"

"As a matter of fact," Sullen began, "I do. Big sale today, a baptism necklace and a silver watch," Sullen smirked. I despised this man.

"Well," admitted Ami, "In that case, it seems as though you are eligible to adopt." Sullen's eyes were glaring down at me. "However," Ami continued, I smiled, "The person who reports a lost animal to the shelter gets first dibs on whether or not they would like to keep them," Ami turned to me, "and the person gets to keep the pet for free. Shelter's policy," Sullen looked livid.

"V?" Ami asked, almost pleading, "Would you like to keep the kitten."

I knew I could not provide her the life she deserved, but Sullen would make her life a living hell. Maybe I could just keep the kitten until I could find her a better home. I looked at Sullen and then looked at Ami. I thought back to the money I

back. The kitten was shaking, she looked scared. Ami came back out with a bag of cat food, a bowl, and a water jug. They passed them to me. This was definitely a lot more than what $18.00 could buy. I could sense Ami could read my mind.

"The old man was a friend of mine," Ami explained, "His grandchildren witnessed him dying, all the while he was longing for the cat. Kept calling out for her on his deathbed. Sullen did not keep his word, charged double what he bartered for her, and the children couldn't afford it, despite spending the summer saving up. The parents didn't see the point in pitching in, they knew the old man wasn't going to last the night, and they did not want to keep the kitten themselves. I always regretted not buying the kitten for them. By the time I thought about it, it was too late. Anyways, the rest of the equipment I'm paying from pocket. I cannot bear to see a man like that keep her. If you tell me you can't afford it and walk out, Sullen will find out through gossip on the street, and I either have to give him the kitten, or I lose my job. You're doing me a service in keeping her, so let me pay you back." Ami was a kind person. I was grateful for their gold heart.

"I will take good care of her," I assured Ami, but it looked as though Ami did not need the assurance. They would not have gone to all this trouble if they thought I wouldn't.

"Kittens need collars," Ami explained, "and frequent visits to the vet. A lot of people neglect their cats, refuse to take them to the vet. Cats internalize their pain. They won't let on when sick. They think it's a sign of weakness and they don't want to be considered a victim. Adopting a kitten, it's like dating someone with trust issues. You can either teach them to trust you, or you can ingrain more severe trust issues within them. You've got a lot of work to do young lady because that Sullen made the trust issues worse in this baby. That's why the poor thing is shaking."

I nodded, "I'll make sure to buy her a collar once I have

the money," I affirmed.

"Oh no," Ami said generously, "I'm paying for that too. You just make sure she gets taken care of. Now, what name am I putting on the collar?"

I considered for a moment what Ami said about kittens with trust issues. I suppose I could identify with that. Kittens were far more independent than dogs, a little more mischievous too. I was not used to independent creatures. For the majority of my life, I had always figured myself to be a dog person, and yet there I was, about to adopt a kitten.

"What did the old man call her?" I asked, but Ami shook their head.

"Oh no, you aren't getting off that easy. I have personally found, in my experience as a vet, that people who name their pets are more likely to keep them. I want to make sure this leery little thing will finally get to have a consistent owner for once." A tinge of guilt hit me when Ami said that. I could promise to keep the cat out of harm's way, but I could not guarantee that the kitten would have a stable home.

'Wait,' I thought to myself, 'Ami just named the cat.'

"Leery," I said aloud, "She is Leery, isn't she?" Ami knew what I was thinking.

"Leery it is. I'll be back in a moment," Ami disappeared into the back for a good twenty minutes. I took the time to observe Leery. The kitten had small white paws and silver fur. Her emerald eyes looked back into mine from her crate, I could tell she was timid. She was still shaking. I was not sure how to soothe her. All I did know was that now she was mine, and I would ensure she would be taken care of properly this time. Leery was a fluffy kitten, her fur was fine, and her ears perked up at the sound of my voice. I did notice though that there was a small chip taken out of the corner of her right ear. It looked as though another animal may have taken a swing at her. I put my finger to the silver rods of her crate that kept her tucked

away from danger. She jumped backward startled. I was surprised to see a kitten acting so timid. I was not used to cats; I was used to dogs. They were usually pretty warm to new people. Hell, Aimless would have left our home for a complete stranger if they were ready to offer a dog treat as incentive. Leery was something different though. I knew it was going to take some hard work to get her to trust me, or anyone for that matter.

When Ami came back out with the little kitten collar, I thanked them, but I had to ask, "Ami what was Leery called before I adopted her? What name did the man give her before he passed on?"

Ami looked startled by the question and was hesitant to answer, "Her name was Genial. Hopefully, that name will suit her again someday," I thanked Ami for their gracious gesture and left the shelter, crate in hand.

And just as if we were in an old country movie; Leery, the silver kitten, and I, the lonely traveler—well, a little less lonely now—rode off on my metal stead and into the silver sunset.

****

CHAPTER VII

FRIGID AIR

"He drinks his coffee black; he drinks his liquor strong." — V

****

Leery and I continued driving even though the tank was nearing empty. We took the scenic country roads passing hills and other small villages on route. We didn't stop to visit any of the communities we passed, they seemed a little too small for us. The car was good on gas, which was fortunate as I was officially out of money and could not afford to refill. I intended to stop off in a city, make some money, then head out again once I could refill my tank. I was still not set on a final destination, but I knew wherever I decided to settle on had to have one thing awaiting me, my dreams.

Leery was still very timid towards me. She waited patiently in her crate as we traveled the hilly country roads. I felt for Leery, if it weren't for Sullen, she wouldn't have so many trust issues. Just one lousy home was enough to instill such a distrust for humanity in her. While Ami was kind enough to supply the equipment to keep Leery settled, they did not provide any toys for the tiny kitten. I pulled out two clean socks from my backpack and balled them up for her and threw them into the crate. At first, she pretended they were mice and pounced on them in the tiny enclosure. She was a clever girl, and it did not take her long to realize the small sock balls were nothing more than inanimate objects. Instead of

treating them like mice, she began to use them as a pillow. I knew I couldn't keep Leery, even though Ami wanted me to, it was clear that this was not the type of lifestyle a feline deserved, especially not one with such a timorous disposition to humankind. She deserved to have a stable home in the suburbs, or perhaps the country, or maybe a tiny apartment would do, regardless, it should be permanent. Consistent. How better to revive trust in a creature than with a sense of security? In knowing I could not provide that for Leery, I hoped to find another who could.

Country hills began to mesh with the mountains. The climate around us began to grow rather cold. I was familiar with this frigid air. Thankfully, the car had a working heater, I cranked it high to offset the chilly atmosphere. I noticed a fork in the road up ahead. It looked as though I had the option to either continue down the country road or turn left onto a winding road. I considered for a moment where to turn. I looked to Leery who was now clawing at the sock balls she was previously cuddling with. The red light on the dash illuminated, indicating we were low on gas. I suppose the car made the decision for me.

"Up for a detour?" I teased the cat who remained unresponsive to my acknowledging her; instead, she continued to claw away at her newfound toy. I decided to interpret her silence as a yes. I swung left, rather abruptly, and my backpack on the back seat shifted, and so did Leery's crate, to her discomfort.

"Meow!" she exclaimed in annoyance.

I grinned to myself and continued on the road. I drove the car up the winding road. I quickly realized that the escalation of the front of the vehicle indicated an incline in the street. We were traveling up the edge of a mountain. I noticed a ski lodge to my left parked at the bottom of the sloped mountainside. There was a machine that emitted fake snow. Despite the

decline in temperature as we moved up the mountain, the environment was not cold enough to produce its own snow. There was an unsettling air to this quaint little lodging. Something about it intimidated me from venturing into it, and so I decided to pass it and keep driving up the winding roads.

I decided to drive the car until it was almost entirely out of gas. I decided to roll down my window and soak in the frigid air. This bothered Leery who curled herself into the back corner of her carrying case, wrapping herself in the towel lining her floor. I laughed and rolled my windows back up. When I finally considered the car to indeed be on the verge of running completely empty, I decided to pull into what looked to be an abandoned lot. There were no other vehicles in sight, and when I got closer to it, I realized it was the lot belonging to a nature trail that a hiker could trek up the mountainside. I looked to Leery, and she stared back at me. It seemed the two of us were thinking the same thing, though it would be impossible to tell. Still, I liked to imagine we were.

'What's next?' we both thought.

Leery and I only differed in one sense. I approached this question with a childish giddiness while Leery seemed quite dubious by the uncertainty of that question.

In exiting the car, I was sure to lock the doors and keep track of any landmarks that caught my attention so I could relocate the car again. I noticed a few, there was a small outdoor proscenium stage to the right, it looked abandoned. I imagined it served as an outdoor theatre for local musicians or artists to perform for community events. There was also a small outlook across the road that seemed to overlook the view of the trail. Once I was confident that I would be able to find this location again, I picked up Leery's carrying case and began to walk along the winding path up the mountainside and far from that eerie lodging I encountered previously. In venturing through the winding road, I noticed that not many

an overtly pretentious appearance like Yippie's love interest did, overall, she seemed like the type who drank her liquor strong.

"Can't play the games without buying something," Leery hissed at the barista, she arched her back, and her tail jetted upward, "and no cats," continued the woman narrowing her eyes as she glanced down at Leery.

The barista had her hair pulled back into a tight bun, and her arms were decorated with intricate tattoos. I scanned her arm quickly and noticed a massive paw on her left shoulder and a small cartoon dog beside it. She was a dog person.

"Um, well," I began, if I had the funds, I would have been quick to purchase a coffee or a small meal, at this point I was quite hungry, I had not eaten for the bulk of the day. My last item of canned food went to Yippie's stray dog Frivy. A tinge of regret hit me as I thought back to how quickly I consumed the canned food I had earlier in hopes that it would lighten my load. If I had suspected then that I would run into Sullen and attain a vehicle of my own, or if I thought for a minute circumstance would require that I adopt Leery, I would have saved every last spoonful of Campbell's soup my mom had given me. "I would purchase but, um..." I quickly looked across the room and scanned my surroundings. It was a board game café, there was not much else to see. It was by a stroke of luck I noticed a posting on the back wall. A Scrabble competition. Perhaps that would be my way out.

"I'm actually here for the Scrabble competition," I said quickly. The barista looked surprised, "The cat is, uh, my mascot."

"Oh," said the barista, she walked behind the front counter, "Name?"

"Um it's V, but I'm, I'm late to register, I might not show up on the list, it's just that I was having computer problems and I just..."

"I just put your name on the list," interrupted the woman impatiently, "It's casual there's no need to register. What can I get you?"

"Um, do you have to order something to play?" I asked timidly.

The woman did not look amused, "No, I suppose not." She rolled her eyes.

I nodded gratefully, "Do you, umm, have a washroom?" I felt as though I was tempting fate in asking to use the amenities in addition to my many other requests.

"To the right," pointed the woman. Leery began to hiss at the woman, and I was confident that the woman might have hissed right back if she were not working.

"Leave the cat at the table. And keep it away from the food!" The woman pulled out a wash bucket from under the counter and began to wipe down the tables. I was hesitant to leave Leery as she was hissing up a storm. I noticed that she was starting to frighten others in the café. I wanted to respect the woman's request, so despite my hesitation, I left her at the counter.

I stepped into the washroom and examined myself in the mirror. I looked as though I had been driving for a couple of days. My hair was oily, and some of the eyeliner I was wearing began to smudge. I decided to touch up my makeup a bit. I took a paper towel and drenched it in warm water. I ran my wrists under it for a moment to warm myself. The circulation in my hands always sort of sucked, my hands were always either freezing or clammy. Kind of gross to think of, but the crisp air here left my hands feeling quite cold. I ran the paper towel across my face. I pulled out my toothbrush from my backpack and began to brush. Within only a few moments of grooming, I began to feel more like myself again. I did not realize I did not feel like myself until I began to feel more like myself again. If that made any sense. A part of me thought that maybe that's

how life was. As an example, sometimes we lose ourselves in a relationship or hobbies, or any other activity we can obsess over. Until we lose the thing consuming us, only then will we begin to feel more like ourselves again, without realizing we lost ourselves in the first place. As an example, someone might not be aware that their occupation is interfering with their dreams until they lose their job. Or, a person gets lost in a love interest only to find themselves again after a breakup.

I looked at my reflection in the mirror. Now I was wearing a thin black winged eyeliner, gold eyeshadow from a pallet I bought for my sixteenth birthday, and a pink lip gloss. My hair was longer than I last remembered it. It curled in spirals down my red leather jacket. My jacket was drenched in perfume, I wore a vanilla-lavender scent. Something about my reflection looked different from how I remembered it a few weeks ago when I was living at home. Something changed in the reflection, the change was in my eyes. They were still a hazel green in color, but something about them changed. I couldn't tell if it was for the better or worse, but judging from the fact that I couldn't stop smiling in noticing this slight change, I had a feeling it was for the better.

It was then that I noticed that Leery was hissing much louder than before. I could hear her from the washroom now. I worried that something had happened to her. I briskly left the restroom to make my way back to her. Leery was still in her carrying case, but now there was someone in front of her. She was hissing, and her back was arched again. This poor cat. Would she ever learn to trust anyone again? A boy was in front of her, it looked as though he was trying to calm her. He had charcoal hair and piercing green eyes. I started to walk over to them.

"Hey, sorry about that. Leery is a little shy around people she doesn't know..."

The boy looked up at me. His eyes were just like marbles,

like Leery's, but his eyes were sharp whereas hers were timid. His brows were thick, and in this contrast, his eyes were like emerald stones. I looked down quickly at Leery. She looked quite uncomfortable in the board game café; I wondered for a moment if it was a mistake to stop here.

"It's alright," said the boy, his eyes did not break from me, and it was somewhat intimidating, "I was trying to calm her down." Leery looked anything but calm, but I could hardly pin it on the boy's lack of effort, I could barely sooth Leery when she got into a fit. I suppose I needed to take more time to get to know her.

"Are you a local?" I asked, attempting to change the subject, Leery was not getting any calmer, and it was sort of pointless to keep trying to soothe her. Perhaps if we left her alone for a few minutes, she would settle on her own.

"Yeah," he said, his eyes were very distracting. I'm sure he got that a lot though, so I wouldn't make a point in complimenting him on them. I found the best compliments were those that a person might not expect. The whole point of compliments was to be original. Original compliments make people feel important.

"So, I'll be honest, I actually don't know much about this area, I'm not from here."

"Oh really," said the boy amused, "Any moron could have figured that out. It's a small town," something about this boy was very mysterious. I felt like I would have to work hard to try and figure him out. Was he an artist like me? Was he nonconforming like Yippie?

"So, I'm assuming you've lived here a while then," I said, "If you know everyone in the area."

"No, I moved here for work. I was born in London," he explained, "It only takes a few years to figure this town out."

He was a traveler like me! Something about this boy captivated my interest. Perhaps it was his eyes, maybe it was

how he carried himself.

"Heathen, you're up," said the barista. The boy, who I now knew went by Heathen, got up and walked to the Scrabble table set off to the side of the room. There was another person there, probably two times his age, they shook hands and sat across from one another. There was a third-party keeping score to the left of the table. I watched the game magnetized.

It seemed as though the two were very strategic in the game. It was clear the two competitors were both avid Scrabble players. They analyzed their opponent's last move and scanned the board. They took several minutes to deliberate each step. Something about the trivial act of pondering one's next move was alluring to me. I watched them both contemplate their next move across their stage. I found something about this competition to be mesmerizing. They were each determined to win, and I waited eagerly to see whom that winner would be. Though I had just met him, I placed my bet-on Heathen. He seemed competent in his match, and I could tell he was ambitious in his pursuit of success. He was coming for the win, this was apparent. His opponent also seemed skilled, but something seemed unnerving in his demeanor. I could not quite pinpoint it until I noticed his hand shaking as he lay his squares on the board. He was anxious.

Then, I saw something new in his eye as he contemplated his move with regret. It was self-doubt. Yes, he wanted to win, though I think he was not fully aware of this drive within him. Still, he told himself it was not about the win; it was about having fun. He was there to have 'fun' he tried to convince himself. But he wasn't solely there to have fun. He wanted to win. Being there for 'the fun of it,' was a falsehood he would tell himself to reassure himself when he would lose. He was confident he would. Despite my confidence in Heathen's ability, undoubtedly, he was no competition for a man twice his age, with twice the experience. His diction was impeccable,

in fact, for his first three moves, Heathen's competitor was in the lead, but the look in his eyes shifted to something unflattering. He was consumed by self-doubt. It was apparent that he was more skilled than Heathen, but he did not believe it to be so, so his game suffered for it.

Heathen's eyes were consistent. He seemed ambitious by nature. He was there to win. He, also a skilled player with impeccable diction, trained immensely for this day. I could tell. I don't believe Heathen figured the man across from him to be more skilled than him. In fact, I think he thought the opposite, he judged him by his last move, not by the look in his eye. While his opponent faltered under pressure, Heathen knew better than to doubt himself. Why should he? He was winning. He was skilled. He did not consider the look of self-doubt in his opponent's eye; instead, he convinced himself he was superior to him. If Heathen did not underestimate his opponent as much as he did, he would be quick to discover that his competitor's intelligence and skill far surpassed that of the average contestant. In fact, despite him losing, I think his opponent could have trained Heathen. He was clearly more skilled of the two, but he faltered under pressure.

Heathen maneuvered his pieces onto the board in his final move. Impressed with himself, he stifled his opponent. The lack of confidence of his opponent had granted Heathen the win, and Heathen was crowned champion of the round. The scorekeeper announced a fifteen-minute break. The nervous runner-up nodded and looked as though he might have extended a hand to Heathen if Heathen did not turn his back from him and walked away.

'Perhaps Heathen did not notice the gesture,' I thought naively to myself. I looked to Leery who had calmed at Heathen's departure from the table. She was sitting patiently in her enclosure and looked as though she tired herself out from her previous state of distress. I pitied the cat.

coffee?"

"With honey and cinnamon," I said.

"With honey and cinnamon?" he laughed, "Okay."

"Well, I don't like things too bitter," I playfully retaliated,

"How do you drink yours?"

"Black," he winked, I got chills, "I like mine bitter."

Leery seemed very irritated at this point, so despite the discontented barista from behind the counter, I released her from her enclosure, and I began to stroke her. Every time I showed Leery some affection; she began to trust me a little more.

Heathen got back and handed me my honey coffee.

"Enjoy your bitter coffee," I teased as I watched him take his first sip.

"Honey is for the weak," he protested, "Your coffee is no match for mine."

"Interesting," I began, "I can drink my coffee black, you know, I just choose not to."

"But the real question is, can you handle the extra espresso shot?"

"Holy," I remarked sarcastically, "A real tough guy."

"Not really," he admitted, "I just feel awkward drinking coffee without a shot in it. Espresso makes up for the lack of vodka." He winked at me, I tried not to blush. Leery hissed simultaneously. I tried to hush her by stroking her fur. It didn't really work.

"So," he said, "What's the deal with you, you're a traveler, right? Cool, but what are you running from?"

I was taken aback by this, "I'm not running from anything," I said defensively, "Not all who wander are lost."

"Alright, Tolkien," he chuckled.

"Pardon?"

He rolled his eyes, "Don't tell me you're one of those girls who quote shit they don't know the reference to."

Leery hissed, and I became defensive, "Pardon me? It's a common saying, 'Not all those who wander are lost,' what's the problem here?"

"Because, that quote has become a mantra for the wanderers, all these wanderlust girls who want to sound like they know shit get that quote tattooed up their arm. They pose in front of the Eiffel tower, all holier than thou, then when you ask them if they've read the "Lord of the Rings," they scratch their heads," he reached into his pocket and pulled out his cell phone, "Here, look, 'All that is gold does not glitter,' J.R.R. Tolkien."

"Give me that," I snatched the phone from his hand and read the poem, "Well, it's beautiful."

"I don't think it was meant to be," he retaliated, "It's supposed to be informative. So cool, you're a wanderlust, I get it. But if you're not running from something, what are you looking for?"

"Honestly," I replied, "I don't know."

"You don't know. So, you're traveling without a destination? That's dumb."

"Perhaps," I admitted, "but I would match rather be dumb and young than corrupted and bitter. Besides, the foolish aren't all fools. Do you know where that one is from?"

"I don't know," he averted his eyes.

"Up here," I said, tapping my temples.

"Alright kid," he diverted the conversation, "So where are you staying the night?"

Oh brother. "I'm not sure," I admitted. "My car is out of gas; I'm stuck here until I find a gig."

"A gig?" he started, "For what, are you a model or something?"

"No, a vocalist. And a writer. But I have writer's block, and I can't find a gig. So right now, I guess I'm neither."

"You're funny. Cool, you'll stay at my place then."

"Wait, pardon?" I asked

"Yeah, you can stay until you find a job. You can chip in on the rent once you do. I'll help you look for something."

My eyes widened. I've only known this boy for a brief period. He was already offering me a place to stay, and he offered to help me find a gig. Was this even safe? I looked at Leery, and he caught my gaze.

"The cat can come too. I like cats," Heathen was sweet. He was offering me a place to stay, I really couldn't afford to say no. Although I had only just met this young man, sure he seemed nice and all, but I wasn't sure if him appearing to be helpful was enough to suffice my concerns.

"I don't know," I replied.

"Alright well, you need dinner," he said, "Come to my place. I'm drinking with some friends tonight. We'll order pizza and chill."

"Sure," I said, that was an offer I couldn't turn down. Just then the café's bell chimed and in stepped a tiny woman. She had a tattoo sleeve up her right arm, and she wore a meek smile as she entered. She looked to be a couple years older than Heathen, and Heathen was a year or two older than me. She was quite beautiful. She captured Heathen's attention as soon as she entered the café. The barista smiled and nodded at her. She waved to Heathen, and he nodded back. She walked to a group of people in the back corner of the café; there were two women and a man around Heathen's age there as well. The man wore a cartoonish suit with monsters decorating the sleeve. He wore a white fitted t-shirt that revealed he was very fit. He was also handsome, tall, and slender. The other two women were also stunning. One of the women was of South Asian descent, she wore her long black hair draped over her right shoulder. The woman with the long hair embraced the tiny framed woman that so captivated Heathen. The third woman was white and wore her short blond hair in a ponytail.

They all conversed together in the corner of the café.

Heathen licked his lips as he looked toward the woman with the tattoo sleeve. I rolled my eyes at his attitude.

'Disgusting,' I thought.

"Alright," he said, "Want another coffee? They're going to call me up soon. That woman who walked in is my competition."

"Are you nervous?" I asked he shook his head, "No, I can beat her. If she lets me win. Want another coffee?" I shook my head. He put five dollars on the table.

"If you change your mind," he said, "You'd better cheer me on."

Heathen walked to the table and shook hands with the man in the cartoonish jacket. I did not see him enter, but he must not have been here long. The blonde woman and the woman with the long hair welcomed him also. This group seemed close. I assumed that these were the friends Heathen was planning to invite home for pizza. I watched as they conversed. I was not asked to enter the conversation, so I took the opportunity to stroke Leery. I desperately wanted her to trust me, though building that connection seemed to be quite the task.

Further still, I wondered if it was even worth making that connection with Leery. Why have her build a sense of trust with me before giving her to a new owner? I knew it would be unfair of me to keep her. Cats enjoy consistency, and my life was far from that.

"Heathen and Elfin," the barista called, the scorekeeper also resumed her seat at the desk. So, the tiny woman who captivated Heathen, who I now knew went by the name Elfin, sat across from Heathen. The group all crowded around the table. I placed Leery back in her enclosure and moved my chair closer to the match. Heathen winked at Elfin, Elfin blushed.

Elfin let Heathen take the first move. He put down the

word QUICKLY collecting some points. While I would suppose most would be intimidated by this initial first move, Elfin simply smiled. We all figured that Elfin was bluffing, though I think Heathen knew full well she wasn't. She built off of QUICKLY placing down the word QUIXOTIC pulling in the lead. I was dumbfounded, just like the rest of the onlookers. Perchance it was nothing more than luck, but the match continued as such. Elfin demolished Heathen in the beginning round, in the second, she could only fit STAR in the blocks while he managed to pull ahead with ZEBRA. The two took turns intermittently de-crowning the other with superior moves to their proceeding. We initially considered it a close call until Elfin cheekily dropped an A creating the word ZA a slag for pizza, to the annoyance of her opponent and to the amusement of the group holistically. She pulled ahead and ended the game. Heathen shook her hand out of courtesy and to show good sportsmanship.

We all applauded Elfin. Heathen watched as she made her way to the bar stools to sit by the barista, he offered her a coffee as a prize for her win in a sarcastic manner. She denied him and offered him a coffee as a consolation prize. He laughed and declined also. He returned to his seat across from me, but he would not break his gaze from Elfin.

"She's very talented," I remarked. Leery was unamused yet again with Heathen's presence. Heathen was neutral to Leery's presence, and despite her attitude, he was even kind toward her. I decided Leery would simply have to overcome her false preconception of Heathen.

"Yes," Heathen nodded, he turned back to face me, "So, what's the deal with your name?"

"I'm sorry?" this boy had an odd way of speaking.

"I mean," he laughed, "What is it, you haven't mentioned."

"Oh," I replied, "My name is V."

"V, what does that stand for?" I wished he wouldn't have

asked. He didn't seem the type who would.

"I don't know yet," I prepared myself for the ridicule.

"You don't know your own name?" the boy teased, "Your parents never told you what your name stood for?"

"No," I replied, "My mother told me I would discover what it stood for in time."

"Your father couldn't give you a hint?" he pushed.

"I don't get along with my father," I explained.

"Is that why you left?" he questioned.

"It was a motivator," I admitted, "but it is not why I left. The cul-de-sac was too small for me."

"I see," he nodded, "Hey, do you smoke?" this took me off guard.

"No," I replied, "Why, do you?"

"Only when I'm bored. I'll be right back," he got up from the table and made his way to the exit.

'Astounding,' I thought to myself, 'This boy is rude. Maybe I shouldn't stay..." I looked to Leery, and I felt as though if she could talk, she would be echoing the same statement. She seemed all the less inclined to stay. But she had no grasp of finance. Nor could she possibly understand the urgency that we were under to find food. Leery's food supply was well stocked, but that was to my sacrifice. I decided that dinner with Heathen would be the most strategic next step. Heathen eventually stepped back into the shop and pointed Leery and me out to his group of companions. Elfin was amongst them. She looked over and waved at me, it seemed as though she was inviting me over to sit with them. It was very thoughtful, and I accepted the offer.

"Nice to meet you, V," greeted Elfin, I've never met a woman so equally humble and fierce, especially one who had such a tiny frame.

"Congratulations on your win," I said, gesturing to the Scrabble station.

me.

"I guess that's us," Elfin tucked in her chair, "Come on, V." Heathen was laughing behind her.

I felt like a prisoner walking to the end of death row. This was going to sting. Elfin, fit the quote, "though she be little, she is fierce," to an absolute tee. Elfin noticed my hesitation to play and she attempted to soothe me.

"It's literally just Scrabble," she laughed, "It's supposed to be fun; I don't care if you're skilled, I don't care if you're not. Let's just have fun," I smiled, she was right. Games were meant to be fun, as long as neither party was hurt in the end, everyone was a winner.

The scorekeeper smiled and instigated the match. We competed.

Elfin started the match with AERIE beginning the game with four vowels on the board. I looked down at my tiles S, W, E, L, L, P, O.

'Well I'm off to a great start,' I thought to myself. In all actuality, I had only played Scrabble a very finite number of occasions. All of which I had lost despite being a writer, my everyday use of diction was okay. Nothing impressive, and I often depended on word checkers when I wrote a piece. So, needless to say, Scrabble was not my forte. I looked at my pieces again. I guess I could play ALL off of Elfin's A. I collected three points for the move. I could hear Heathen laugh as I did. This irritated me.

'Elfin isn't in the lead by far,' I thought to myself, but in reality, I knew she was likely playing a strategy, and I, transparently, was not. But Elfin just smiled reassuringly toward me. It was encouraging and thoughtful. I picked up two more letters, another E and N, I was clueless as to how I would use them.

Elfin linked on an S and an M to my ALL earning herself another four points. I decided to play SEW, earning myself

seven points because I got a double point on the W. I was impressed with myself, I pulled in the lead with ten points to Elfin's nine.

Heathen laughed, "Letting an amateur pull in the lead?" he winked to Elfin, "Quit going easy on her," I became angry. No one was going easy on me, SEW was a great play! It got me seven points! I could sense Elfin saw my frustrations.

"Don't listen to Heathen," she stated, "I never do."

'So, he teased Elfin too?' I thought to myself. 'How could someone tease another more skilled than them?' Maybe it was just the way he spoke. Still, I wouldn't let it throw me off my game, quite literally in this particular circumstance.

I looked over to Leery, though she was a cat and incapable of comprehending what was proceeding in the match, one might have confused her as captivated by the game. Just as everyone else in the café was. She seemed to be looking right at me. It was quite encouraging. I picked up a Q and a U. I already saw an opening, QUEEN, the letters I needed were on the board, I would just wait until my turn and impress Heathen. Elfin took a moment to scope out the board, she took several minutes.

'Ha! I've stumped her,' I thought to myself, 'Guess I shouldn't have doubted myself after all.'

Elfin took several more moments to contemplate her move. All the while I was attempting to mask my sense of superiority and offered her a meek smile as a means to reconcile any negative disposition my last move might have left her in the game. I was grateful that Elfin did not pick up on my competitive edge, nor on my cocky attitude toward the match. It was, after all, just a game, and I never pegged myself to be the competitive type. Elfin looked very concentrated on the board. The silence extended for quite some time, and I figured maybe I should consider my next move too. Though, I had no way to tell what Elfin might play next. Finally, Elfin

played ZEX and tagged it onto the E I was going to use for my next move! What does that even mean?

"What does Zex mean?" I outburst.

"Dumbass," Heathen called from the back, I shrunk a little, "It's a tool for cutting roof slate. It counts."

Elfin saw how embarrassed I got and told Heathen to shut up.

"I was just trying to help," Heathen muttered back, "If she called to check it, it would have ended the game. Then all this fun would end."

"No interference from the crowd," called the scorekeeper hushing Heathen. This shut him up for a little while.

"V, don't feel bad," Elfin smiled, "I play competitively, remember? I actually train for this. For someone untrained you are doing very well."

Despite her efforts, this small reassurance did not help to offset my stagnation in confidence as the scorekeeper tallied up the points. Z is ten points, E is 1, and Elfin got a double on the X, giving her a total score of 36.

'I can catch up with Queen,' I thought to myself, 'I mean I'll still be behind, but at least I can start catching up. I began to place my tiles onto the board, stealing the E from Sew.

"No, wait," said Elfin, "You can't tag that onto Sew, it'll sandwich the N between M and Z. 'Mnz' isn't a word."

My blunder made me blush. I stuttered an apology and recollected my tiles. Great, now not only did I expose some of my letters, but now Heathen was laughing at me again. I had no idea what to play at this point. I was entirely lost. Elfin smiled back at me.

"O and A are pretty common," she started, "and Z is on the board, do you have either of those letters?"

I did see Elfin play Za in her last game, I didn't have an A though. I looked back down at the tiles in front of me. I did have an O. Though I've never heard of the word Zo I decided to

take her advice and play it. At the risk that she might be sabotaging me, I placed the word down, and sure enough, it counted, and I collected 11 points, leaving me at 21 points. Still a good fifteen points behind Elfin, but it was better than nothing. The game persisted, and even with the occasional aid from Elfin, I lost quite brutally. We shook hands, and Elfin offered to buy me a coffee. When I declined, she explained it was customary that friends buy each other coffee post game to ensure there was no hardship between them. She told me that she liked me and insisted, so I accepted.

"You and Heathen didn't exchange coffee after your match," I chuckled after she handed me my second coffee with honey and cinnamon of the day.

"Yeah well Heathen and I butt heads too often for customs," she teased, "I never let him buy, he never lets me. And I win more often than him, usually, that leaves him bitter for a little while, so I try to steer clear of him for an hour or so postgame," she giggled to herself.

"What got you into Scrabble?" I asked her, she just chuckled.

"Oh, I don't know. Probably my competitive side. I like playing things I'm good at. I've been enrolled in spelling bees since I was a kid. Words are my forte," she smiled.

"That's valid," I smiled back at her, "I really like your tattoo sleeve by the way," I gestured to her right arm.

"Thank you!" she exclaimed, "My friend Able designed it for me. She's incredible. The barista and I are going again next week, I want to touch up one of the octopus' tentacles, it's starting to fade a bit. And I really want a seahorse, I'm going to see if she has time to fit one onto my shoulder here," she pointed to the only bare space on her left shoulder.

"You really like the ocean," I exclaimed examining her arm, "I see like a million different sea creatures," I exaggerated.

"Yeah! Let me show you," she pulled the sleeve of her t-

shirt back up and exposed several tinier cartoon sea critters.

"I love whales, that's why I have three," she laughed, "I got this coral reef a while ago, my first tattoo ever was this blowfish. This mermaid I got on 'International Women's Day' two years ago, and I got the shark fin during my fifth-year competition in International Scrabble. I placed third that year."

"Wow, that is really impressive," I stated, "So, what sparked the interest in sea creatures?"

"Oh, I'm an environmental advocate. Actually, I studied environmental engineering in college. I study the science behind pollutants, and I'm working as a research assistant to save the coral reefs. I just always sort of connected with sea life. Something about the ocean is exciting to me. It's mysterious."

"Yeah I guess it is, I always had this fascination for the sky for the same reason," I said. I reflected back to my nights at the ravine. I was reading poetry from my thoughts to the stars. Something about the sky truly did intrigue me, it was mystical and unknown. I liked hidden things; it instilled a sense of wonder in me. It seemed as though Elfin and I were similar in that sense, she thought the sea was mysterious, and I got my sense of wonder from the stars. I also got an inkling from the way Elfin smiled at others that she also liked the mystery of strangers. I figured that was why she invested her time in getting to know me. She and I were also similar in that sense.

"People are mysterious too," I said aloud.

"I'm sorry?" Elfin asked.

"Oh no, you just got me thinking. I love the sky, and you love the sea, but I think the real mystery is in people."

"Oh, how so?" she asked.

"Well, for starters, you can never really know a person. Isn't there a proverb that speaks to that ideology? Each person has three faces; the first they show to the world, the second they show to those closest to them, and the third they show to

no one. I guess people are kind of like the sea, we're just as mysterious."

"There definitely is some mysterious components to human beings," Elfin laughed, "I don't know if I can say we're all as mysterious as the sea. Some of us are pretty shallow." She rolled her eyes, I imagined she recalled to mind a few specific people that fit that statement.

"Yeah, I guess," I said, "Anyways what do you think about the proverb? I don't know why I'm going off on this," I laughed.

"No that's quite alright! I like having deep conversations with philosophers every once and a while," she nudged my shoulder, and I smile. That was not my name.

"I mean sure," she continued, "We have different versions of ourselves that we reveal to others. As an example, I just met you. So I don't know that much about you, but I'm sure your mom knows a great deal more about you than I ever would. Maybe you know even more about yourself than she ever would. Though the point remains, can you ever show your full self to another? Like your inner thoughts? I would say yes."

"I would say no, why would you say yes, though?" I asked.

"Okay, well because of this. When you write in a diary, you are writing your inner thoughts. Sure, your exact thoughts may not exactly translate to the page, depending on your skill level. Let's assume that someone is really good at writing. They might free write for a bit, scrummage through their thoughts and make sense of whatever they're feeling in the moment. Then someone reads the entry. Their third face becomes apparent to that reader."

"I mean true," I thought, "but can one really project their inner selves in being bound to tactile concepts and realities? Okay, as a for instance, if your diary entry mentions your relatives, then, you single out one specific person and discuss an event that procured that caused you either enlightenment or turmoil. So, that person then finds the entry and reads it,

from the word. Tattoos fit your description of a tool to communicate one's self-conscious perfectly. It is not exactly tactile in the traditional sense, tattoos are very abstract, and yet still real. Still human. A reflection of one's subconscious."

She had a point. Elfin was very intelligent. She could blame her Scrabble win on training and skill all she liked. While I am confident that did contribute a substantial part to her success, it was not enough to beat Heathen. He had similar training to her, perhaps even more experience in actually playing Scrabble, still, though, she won. That win she could credit to her intelligence. She had a humble disposition to match her competitive edge. She was willing to help me save face while she could have quickly demolished me in our match.

Though humble, she did not doubt herself the way Heathen's first opponent had. Elfin was self-assured, and I think that is what made her so successful.

The barista walked over, holding Leery's enclosure. I had left her on the table with Apt, Staid, and Dote.

"Take your cat," the barista stated, placing Leery's enclosure onto my lap.

"Oh! She's yours?" Elfin exclaimed she was swooning over the scared kitten in her crate, "I adore kittens!" and to my luck, the barista adored Elfin. So, she smiled at Elfin. When Elfin asked the barista and I if it would be alright if she held Leery and took her out of the enclosure, just for a minute, the barista and I both agreed. Elfin carefully opened the cage and pulled Leery out from the back corner of the crate where she was curled up into. She placed the bundle on her lap and began to stroke the kitten. Leery warmed up to her almost instantaneously, and I was amazed by this. It had taken me an entire day to get Leery to let me pull her out of her enclosure. Elfin, on the other hand, was able to establish trust with Leery in only a moment. I observed them so I could see how Elfin

interacted with Leery so I could later mimic the same actions to develop the same trust with the cat.

Elfin was not handling Leery any differently than I had been. Then I realized what Elfin's secret was. Just like in the Scrabble match, it was her level of self-assurance that made Elfin so successful. Elfin was not anxious the way I had been in handling Leery.

I really liked and respected Elfin. Apparently, I wasn't the only one because across the room I spotted Heathen looking over at her too. He flashed her a half smile, and though Elfin didn't see it, I noticed.

"If you had to get a tattoo, what would you get?" Elfin asked me, continuing our conversation from before.

"Oh, I have no idea," I responded, "Maybe something to do with the sky," Heathen walked up to us and took the kitten from Elfin's lap.

"What the hell, Heathen?" she exclaimed.

Despondent to her reaction to his trek to the table, he rolled his eyes. "I came to formally invite you to my apartment," he said sarcastically, "Consider this your invitation. We're drinking, maybe smoking, maybe ordering pizza. Are you two coming?" He rolled his eyes again.

"Yes, Heathen, I already said I was coming," Elfin snatched Leery back from him.

"Well, we're leaving now. Bring the cat if you want, just come." He stormed out of the café.

"What's up with him?" Elfin questioned.

"I have no idea," I admitted, "You've known him longer."

"Yeah, he gets moody sometimes. Guess we better go then. What's her name?" Elfin asked gesturing to the kitten.

"Leery," I said.

"Come on, Leery," she spoke softly to her, "Let's go get some pizza. I love cats so much."

Together, we walked out into the streets. The frigid air

from the mountains tickled my spine. We decided to cab to Heathen's, Elfin told us it was on her. The barista looked as though she wanted to come but all the same, she had to work late. I glanced up at the stars before getting into the cab.

'I wonder what this night holds in store for me?' I thought to myself, 'Aside from the frigid mountain air.'

CHAPTER VIII

HEAVEN-LESS SKIES

"Passion drives us mad, but it's that brilliant kind of madness that brings us sanity." — V

****

Did you miss me, dear reader? V has been fortunate enough to do without me for a while. Though uncertain and oftentimes directionless, V's life has thus far been smooth sailing. She has not met any immediate threat to her well-being or mental state. Aside from her quarrel with family, but she recovered from that with ease. That is not to say her state of serenity will remain consistent for long. Frigid air does not exactly complement warm hearts. At least from my experience. The mountains are too cold for her and Leery. I hope, for her sake, she discovers this sooner rather than later. But in being an optimist, she can see the light in the darkness, even if it is dim and fading. This was perhaps her third greatest folly.

But let me not spoil it. No one likes a spoiler, not in life, nor in novels.

****

Heathen's apartment had a lot of leather furniture. Black leather, nothing too frilly or overtly feminine. His apartment fit the stereotypical bachelor pad to the dictionary's definition. There were several trademark objects of a typical dorm, a magnet dartboard by the refrigerator, a bong by the sofa tables, quite a few empty beer cans crushed on the shelves, almost as if a house party had taken place and everyone placed

their empties around the room. There was, to no surprise, a shelf stacked with board games at the back of the room. The room had an underlying stench of cigarette smoke. I loved the scent; it was a guilty pleasure, but I craved the smell of a smoker. Booze and the stench of marijuana were far less appealing. I sat on the coach by Elfin.

Heathen, to my content, took the spot on the couch beside me. He passed me a Corona, and I drank it back. I didn't often drink so I would only need two or three more beers following this to feel a substantial buzz. Elfin was petting Leery until she began to purr. I was impressed with Elfin's ability to calm her so quickly. Perhaps Elfin would be the one to accept Leery into her permanent home. Leery would be happy with her.

The chatter of the party commenced, Staid, the stoic zany of the bunch, offered his contribution to the party's conversation.

"Yo everyone," initially the group continued their mundane chatter, completely ignoring Staid, "Everyone listen up," he projected in a drunken slur. After calling the group's attention two or three more times proceeding this, Elfin urged everyone to silence themselves. Staid looked amused.

"If you could use one eating kind of utensil for the rest of your life, a spoon or a fork, which would you pick?"

"Chopsticks," responded Elfin nudging me.

"No, that wasn't one of the options," retorted Staid slightly annoyed.

"Okay fine, I chose a fork," said Elfin.

"Spoon," blurted Dote who just got back inside with Apt, each slightly high.

"Spoon," agreed Apt, "It's more feminine."

"Oh, what now we're gendering cutlery?" Staid remarked, "How is a spoon feminine?"

"It's more elegant," Dote noted.

"You both think it's feminine? Am I the only one who

knows that cutlery doesn't have a gender?" Staid was a little intoxicated at this point, not everything he said made much sense anymore. At this point I was also reasonably drunk, though I can't remember who it was that blurted out spork, I did remember, quite clearly, that this remark sent Staid into a frenzy. He had to leave the room for a few moments to recollect himself. Elfin giggled, and I smiled at her.

"You know," I said in a drunken slur, similar to Staid, "Leery needs a permanent abode."

I thought I was coming across as intellectual by saying 'abode,' rather than 'home.' It was a sad attempt at overcompensating for my glaringly apparent intoxicated state. When I looked back at that conversation the next day, I determined that I, most certainly, came across as a pretentious drunkard.

"Oh, does she," Elfin laughed.

"Oh yes," I reaffirmed, "Cats get car sick, apparently. I can't keep her."

"What do you mean by carsick?" Elfin asked, "You aren't staying? I assumed you were a student here or something."

"No, I'm a Nomad, that's what Realist's mom calls me."

"Who?"

"Realist's mom," I said, "She likes me. She always asks what I'm reading, I miss that."

"Oh, I see," smiled Elfin, "and what are you reading?"

"Nothing, that's the problem. I'm not reading, and I have no gas."

The room was beginning to spin around me, I stood up for a minute, with no particular motive other than to test if the spinning would ease in a new posture, but it didn't. If anything, it got worse. I sat back down and tried to recall what I was just talking about with Elfin. I was just a little buzzed. Heathen kept handing me drinks, I think I only had three beers and a couple shots. I don't really remember anymore, though.

Was he staring into an abyss like Winnie in "The Secret Agent?" Why was he looking into the abyss? Was he waiting for it to look back into him? Intriguing. Mysterious. I needed to grasp him. I needed to vomit. Oh, no. I needed to vomit.

"I'll be back momentarily," I told the mystery man. Heathen looked equally intoxicated, so he did not initially protest what I told him so. He witnessed me run to the restroom and I think that he got the hint.

I looked at myself in the mirror. The room was spinning so much that I could hardly recognize my own reflection. I looked into it again, and I saw a stranger looking back at me. She also wore a red leather jacket and smudged eyeliner, but she did not look like me in the slightest. I heard a light knocking at the door, I told the person I would only be another minute.

"V, it's Heathen," said the low voice, "I have water for you when you get out. Hurry it up I want to show you something." What could he possibly want to show me right now? My head ached. I splashed some water on my face and tried to ignore my queasiness the best I could.

I opened the washroom door, Heathen threw a damp towel at me and instructed I put it on my forehead. He handed me a glass of water and offered me some salt and vinegar chips. I accepted a few. He didn't say another word aside from taking my hand out to the balcony of his bachelor pad. He closed the door behind us.

"Sober up I want to talk," he threw the chip bag back at me.

"I am sober," I lied accepting a handful of chips from his bag.

"Yeah, and I believe in angels. Please drink water," I did as he asked.

"You don't believe in angels?" I asked in shock. Everyone in the neighborhood of the cul-de-sac with the yellow house

believed in angels.

"No, and I don't believe in the tooth fairy either."

"But that's nowhere near the same thing," I said, doing my best to concentrate on what was happening in front of me.

"Well, both are stories, so yeah I think they pretty much are exactly the same," I rolled my eyes. I was beginning to feel myself sober up.

"So, you mean to tell me you don't believe in angels? That's a little despairing, don't you think?"

"No, I don't think that. Drink the water."

"You don't think completely disregarding the idea that our loved ones come back to watch over us is despairing? Alright, then."

"I don't. Why would I find that despairing? I don't believe people come back as ghosts."

"Okay, well do you believe in an afterlife? Because if you don't, I would also argue that it is pretty despairing."

"I don't though," he said, "and I think anyone who does is naïve."

"Naive?" I spat, "What about hopeful? Faithful?"

"You didn't strike me as the religious type V," Heathen sounded disappointed.

"I'm not religious," I corrected him, "I'm spiritual."

"The difference?"

"Okay. So, I believe in faith. I believe in hope; I believe in an afterlife..."

"Why?"

"Why do I believe in shit?" I asked.

"Yeah."

"Well, because I can't imagine a world where when my loved ones died, they didn't have a place to go."

"So, you're not afraid of an abyss yourself, you're just afraid your loved ones would suffer non-existence."

"Yes."

"Okay, so let's play a game," said Heathen.

"What kind of game?"

"21 questions. I'll start. If you could guarantee heaven for one person, and one person only, who would you pick?"

"Zeal," I answered, "My sister. She's the one I worry about the most."

"Worry, is she reckless? I like reckless girls."

"She's three years younger than you," I spat.

"So? My mother's five years younger than my dad."

"My sister is still in high school. You graduated College; you prick."

"It was only a three-year program. Your turn."

"Oh, so you're not going to answer your own cynical question?"

"Sure, I chose myself."

"Wow."

"Want to know why?" he asked smirking.

"Not particularly."

"Because I don't want to stop existing. People always assume atheists are fearless moguls, these fearless martyrs just because we don't believe in an afterlife. They think facing the truth makes us strong, cynical as you put it. People always need to glorify something nowadays. What you 'spiritual' dumbasses don't realize is that we're just as scared as you are. We just chose to face reality head-on. What's the point in living in ignorance? You all get so defensive when someone even mentions atheism. If you really had legs to stand on, you wouldn't need to preach."

"You're an asshole," I told him. Those damn heathens.

"Your turn," he said unphased by the insult.

"Fine. I'll play. Master of games. What's your preference, death by ice or fire?"

"Ice. You?"

"I'm not surprised. I'd chose fire."

"What because it's red?" he gestured to my jacket, "Or because you like the attention."

"No. Because I'm the flame," Heathen's piercing eyes sobered me, "Your turn, go."

"Do you believe in soulmates?" he asked me. I blushed.

"You would have to be pretty hard-bitten not to, yes. Wait, don't tell me you don't."

"No. I don't believe in soulmates. I think anyone can be your 'soulmate' you just have to work hard enough. Nothing jaded about that, even you would have to admit it. I just believe you could love anyone, and anyone could love you."

"You're a blast at parties, you know that right?"

"I'm the shot that sobers you," Heathen gazed back at me.

"That's not the kind of shot someone would take willingly," I said, scanning his face.

"People like reality," he said, "That's why you're talking to me now. There is something that intrigues you in pessimists. I know your type."

"Oh, I'm a type now. Lovely."

"No, not quite. But you're the person who poses as an optimist hoping no one will ever find the pessimism buried deep inside. Because you think it's ugly and you hate yourself for it. But it's there, and you're not a kid anymore. You need to learn how to embrace it. I'm tired of seeing smart people praying for false hopes. Why not save the effort and do something productive about whatever it is you're hoping for? Okay, your turn. Go."

"Do you believe in fate?" I asked he's got to believe in something.

"No. Not in the traditional sense."

"What do you mean by that?"

"I mean you make your own fate," he started, "I don't believe in destiny. Fate, soulmates, afterlife... nothing. It's just a bunch of stories and false hope. You know what I want to be,

V?"

"The shot that sobers people?" I rolled my eyes.

"As a matter of fact, yes. I want to be the guy that pisses people off and shows them that luck and fairy dust and all that shit they were supposed to grow out of when they were ten, is nothing more than a bunch of stories and pointless myths."

"If I were sober, I would fight you on this a little better, but I can't think straight right now. I'm having trouble even seeing straight in all honesty, but anyways, next question, go."

"What do you do in your spare time?" he asked. This one caught me off guard.

"I read, write songs then I sing them. Why?"

"Just trying to get to know you V. What do you read?"

"Shakespeare."

"You read Shakespeare? Don't you think you should be using your time to do something a little more productive?"

"Like?" I asked.

"I don't know, just something."

"What do you do?" I asked.

"I sign up for math competitions."

"Nerd," I smirked.

"Rather be a nerd than a dumbass,"

"Too bad you're both," I retaliated, "What's an overused mantra, something you consider to be a mob mentality."

"Oh, I know exactly what mine is, the myth that girls mature faster than boys. Mob mentality."

"Forget I asked," I wanted to go back into the party, "I should probably go check on Leery."

"What's your pet peeve mantra?" he asked, I signed.

"It's far too overused. Einstein's quote that the definition of insanity is when someone repeats the same action over and over expecting different results. Everyone believes themselves to be so intelligent for quoting Einstein and it irritates me."

"It's funny how they all repeat the same quote over and

over again, expecting a different revelation each time they do so. How insane does that make someone?" I smiled. That was a witty comeback.

Heathen was an immature asshole, that much was certain. But he was intelligent. Not as bright as he let on to be, not as talented as Elfin or me. Still, he did have something interesting to contribute to a conversation. Even if he was only skilled at being perceived as intelligent, that took some level of competence to maintain. At least I wasn't engaging in small talk. Or worse yet, sitting in on a group gossiping about one another.

"Okay, the last one," I said, "What's a philosophy or theory you were always curious about trying. I want to live minimalist like a Monk does for a month. I want to see if I can do it. What about you?"

"Have you ever read, 'The Stranger," by Albert Camus?" I nodded.

"You're curious about existentialism?" I chuckled, "and you don't believe in fate or destiny, and you want to die by ice. Sounds about right."

"Hear me out before you cast your judgments," he started, "Existentialism is basically the ideology that one takes life as it is. No attachments. Companionships are formed when mutually convenient, and they end when they no longer serve either party. I really only see pros to existentialism. You are not allowed to be materialistic, which means you can't contribute to the environmental epidemic; you aren't provoked into passionate disagreements, nor is mourning a loved one considered such an aggrievance. It really is the simplest, most intelligent way to live out one's life."

"Simplest sure. Not the most intelligent," I retorted.

"Oh, don't give me that liberal bull V. Emotions holds us back. Think of how much more productive we would be without them? Without empathy, we could all individually

quite the time.

"V I'm so sorry about Leery. I thought everything was going fine. She looked as though she trusted me, alright. I don't know what happened aside from the fact that I placed her down on the couch for less than a minute. I swear it was such a brief timeframe. I didn't think it necessary to put her back in the enclosure."

"It's okay Elfin. It really isn't your fault. Leery has a lot of trust issues. She would have run away from me too. Let's just try to find her."

Elfin and I searched the house for Leery, after we scanned the room and found no sign of her, we called the party to a halt and pulled the cord on the music.

"We can't find Leery. Can everyone please help us look for Leery?"

"Who?" asked Staid.

"Leery," I replied, "My kitten. The grey tabby in the café from earlier."

"Of course, V, we'll help look," Dote and Apt started looking around the place. Heathen continued to smoke on the balcony, he said he would be in soon to help search as well.

"I'm sorry we lost Leery," sighed Elfin.

"I trusted you with her Elfin, with all of you," I outburst, "but it's okay, I'll find her. I have to."

This was not the case, after several hours of searching we still couldn't find Leery. Heathen suggested we break for the night and search again tomorrow. I tried to explain to him that kittens are more likely to come out in the night as they are nocturnal and that we should keep looking, but everyone seemed quite exhausted.

"Kittens know when they're being searched for V," said Apt, "They can sense you looking. It's when they finally feel as though you have stopped searching for them that they will come out of their hiding place."

"The more you interfere," said Dote, "The harder it is to win her back. If you let her roam free a little while, she will come back." I was crushed to hear of Leery's disappearance, but my fear was relinquished when Heathen was kind enough to offer me a place to stay in the meantime as we looked for Leery. He showed me his roommate's room and explained that he was not in town frequently because he slept over at his girlfriend's place quite a bit. He ended up messaging him, and he agreed to let me sleep in his room for the time being. Heathen brought me bedsheets with flowers imprinted on the blanket.

"You know," I teased him, "For a boy who doesn't believe in anything, you have a soft side." I gestured to the sheets.

"As I was saying," he started, "Being rational and being human are two entirely different things, V."

"What is your favorite flower?" I asked him.

"Why do you want to know?" he asked softly.

"21 questions remember, we were stopped midgame."

"White roses," he responded, "They're a classic."

"I like red roses," I smiled.

"Such a cliché," he said, "This is coming from the girl who didn't like the Einstein quote because it was 'too overused.'"

"Well, it was," I laughed.

"Oh V, I should probably let you know, while you're here if you want to keep busy throughout the day, the board game café is hiring part-time workers. I talked to the owner, and they said they will hire you on. You can start tomorrow. They aren't looking for someone with a lot of experience per se, more of a busboy. They're desperate for workers, so even if you only stay a week or so you'll be doing them a favor."

"Heathen, that's very thoughtful of you, thank you, but I don't intend to stay for a week, I just want to stay long enough until I can find Leery, and besides, working at a coffee shop is not exactly what I had in mind when I left my home to follow

my dreams. I want to find gigs, and I am worried that my job with the board game coffee shop will interfere with that."

"But there is nothing wrong in having a stable income is there? Plus, I'm not really sure how much these local vocal gigs pay. You'll make more as a barista, the tips are excellent too."

"It's not really about the money Heathen, it's about the art, I'm trying to get a little exposure so I can keep making music."

"V, remember what I told you? Let me be the shot that sobers you. Vocalists don't get paid a lot, and a lot of you guys don't even make careers out of it. This job is consistent, and it'll allow you to save up some cash. Plus, they have an open mic night on Tuesdays, I think. You could do karaoke."

"Heathen don't tell me where I should or shouldn't be working, if vocalists work hard, they can make a career out of it."

"Really?" he mused, "Then why haven't you? I'm just trying to be logical V. If you want to stay here, you'll eventually have to start chipping in on rent."

"I don't want to stay here," I barked, "I would leave tonight if I could."

"But what about Leery?" he taunted. I despised him for it. If Leery hadn't gone missing, I would never have the heart to leave. He smirked at me and turned toward the staircase. "You start at 8:00 am," he affirmed, and then he disappeared into the shadows.

****

When reading a story, one can pick out the antagonist with ease. In one's own life, the differentiation between hero and villain is far less clear cut. This is because, while people are not all good, no person is inherently bad either. Who is Heathen of not the Heathcliff to this story? The jaded man with a tumultuous past, or rather the cleverly keen villain who utilizes his intelligence for brutality in those he projects his insecurities? We can only hope for the prior, but hope alone rarely suffices. No

matter how cruel the villain in the books she scrutinizes, V always reads the villain with an empathetic lens. She often falls victim to their past and wishes them a more enriching future.

Rather than lift her in the way she lifts them, the villains in V's story always attempt to drag her back to their lowly grounds. Thereby V must collect herself again, and again, placing back together the pieces that her antagonist once disserved from her. Despite her antagonist's ill-treatment toward her, V always rises. Better still, this time, she will not be alone. Dear reader, we are with V now. If we pity her, she will stay safe. But let her learn first dear reader, let her learn so she may thrive.

****

That night, when the day broke, and Leery was still nowhere to be found, I wandered to the café, and began my first shift. Initially, I expected to only work a week, perhaps two at most. Then two turned to three, and three became five, five became nine until three months had passed, and still, I catered to the customers of the board game café. Most were rarely in high spirits, and oftentimes they were quite pointed in their orders. I found discomfort in the way they groveled into the shop. We were frequently overcrowded with customers midday on lunch break. They were rarely in the mood to converse, and patience was rarely a motive in them. They would often enter with the intent of belittling the servers. I had gotten rather close with the barista with the tattooed sleeve. We often joked about the first night we met. That awkward first meeting blossomed into a swift forming friendship. Her and I, this afternoon, took out lunch break together at 2:00 pm. As anyone who works at a café would know, you cannot take your break at the hour of noon because that is the time customers bombard the shop. One is either to take their break marginally early or unsettlingly late. So, I chose late, as did my friend.

"Busy day," she said, looking at her watch, "and with

karaoke night tonight, this place will be packed."

"I know, I've been dreading it," I admitted.

"Me, too," laughed the barista, "Will you be performing?"

"No," I stated adamantly, "I'm far too scared to perform in public."

"V, you sing. And you're good. Every karaoke night that comes around I beg you to sing and you always turn the offer down."

"I just haven't really been motivated to make music," I sighed, "I would need more practice if I were to perform again."

"You sing beautifully, V! I think the customers would love if you were to sing. We have a lot of slots still open for you."

Just as I started, I saw Heathen enter with Staid.

"Hi babe," he smiled at me and kissed me on the cheek.

****

Oh reader, how silly of me to forget to mention. Heathen and V began to date. For two months now they have. V doesn't remember this time very well as it was insignificant to the grander plan, but at the time, the relationship was important to her. I spoil again! Let us resume without my protruding into the plot any further.

****

"Heathen, tell your girlfriend to perform tonight at the open mic," the barista said, and he smirked.

"Oh, you want V to perform? Yeah okay, she has stage fright, she doesn't like crowds. She's too humble for that shit, right V?"

"That's what I have been trying to tell her," I turned back to the barista, "See?"

"That's it, I'm going out for a smoke. V, you're coming," she grasped me by the arm.

"Woah, she doesn't smoke," Heathen started.

"She can keep me company," said the barista, "Girl talk."

She dragged me out of the shop. With her hand firmly grasping my left arm, I had very little say in the matter.

"Lunch ends in like two minutes," I said.

"Work can wait, we're always dead anyway," the barista looked into my eyes in a way I had never seen someone look at me before. I could not describe if it was pity, or anger, or pain that she projected to me through that look. All I knew was that I would never forget it.

"V, when I first met you, I didn't like you." I laughed, "No, I'm serious, hear me out. When you first walked into my café with that tattered red jacket and that damn cat, and you know I hate cats, I looked at you, and I thought, Nomad." I shivered in hearing her call me that. Flashbacks to Realist's mother ensued. She continued and urged me to silence when I attempted to interject.

> "I thought to myself, 'Directionless Nomad. Coming into my café with that smug look on her face, wearing those worn out shoes and that broken, aged ukulele.' Then you spoke. And I thought, 'No, not a nomad, an artist.' There was something in the resourceful way you approached me and asked to be signed to the Scrabble match that I was sure that you had no idea how to play. I watched you bitterly because I hate both nomads and artists. Both cause a nuisance to me. Then I saw you leave to freshen yourself up. When you came back, you looked about the same on the surface, but something was different. At first, I didn't know what it was, but then I saw it. It was confidence. Unwavering confidence and sureness, something that others lack. I saw those traits in you."

"Thank you, that is probably the sweetest thing anyone has ever said to me, then we became friends when you saw I

requested an interview. It was in New York, so I got all dressed up and spent the money I had saved up on a plane ticket, and I flew out to New York City. I got all dressed up in my formal attire, and I printed off paper resumes, and I rented a cheap motel for the night before, so I knew there wouldn't be any complications. I practiced my interview over several Skype calls with my brother, and he told me I would ace it. In the morning, I walked to the studio office in my little kitten heels, and I shook hands with my interviewer, and I answered every question correctly, and they all saw my potential. It was clear that they were very interested in working with me. I was certain I would get the job."

"And you did right, but turned it down?" I asked.

"No, I was rejected. The company informed me they were no longer interested in offering me the position as my qualifications did not match those the requirement official was seeking in its candidates. V that rejection email dismantled me. A few weeks later, a prof who was in with the company reported back to me, they gave the position to a previous intern. Male. Who was in the exact major as me, attended the same school, a year or two older, but with a horrendous work ethic. He had little ambition and worked to complete tasks with minimal effort. He graduated with a substantially lower average than me. I was heartbroken and dissuaded from my ambition. True I got other interviews, but I canceled each of them. Eventually, I gave up canceling and simply stopped showing up to the interviews I had pre-scheduled, permanently damaging my reputation with each company. A few weeks after sluggishly staying in the house, my parents become frustrated and offered me an ultimatum. I could either work for my keep, or I would have to find another place to live. So, I had to find a job

quickly, and I started waitressing at some restaurant uptown. I hated it there, so I started applying to other local coffee shops and restaurants. Now, I am here, and I have been here for the past three years."

"I don't know what to say," I started.

"I do. I realize now why I didn't like you when I first met you. You reminded me of my actors. When I would do set design, I would hang out in the green room with the actors, even though we weren't supposed to. They were full of life and ambition. They would sing inspirational Broadway songs on repeat, compliment each other, rather than envy one another. They would talk about the local shows they were performing in, talk about their ambitions to go to Broadway, and perform as a soloist in 'Les Miserable,' or some wanted to switch to film after they graduated, some wanted to delve into the opera. V, they were like you. I loved them once. Now when I see an artist or a Nomad like yourself, I loathe them, not because I hate them, but because I envy them," I was speechless.

"I am no performer," I said after a moment's deliberation.

"V, when you first met me, you told me you were a writer. Yet, you have not written anything substantial aside from a few poems on your breaks when you think no one is noticing. You started dating Heathen, and he started telling you your poems made no sense and that your dreams and ambition to travel was childish and absurd for someone of your age to pursue. He used the cat to manipulate you in stay put. You have been here for three months, and have not sung one note. And you stopped looking for Leery. Don't give up on your dreams, V. Perform tonight."

I could not believe this. The barista who despised me on the very first day was now giving me life advice.

"I am happy with Heathen," I told her, "I love him. I am happy with a starless sky; I see no need to fix what is not broken."

"V, that's an overused cliché. You never would have said that before you came here. Don't get stuck in this small town. It is a town designed for the small-minded, and I believe there are better things in store for you."

"I'm not performing tonight," I said, cutting her off, "and I think our lunch break is over. Let's go back in."

I stormed into the café and went behind the counter. I operated the cash register while the population of the shop increased. Since the weather had begun to get a little warmer, we opened up the patio. Everyone seemed to be a fan of it. I didn't see Heathen and Elfin in the café anymore, so I assumed they were out on the patio.

"Excuse me," exclaimed a woman, she was in her forties, and she held an empty mug in her hand, "I dropped this on the patio. I tripped on the step by the door. Can I please get a refill?"

"Oh, of course!" I said quickly, I began to get the lady her dark roast, and I left a little room at the top for creamers. "This one is on the house. Where did you spill it? Do you mind letting me know? I will go to mop it up."

"Just by the door of the patio," she began. So, I walked to the patio. I was right about Heathen and Elfin sitting out there; it was likely to talk strategy for their next Scrabble match that was coming up in an hour. But then I began to hear some strange whispers interchanged between them, I stopped my mopping. I loomed a little closer in, suspicious, but also ashamed of my jealousy.

"Elfin, you know it's you."

"Then why are you still with her? You told me you would break things off."

"What do you want from me, Elfin? We're not together anymore." Anymore? What were they talking about? He continued, and I listened in the shadows, "You're going off to college again for your masters, and I'm going to be stuck here

again, I don't want to be alone," Heathen admitted.

"Yes, but if we aren't together anymore, then why do you keep doing this? I'm not your girlfriend, she is. Go be with her."

"I love you Elfin," he burst out, I felt my heart split into two, "You're smart, funny. Look I just can't let you go. I want you tonight. V doesn't have to know."

"Heathen stop it, I can't do that to V."

"So, you barely know V, and you've known me for two years. You're going to put someone's feelings you've only known for three months over mine? Wow."

"It's not like that Heathen—why don't you just give her the damn cat back and let her go. Why do you always have to be so childish?" What did she mean by that, did Heathen know where Leery was?

The two looked at each other. Elfin bit her lip, and Heathen did not even bother to look to his right or left to check to see if I was anywhere in sight. In my café. In my place of work. He leaned into the beautiful Elfin, and she reciprocated his kiss. It lasted thirty seconds, which was enough time for me to drop the mop to the floor and run out of the café in tears unnoticed by the two. The barista saw me and looked as though she wanted to reach out, but yet knew nothing to say. What can one say in a moment like that?

Now I saw the heaven-less skies Heathen warned me about.

CHAPTER IX

BURSTING STAR

"I will always be myself; it is the only way I know to be, and the only way I would want to be." — V

****

All I wanted was to run to the ravine with the bridge that overlooked the night sky, but I couldn't. I was miles away from the cul-de-sac, and the ravine, and the conservative downtown I grew up, with its roads lit by a combination of streetlights and star-lights. Instead, I found myself alone in a tiny town on a mountainside. I ran. I ran without intention into the afternoon. I wish I could say the weather mirrored my mood that afternoon, just like in the movies when a storm erupts just as the lead actress begins to cry, but this was not the case for me. It was just an average day. There was nothing special, nothing extraordinary about that day. The people of the town continued on with their daily lives, the sun was shining, birds sang in the streets, but I didn't notice because my eyes were drowned by tears. Perhaps it was because that day was so average, so ordinary, that it felt so sad.

I idly scattered through the forest, through the trails, through the cobbled roads, and down the spiraling staircases. I saw nothing beautiful in that midday. Instead, the streets looked dull and dying. My heart felt as though it was decaying in my chest, and I was fading with it. Who was Heathen to love another? While vowing to stay loyal to me, while making

promises he could not keep. Who was he to devalue me? Who was he to leave a scar? I sobbed as I ran. The locals who knew me did not dare approach me, nor did they ask what was wrong. They already knew.

I wanted to vomit, I wanted to sob, but most importantly, I wanted to get out of this town. I ran until I could no longer see the plaza. The trail I traveled on looked familiar, but I could not determine where I had seen it before until I saw a red car pulled into an abandoned parking lot. I also saw an entrance to a trail across the street from that parking lot. I knew that trail, and I knew that red car. It looked foreign now. I once viewed that car as an opportunity, a vehicle that could transport me to my dreams. Now, the car was like a broken promise. It was a disappointment, a broken dream. It was nothing more than a rusted metal tin enclosure. Sort of like a cage, like the one I used to carry Leery in.

I decided to venture down the trail. The trail that piqued my interest on the first day. I recalled Leery, distrustful in nature, once caused a fit as I dabbled with the idea of taking this trail as an alternate pathway. I was not Leery, I did not fear the world the way she did, the world had reason to fear me. So, I decided to enter the trail at my leisure.

The air in the forest was frigid due to the cold atmosphere of the mountainside. I wished I could be free of the cold. I never did thrive in the frigid air. There was something therapeutic in the bare trees of this forest. Not a single leaf decorated the treetops. The wind rattled its branches, and the cold air left my fingers numb. I sobbed into the breeze, and it dried my tears. I could not hold back my tears for much longer as they trickled down my cheeks and froze to my face. I walked the trail until it ended, then I walked into an expanse in the forest, a field was frozen over and bare. It looked the way my heart felt. The snow crunched beneath my boots. I took off my apron and lay it on the ground. I sat there, in the falling snow,

you broken, and it's no fault but his. It is only if you stay broken that the fault becomes your own."

"But I wanted him so badly," I cried, "He was my best friend!"

"V, can I ask you something?" interrupted Angel.

"Yes, Angel," I nodded.

"V, why did you come to the mountains all those months ago?"

The mountains, why did I come? Oh, well, that was simple, I came because... well. Why did I come to the mountainside? My mind went numb. I couldn't remember why I came here; all I could remember was that I didn't want to leave. Something in that question struck a memory. The memory was from when I was driving, a song played on the radio, I don't remember the name of it now, just the tune. The lyrics were talking about the freedom of riding down endless roads. Something in the message of the song intrigued me. I sang along to the tune.

Leery, in being a cat, was incapable of singing along. Instead, she sat silently, but then, to my surprise, Leery began to meow along to the song! If kittens were capable of keeping a tune, I believe Leery would have belted out the lyrics alongside me. Then, I remembered everything.

"I came to the mountains because I wanted to get gas," I said. That was it, that was all, the only reason I came to the mountainside was to find gas money so I could drive onward. The town on the mountainside was supposed to be a detour, but then I met Heathen. I stayed and fell for a boy who never intended on falling for me. Oh, how foolish was I to stay here?

"V, you have not sung here in the mountains for months, nor have you composed any songs, or written any poetry. Why are you still here in the town in the mountainside? You have enough for gas and food now. You have saved from your keep at the restaurant. Now you may go onward, but what keeps

you here?"

Angel was right, she always was.

"But Angel my heart hurts," I cried to her, she only nodded.

"A successful journey mends all broken hearts. Give it time and foster new memories, new memories will soon replace the old."

"But Angel, he was perfect, he was beautiful."

"No, V, you are beautiful. Heathen is not perfect because perfect people do not hurt others. And he has hurt you now. He has hurt you very deeply." I knew she was right. I never intended for my story to become a story of unrequited love. I just wanted to travel and follow my dreams.

"Angel," I started, "What about Leery? I can't find her, and I can't leave without her."

Now, I knew Angel was a wise woman. She looked at me and smiled, and I knew then she had the answer.

"V," Angel began, "Leery is a distrustful creature, and while precariously cautious, that much is certain, her trust can be earned. But it must be earned. She will find her way back to you, cats always do, but you need to learn to put more trust in her hesitation. When she suggested her discontent toward Heathen, you disputed her insight. When she cried, you did not give her affection. You must learn to love her and take her hesitations seriously because there is wisdom in the precautious beings among us. Sometimes a little bit of wisdom can go a long way." I knew she was right.

"I'm going back to get Leery. I'm going back to get my kitten," I told Angel. I turned my gaze from her, for only a moment, and when I turned back again, Angel was gone.

I walked back to the café; I knew Heathen would still be there with Elfin. I entered the coffee shop, apron in hand. I slammed it on the counter. Open mic night had not started yet, so I knew I had to make this quick, I walked straight up to

Heathen and looked into his green eyes, they no longer looked piercing to me. I had a fierceness in me that I knew he had never seen before. I was a flame.

"Heathen. I know what you did, and I only want two questions answered. This much you owe me. Can we not agree to that?" If it weren't for the passion in my voice, I felt as though he may have dismissed my request, but something in me scared him. It was the very same thing that intimidated the barista on the day she met me. So, he agreed to my demand.

"I didn't want to believe it, and I did my best to dismiss it as best I could. But I noticed it, and I have to ask. In your room, there are two nightstands. The one on the left, and the other on the right. On the left nightstand, there is a scrunchy doesn't belong to me, it has been there since the night I moved in. Now I know it is Elfin's, but on the right Heathen, on the right of that scrunchy, there is a tiny figurine. I thought it was odd at first, and I never asked about it.

"It's a fairy Heathen. A tiny fairy ornaments. In my travels, long before I met you, I befriended a pregnant woman in a little town. She had blondest hair and the biggest heart I have ever seen. Here is the first question, and you had better answer it. Do you know the woman I speak of?" he looked into my eyes and he saw I was not wavering.

"Yes," he muttered. I smacked him hard across the face and left a large red mark across his cheek. I was never one to resort to aggression, but it was deserved in this one instance. He caused so much damage, he broke the heart of the naive Caprice, the mother to his child. I had tried to suppress my suspicion, but deep down, I always knew, this was the man who Caprice lights a candle for each night on her doorstep.

"I gave her my word," I continued, "That if I met the man with the green eyes, with the raven hair, and the angelic smile, that I would tell him that she keeps a candle lit on her porch for him and a key behind the plant in her urn. Caprice waits for

you, and you don't deserve her gratitude. Second question. Where is Leery? I know you have her. I think I have known all this time. You kept her from me to keep me trapped here in this town on the mountainside. Tell me where I can find her." The boy was scared, he decided to confess.

"Yes. I took that damn cat. I figured, what was the point in watching her? You can't travel forever, Nomad. Eventually, you'll have to settle like the rest of us."

"You did not answer my question," I began to raise my voice, "Where is my cat?!" Heathen was caught off guard by this surge of aggression.

"She's in your goddamn car!" he blurted, I felt I would faint, "In your car, I put her in there, that red tin piece of scrap metal by the trail, I put the crate in the trunk."

"Oh my god, Leery!" I exclaimed.

"V, it's okay, please she's okay," Elfin tried to calm me down, "I've been going out to feed her once a day to ensure she is okay..."

"You mean you knew she was in there Elfin! And you kept this from me? You can have Heathen, but you can never have Leery. Neither of you! Cruel creatures, the both of you. The lot of you!" I gestured to the rest of the friend group.

"Go, Nomad," exclaimed Heathen in a frenzy, "I never liked you anyways. You wanted to be my girlfriend, yeah that ain't happening. Ever. I don't have time for people like you in my life."

"You know what Heathen," I said, stepping up to him, I looked him straight in the eye, "I'm getting tired of the games," he sat down.

I nodded to the barista, she smiled back at me. I ran out of the coffee shop and ran to the car. I opened the trunk and saw my Leery safe, but she was scared. How could they be so inhumane! I stroked her fur until she was calm. When I was sure she was safe, I walked on foot to the gas station and filled

a carton, I fueled the car and took to the road.

****

V made it out from the depths of her own hell. Thankfully too. She is a strong woman and a bright one at that. So, when someone told her to hit the road, she took it quite literally and traveled so far from them in hopes she would never see them again. V drove back down the mountainside and saw the little cabin she had passed earlier. V decided to venture into it now that she was no longer scared of it.

****

I pulled up to the cabin. It seemed to be calling to me. I couldn't help but wonder what it was about this cabin that I feared before? Leery, on the other hand, was never intimidated by this cabin.

'Strange,' I thought to myself. Leery feared most places and people, and still, she did not fear the cabin. I considered for a moment what Angel had told me previously: "Leery's trust must be earned." Rather than earning Leery's trust, Heathen and Elfin hid her, oppressed her, rid her from their sights. They did so hoping that I would forget about Leery entirely.

I decided to wander into the cabin, it neighbored a ski slope. I could see the hills out from the cabin's gaping windows. I saw a tiny café within the cabin. People were ordering hot chocolate from it.

There was once a time that I would have been more frivolous with my money. I might have ordered a coffee with honey and cinnamon, but in seeing that a lack of funds could result in a detour to a town like the one on the mountainside, I decided I was better off saving my income. The more I saved, the longer I could travel without taking a lengthy detour.

I sat alone at a table and watched as a violinist performed for a crowd. He was of South Asian descent. He looked

talented, and from the way he played, I could tell he was intelligent.

He looked at me and saw I sat alone. He wanted to come to sit with me, but I was not ready. Yet, he played sweet, sad songs for me. I felt them, and I cried for him. But, I could not go to him because he was not mine to keep, and I was not his. And though he played a melancholy tune that I loved and pitied, I could not go to the violinist who composed poetry into song. Who listened to jazz like it was gospel. Who saw art in my eyes first. I nodded to him as he played his sad song, and he smiled gravely back at me. I felt for him, but I knew I could not put his blues into the robin eggs of Spring, and I knew I could only make him bluer in staying.

"Can I buy you a coffee?" I jumped and looked to my right, an older woman was standing by me. Like Elfin and the barista, her arms were decorated by intricate tattoos.

"You want to buy me a coffee?" I asked.

"I always offer to buy glum newcomers' coffee, it eases the soul," said the mysterious woman.

"I'm not glum," I exclaimed.

"Well, you aren't exactly cheery either," said the woman, she extended a hand out toward me, "My name is Able, I like to get to know newcomers over coffee. Can we talk?"

I ended up accepting the woman's offer, and we chatted over coffee. I'll spare the details of the more mundane parts of the conversation. I learned her name was Able, and I told her mine was V. Able asked about my disposition, and I told her about the town on the mountainside, and I told her about Heathen and Leery and all of the others who contributed to my broken heart. She asked to hold Leery, she warmed up to Able quickly. I learned that Able was a tattoo artist, I supposed she was the one Elfin, and the barista went to, I understood why she was very personable. I did not realize then that Able would be capable of shifting my entire perception of the events that

unmotivated and exhausted chapter at that. I almost stopped writing entirely during those two, three chapters I gave them."

"Well, it's like this V," started the wise Able, "Why do all fairy tales end in happy endings? Ask anyone, most will say it is because we tell fairy tales to children, and it is important that we end on a high note to teach them about hope. Still, I wonder, why don't we begin every fairy tale with a happy start? Why do we tell stories of characters who endure struggle and pain before they finally attain that golden ending? Well, V, the answer is simple. It is because the story is in the struggle. Forgive yourself for writing long chapters about those who meant the least to you. Those chapters were meant to teach you to be more attuned to the people who mean the most to you. The people who hurt us redirect us to the friends in our lives who actually mean something to us."

"Why do you live on the mountainside Able?" I asked her, she smiled.

"Because V, I am an old woman now, I have lived my entire life grazing mountaintops, and I have spent even more time clambering their sides. I know the view of the mountaintops like the back of my own hand, and I want nothing more than to encourage the mountainside dwellers to see the view for themselves. I give them art, little tiny pieces of art to carry with them in the hope that someday they will look down at their bodies and see the symbol. The symbol that's meant to remind them that they do have what it takes to see the mountaintops. They had it with them all along. Some dwell the mountainsides for an eternity, and they keep traveler's hostage there with them. I, on the other hand, hope to free the traveler from the mountainside so she may rise to the mountaintop."

I considered Able's soft warnings, and I valued her for them. The mountainsides did trap a lot of people with potential, like the barista and Elfin, I wished them the best. I

looked to Able's arm and noticed one particular tattoo that I felt the need to ask about it.

"Your tattoo is very beautiful Able, 'If the artists don't praise our art, then who will?'"

"Thank you, V, it's my own design. When I am not decorating the arms of mountainside dwellers, I draw on my own," she laughed to herself.

"Did you do the sleeve on a barista in a board game café, and do you know a woman named Elfin?"

"Yes, I most certainly do," Able smiled, "V, you fear losing yourself to the mountainsides, but I know better than to fear the inevitable. We all fall victim to the mountainsides every so often. Mountainsides can be towns and cities, even places of work. People can also be mountainsides. There is nothing wrong with taking leisure on these mountainsides. Only as long as you keep moving upward to see the starry sky. I do not think you have to worry about losing yourself to a mountainside again. I will give you a little permanent reminder, a symbol, one for you to look down upon in times of stress so that you will never forget yourself again."

I smiled, she wanted to give me a tattoo. I never thought I would have the courage to get one. Tattoos are art on the body, maybe it would serve as a reminder that my body is art. My soul is art. My intentions and ambition are also art. Who was I to deny an artist? But finances were a concern.

"Able, thank you, but I am trying to save money for the road."

"I never said that I would charge you," Able cut in, "In fact, I believe all I said was, would you like a little permanent reminder of who you truly are? I charge for my designs. In seeing the tattoo is not meant to represent my true self, but rather yours, you should design it, and then I will ink it onto you."

What a compelling proposition! But now I was left to

consider what best represented me. What symbol could help me the next time I found myself on the mountainside, to encourage me to break free from it and clamber upward. Then it hit me, I knew what I wanted.

"Able, I want to be reminded to climb upward. To always look up to the stars. Of all the symbols in the world, a star, bursting with energy, would best represent me." I took a napkin from the coffee counter, and Able passed me a pen. I drew my star design onto it, and she examined it wide-eyed.

"I give bumblebees to feminists," she started, "To remind them even nature reflects their strength. I give tornados to those who overcame trauma, to remind them it's only tumultuous winds that will eventually subside. I now give bursting stars to the dreamers. Is that your name V?" I thought it over, it seemed to fit, but it did not start with V, so it couldn't be my name.

"No Able, it's close, but 'Dreamer' is not my name."

"Just as well, tell me when you find it. I mean, when you learn what your name stands for. In the meanwhile, I'll give bursting star designs to those who dream of seeing the views on mountaintops."

Able took me to her studio in the cabin. The walls of the studio were decorated with symbols and potential tattoo designs. It was clear to me that Able was passionate about her work, perhaps it was because of the way she spoke of tattoos, maybe it was because of that sparkle in her eye.

'Dream-catalyst,' I thought to myself, 'Able, you're a dream-catalyst, I would recognize that sparkle anywhere. I wondered why your eyes looked so familiar.'

Able put her needle to the skin over my right rib, the pain of permanence surged onto my side. I knew better than to cry out in pain as Able inked my side, after all, I left my true source of pain on the mountainside. No, that true source of pain was not Heathen; instead, it was complacency that pained me so. I

left complacency behind with the people on the mountainside.

"Able," I said, "Thank you." She smiled and continued to work. There on my right side, Able left a small bursting star.

I sat and contemplated these past three months as Able began to bandage my new tattoo so it can start its healing process. What did I ever see in Heathen and the people on the mountainside? I did love something about Heathen, despite his many faults, but what was it that allured me to him?

After reflecting, I came to a revelation. I knew what it was that I loved about him. I loved Heathen for the man he was before he got stuck on the mountainside. It would shine through the walls he built for himself from time to time. Somehow, I knew he was a nomad, even before I discovered Caprice's fairy on his nightstand. I knew he was a traveler like me, a more experienced traveler than I. I was trying to live vicariously through him. I lived through his adventures through his alluring stories. He would frequently tell me about the lands he had roamed the people he had met. He was an adventure before he settled on the mountainside. I did not love him; I loved his stories.

Was Vicarious my name? It does start with V after all. Maybe Able was right, my novel was beginning to turn very dialogue heavy. I was living vicariously through others. Everyone had so much to say, everyone had their story to tell, but finding someone to listen to mine was a challenge.

No. No, it is not. I knew for sure that Vicarious was not my name. I would know it instantly if it was. No, I knew better than to believe I was vicarious by nature. I was much more than that. People told me their stories because I listened to them. I was not vicarious for listening to others, I had my own adventures to live. In reality, my life was nothing like the mountainside dwellers, I was going to see the mountaintops.

"V," Able asked after she finished cleaning her tools, "Did

you see the tattoos on Elfin's sleeve?" I nodded, "I know you may want to forget Elfin, but you have to remember to have reverence for the fallen ones. She will rise again someday. Every tattoo comes with a story, and I tell one to Elfin as I decorate her arm. Same is true of the barista. That is why both keep coming back as my clients, to hear my stories. I know you feel betrayed by Elfin, but you've got to remember, she is your sister, and she is gentle. Elfin is not a mountainside dweller, neither is the barista, Heathen keeps them, hostage there, but in reality, the two are meant for much greater things."

"I never stopped liking Elfin," I admitted, "Nor did I stop respecting her. I just wish she had become the activist instead of the bystander, but she hasn't yet, and it broke my heart."

"V, invest time in those who do not need to grow into their good character, but instead, have already developed it," I nodded and told Able I would from now on, but she knew I was lying. Something about the flawed among us seemed perfect to me. Perhaps because they had potential like a seedling has potential.

Able and I parted ways, and I left the mountainside. I bid Able a final farewell, I took her symbols and stories with me. I drove to the fork in the road I had past previous. I saw what the town in the mountainside had in store for me, and it was not enough. So I traveled onward to the new lands awaiting me. The grounds I was yet to discover. Onward to art! Onward to love! And onward to song!

****

V rode onward down the country roads in quest of her future, but this time she traveled with a permanent bursting star inked on her side.

CHAPTER X

MOON-EYES

"Great minds discuss ideas;
average minds discuss events;
small minds discuss people." - E.R.

... and did he ever have a great mind — V

****

This chapter is beautiful and V hoped that it would never end. In being a believer in happy endings, V thought this chapter would be the last of her story, but she was wrong. If the story is in the struggle, as Able told her, this chapter would be the bulk of V's journey of self-discovery.

V took to the road again. Six months had passed since V had last spoken to Able. She drove down the streets and performed at gigs in the cities she came across on her journey.

V only visited the cities that were large enough for her. V had made a promise to herself that until she found a city that was strong enough to carry her dreams, she would continue to search. V never stayed in a city for any longer than a week or two. She collected income from the occasional paying gig and then continued onto the next city.

People began to notice V. They knew her as the mystery girl with the powerful voice who roamed freely from one city to the next. The mysterious girl with the one-letter name. Everyone wanted V to perform in their city; V began to establish a name for herself. She posted covers of Billboard Top One Hundred

a day she didn't otherwise have it booked. In exchange for the kind gesture, I performed at her friend's pub on the Friday and Saturday of that week, the band originally scheduled to perform bailed last minute.

I was starting to establish a name for myself. People were asking about the mystery girl with the one-letter name. I started to get requests from my steadily growing fanbase. Venues would reach out to me and invite me to perform. I sold my EP and the t-shirts I designed at the venues I performed.

I was working on an album, I was almost done with it too. I just had one or two more songs to record, then it would be complete.

Today I had an esteemed gig booked in Toronto. It was at a well-established concert hall for a semi-annual festival that supported up and coming artists. It would host four of five sets, and it paid its artists. It was famous for inviting high profile local agencies to the two-day festival, and I was in need of representation. If I had someone handling the business side of things, I could continue composing music undisturbed. I would not have to set time aside to handle the logistics of my career. Currently, I was restricted to booking gigs on my laptop and I had no choice but to mooch off of open Wi-Fi networks. I didn't have a cell phone so I relied on social media platforms and my email to connect with venues.

Since I did not have a fixed home, I would barter Wi-Fi from coffee shops and the motels I rented from. While most of the motels did have free Wi-Fi, it was typically a poor connection. This made it difficult for me to search the web for gigs. Despite this, I managed, but still, having an agent would take this burden off of my shoulders.

I was actually surprised to receive an invitation to this exclusive venue. You had to apply online to get invited, I sent in my EP, and I wrote up a resume of all the places I had performed previously. I did not expect to be invited, but when

I was, I made arrangements to settle in Toronto for a week or so.

I was opening for a few well-established bands in the city. One of the bands was called Zephyr, and the other was called Hurl. People are so creative when naming their band. I sort of figured Hurl played heavy metal or something along those lines, but I had no idea what kind of music Zephyr performed. When I looked up the term 'Zephyr' I found that it meant cool breeze in its literary definition. I was still at a loss, perhaps they performed soft rock, maybe? Or classical music? I was still unsure.

I just called myself V, I didn't think of a stage name. Some of my fans compared me to the artist formerly known as Prince because I defined myself by a symbol. A lot of people asked me what 'V' stood for. I never had an answer for them, this kept them speculating.

Some thought that V alluded to the female genitalia; they took this to symbolize either sexual freedom or feminism or both. Some thought it stood for Victorious because I frequently sang about success. One person thought it stood for Vampy because of the red pleather jacket I wore over my black attire. I honestly just went by the name I was born with. When I told this to my fanbase they were discontent. They insisted that V stood for something. I let them keep guessing, it was amusing.

When the traffic driving into Toronto finally subsided, I made my way into the downtown. When I finally reached the venue, I maneuver my vehicle into a parallel parking spot that charged by the hour. I decided to invest in the flat rate to be safe, I locked my door behind me and picked up Leery's cage.

Oh, I forgot to mention, Leery sort of became my personal mascot, everyone who knew me, also knew Leery. Leery was always welcomed into every venue, even despite the regulation, the venues made an exception for Leery. She was a celebrity in her own right.

I took a moment to examine my surroundings. One must always stop to smell the roses, and while Downtown Toronto was not abundant in roses per se, it certainly did offer various attractions to the eyes of a tourist.

A local to the city cannot appreciate the beauty of Toronto the way a newcomer can. This is true of any city. When you live in an area for long enough, you grow used to it.

I never wanted to take any place for granted, I never wanted to lose the butterflies in my stomach as I looked around a new city. To prevent growing familiar and losing the butterflies, I never stayed anywhere for any longer than a week or two. When one stays somewhere for any longer than a week or two, everything starts to blend together. The magnificent buildings they once stood in awe of would begin to mesh into one another. I couldn't handle the idea of losing my lust for a city, so I took the necessary precautions to ensure I never would.

I once had a conversation with a farmer at one of the venues I performed at. It was a coffee shop in the countryside, a detour on my way to the next city. I told him about my fear of losing lust for a city, he shook his head. He told me I should live on a farm, then I would never grow too familiar with the view. I laughed him off and told him the life of a farmer was not in the cards for me.

He seemed unsettled by my response, "Girl, philosophers for years have regarded us the bottom of the hierarchy," the farmer admitted, "Plato compared us to bronze, academics to silver and philosophers to gold. But I have my own philosophies. When the environment crumbles because the academics and philosophers of the system destroy our only home, the Earth, they will praise the farmers. Us farmers will become a rare commodity because we will be the only ones who know how to work the land. Only then will they regard the farmer highly, only then will they take us seriously. Your

corrupted world will burn while ours thrives. Just remember the farmers V, we are not the simpletons you pretentious scholars make us out to be. We are not the slaves of society, no, it is the academics that serve as societies slave. A slave to a corrupted system. Sure, you pay tribute to it now, and you might even commemorate it at its memorial when your precious, corrupted society dies. But as for us farmers, we will never worship your corrupted system the way you do. We put no value in it, just as it puts no value in us."

I was surprised by this farmers passion as he iterated his position on today's social hierarchy. I asked him where he learned so much about philosophy, he laughed again.

"I have all the time in the world to study. I barter books and read them for hours. Academics sell all their hours to the system. Your precious hours are wasted away by fruitless jobs at your corrupted industries. You are a slave to the system. They shame you for not reading enough, while they simultaneously rob you of your time, preventing you from doing so."

I suppose the farmer had a leg to stand on in his criticism of the system. I decided I would write a song for him. I was not sure what I would call it, but it would be radical and lovely.

I looked around the city again with the farmer's lens. Now I saw the truth. The city was only beautiful on the surface, but that was because a newcomer wouldn't notice the smoke clouds caused by pollutants at first glance. A newcomer wouldn't see the plastic bags that littered the streets or the debris that covered the sidewalks.

'I might become familiar with this city sooner than a week,' I thought to myself, 'But maybe that was the point. Maybe the whole point of a city was to embrace its consistency, maybe you were supposed to become familiar with a city so it felt more like home,' I tried not to think about it because 'home' has always been a synonym for complacent

and stagnant to me, the two things I dreaded the most.

It was evening now and the sun was going to set in another thirty minutes or so. I walked into the venue. It was quite lovely, it looked as though it could seat a few hundred people. It was a local theatre, probably attached to one of the colleges in the area. I smiled; it had been a while since I had performed on a proper stage. In the corner, I noticed they had set up a concession stand. They sold soft beverages, coffee, and some snacks. I ordered myself a coffee with cinnamon and honey.

As I sipped my coffee, I noticed a band setting up on stage. Judging from their leather jackets and their studded bracelets, I figured it was Hurl. They already had a table set up in front of the stage with their band shirts and their album available for purchase. There was a girl in a metal t-shirt operating the table.

The doors weren't open to the public yet. The venue wanted to give us an hour to set up before the paying customers were let in. Leery sat quietly as I sipped my coffee. All theatres must have a green room, perhaps I could put Leery in there for a little while, it might be more comfortable for her. I asked the barista if there was a green room and he pointed me in the direction. I asked if I could take my coffee in, he sighed and said yes, but he insisted I bring the mug back afterward.

I found irony in the fact that this green room was painted blue. As I walked in I noticed a boy dressed entirely in black, he was sitting on one of the couches. I placed Leery on the table and smiled at him, he smiled back. I sat on the couch adjacent to him and pulled out my laptop. I had some downtime now so I figured I might as well start booking gigs. I peered over my laptop again at the boy, he wore a black leather jacket and dark jeans, his hair was dark as well. His glasses looked similar to mine and he seemed to be typing

something out on his phone. He was of South Asian descent and he was very cute. I shifted my focus back to my laptop. I studied it for a minute, I was trying to book another gig in Toronto while I was in the city. I was going to be here for the two more days so I figured I might as well be productive with my time.

"Hello," said a voice across from me, I jumped. Oh right, there was another person in the room.

"Nice leather jacket," he pointed to my red jacket.

"Oh thanks," I nodded, "but actually it's pleather. I like your leather jacket too."

"It's also pleather," he replied, "I don't like leather."

He got up from his couch and took the seat next to me. He offered me his hand; I shook it.

"What are you working on?" he asked, peering over my shoulder at my laptop.

"Oh, I'm just looking for another gig. I'm in Toronto for the next two days," I explained.

"You're a singer?" he asked.

"Yeah, and a musician technically," I laughed picking up my ukulele, "I'm assuming you're also a singer? They didn't open the doors to the public yet."

"Yes, and a musician like yourself. I'm the guitarist for Zephyr," his eyes lit up as he mentioned his band.

"You play for Zephyr?" I exclaimed, "I looked your band up online the other night. Apparently, you lot are a pretty big deal around here," he laughed.

"I guess you can say that," he smiled.

"So, what kind of music do you play?" he started laughing.

"You're meaning to tell me you looked us up but you didn't listen to any of our music yet?" he laughed again, "I play soft rock."

'Ha, I knew it!' I thought to myself.

"I tried to find your music but you guys don't post on

thought. I wanted to bite my tongue! I hated being asked that question, and yet I asked a complete stranger the very same question that I loathed. Maybe his mother didn't tell him what his name stood for either. Was he also searching for himself like I was?

"Guess," he said. Guess? Was that supposed to mean he knew what his name stood for, but went by an acronym instead?

"Guess?" I replied, "but I know nothing about you. What is there to guess? What do you like?"

"You know plenty about me V, first impressions give away a great deal about a person. You know I play soft rock for Zephyr, a band inspired by The Beatles. You know I like wearing black," he gestured to his attire, "Okay, fine, I'll give you one more hint because that might not be enough to give it away. I also like traveling," He was a nomad just like me!

"Are you called Wanderlust?" I asked him, he shook his head. He looked a little disappointed.

"No V, I'm not Wanderlust. People always think my name is Wanderlust or Nomad," he shook his head. I could relate to that, people always thought my name was Nomad too, but it's not my name.

"Look deeper. Look past the stigma," what could he possibly mean by that? *Look past the stigma* but what stigma? The stigma of being a traveler? I tried to remove the stigma, but if his name was not Wanderlust, I was at a loss as to what it could be.

"I'm sorry, I don't know," I admitted.

"My name is Wonder-Lust," he said, "Not Wanderlust, I do not lust for new destinations, I lust for the wonder in the journey."

'Wonder-Lust?' I thought to myself, 'but that isn't a word, it isn't a name. So he claims to see the wonder in everything? Well, I suppose that's a commendable trait. Perhaps it's that

trait that makes him such a successful musician.

"So, are you from here Wonder-Lust?"

"Yes, I am a local here, and also in San Francisco, and in New York City too, I'm performing there next month."

"You are a local to three cities?" I asked, how odd. How could a person live in three cities at once?

"Yes," Wonder-Lust replied, "I am also a local in Boston, and Ranchi, and Paris. In fact, I am a local in every city I visit, because I believe the home is where the heart is, and my heart goes wherever I go. But, if you are asking about where I own property, then the answer is San Francisco, I own an apartment there."

What an interesting boy. He took a very optimistic approach to life, and his perspective of the world was entirely different from any other person I have spoken to before. I wanted to get to know him better and ask about his journeys abroad, but just as I was about to inquire about his adventures, a woman wearing a headset walked in and called me to the stage, she was the ASM. She told me it was time for me to set up for my performance, she seemed a little stressed so I closed my laptop and made my way to the door.

"Can I leave Leery in here?" I asked the ASM, she nodded and agreed to stop in and check on her during my performance.

"Her name is Leery? I love cats!" Wonder-Lust exclaimed, "Can I play with her?"

"Sure, but I'll warn you in advance, Leery isn't very receptive to strangers," but just as I said this Wonder-Lust opened the crate and was successful in pulling Leery out. He placed her on his lap and she began to purr as he stroked her fur.

'Interesting,' I thought, 'She trusted him immediately, but it took me so long to teach her to trust me. What a strange cat," I chuckled, I smiled at Wonder-Lust and followed the ASM to

the stage.

****

When V performs, adrenaline courses through her. She fills a room with her soul and lets strangers judge it. Some have asked V how she can show a room of strangers her heart, even despite their ridicule. Many have commended V's fortitude when addressing judgment from the masses. She is equally commended for her gratitude when accepting praise. To be perfectly honest, V doesn't even know how she does it.

V knows that those who judge her soul oppress their own. They package their soul airtight in a tiny box buried deep within them. These critics lack the courage V possesses and they envy her because of it. V has no time to be dissuaded by these shrinkers, she is too busy pitying them.

Though V had many fans in the crowd that night, only one man in the crowd was moved enough by the sound of V's soul to get to know her. No, it was not Wonder-Lust, he could not hear V yet, he was instructed to stay put in the green room until V's set was complete. Though he wanted to, he couldn't sneak out to watch V that night. But another heard her, and his name was Art and Art was an angel. I, of all people, would know.

He watched V with moony eyes from the crowd. This is where their story begins. It is shorter than V would have liked it to be, but as Sunny once said, 'There is something to be said for short books.'

V could write novels for her moon-eyed lover in the audience that night, in fact, she should have. Maybe that would have kept him, but now V can only dedicate one chapter to him because he decides to close their book. But no spoilers! Read on.

****

The audience applauded as I finished my set. Anyone from the crowd would have noticed I was beaming, I loved performing, it made me feel alive. In fact, performing was the only thing that would resurrect my fairy on the days

mundanity murdered her.

The MC took the mic and congratulated me on my opening set. He asked if I was willing to answer a few questions from the crowd, I nodded. One person asked about the inspiration behind the song I wrote for Leery. I tried to explain that my cat had trust issues and I wanted to dedicate a song to her, but once I saw that answer wasn't resonating with him I changed my approach.

"Leery and I, we take a while to build trust. Not because we want to, nor because we were raised to be apprehensive of others, life has just conditioned us to think before we trust. I figured that if I wrote this song, I would overcome my fear of trusting others, writing this song helped me to do so, but it did not help Leery at all."

Another asked about the radical song I wrote in the countryside.

"I wrote that song about a lowly farmer who regarded me as a lowly citizen. His dissentient philosophy valued for simplicity. This idea challenged my views, so I wrote a song to understand him and it better."

One person from the audience, a boy with moon-eyes and raven hair raised his hand next. The MC selected him from the crowd, "V, what does your music stand for?" he asked.

Never, in my life, of all the crowds I have performed for, of all the people I met, I had never been asked a question like this before. I took a moment to think it over, I did not know how to respond. I looked around the room and it seemed that everyone was equally intrigued by the question. They sat at the edge of their seats to hear my answer. I hoped they did not set their expectations too high, because I was not confident, I could come up with an answer that would satisfy them.

I considered his question. Most asked me what my name stood for, but no one had ever asked what my music stood for. I was not really sure what my music stood for; I hadn't really

thought about it before today. I just made music; I just write songs. I don't dissect the songs I write and analyze them the way an English major might. I didn't give the meaning of my songs much thought at all. I just didn't think my songs and poems to page, I felt them. Maybe this boy was onto something, maybe if I could look within myself and learn what my music stood for, then I could learn what my name stood for too. Then maybe when I discovered what my name stood for, and what my music stood for, maybe then I would finally discover what I stood for. What did I stand for? Was it Freedom? Was it Feminism? Justice? Love? Love. That wasn't it, it was not even remotely close, but my mind clung to the idea of standing for love. What would that look like? I sang love ballads at times, the blues at others. Sometimes I would sing about politics or success. Yet, no matter what the story of the song was, love was embedded into it, even if I only sang out of love for music, love was always present. I turned to the moon-eyed boy, I finally had an answer for him.

"My music is a reflection of my heart's emblem," I explained, "This emblem is inked on my mind like a tattoo; before I speak, before I sing, before I talk, the emblem reminds me to consult my heart first. If my heart approves of my music, I perform. If it doesn't, I scrap the song."

He nodded, the ASM signaled the MC to wrap it up backstage. Zephyr needed time to set up their equipment. The MC thanked everyone for coming out and said that proceeding a fifteen-minute intermission, Zephyr would begin their set. The MC encouraged we nourish ourselves with snacks and beverages from the concession stand in the meantime. I stepped offstage and stood by the sales table with my EP on display. The woman manning the table started to put Zephyr's merch on display beside mine. I looked at their album cover and compared it to my EP. My case was underwhelming, I didn't have a logo printed on the cover like them, I put my CDs

in a transparent case while theirs had an intricate cover design. Then I noticed their other merch, they sold t-shirts and stickers. I was disappointed with my lack of merch compared to theirs. But I did not have the means to fund it. Having a logo would require hiring a graphic designer, then I would have to pay to print stickers and t-shirts. Merch was good for people who could afford the initial expenses. Eventually, you made your money back, but I couldn't afford to take that risk right now. Any money I made went to food, gas, and back into my music. I couldn't hire an artist right now.

"I need a logo," I told the woman at the table, she was a few years younger than me, she nodded and said that if I had a logo it would help in sales. She said a lot of people were asking for my EP, but some of them didn't buy after seeing the transparent case. They thought I was lazy or that I wasn't detail-oriented. They thought the music would reflect the empty cover. I was disheartened to learn my EP would have sold if I could afford a logo.

"I can design you a logo," I turned back to see the moon-eyed boy with raven hair behind me.

"Sorry to eavesdrop, but I am an artist, and I can design a logo for you." I was startled by this. It took me a minute to recall his familiar eyes. Then I remembered that he was the boy who asked what my music stood for.

"I would love that, thank you. What's your name?" I asked turning back to him.

"I'm Art, and you're V, right? Can I buy you a coffee?"

"Yeah sure, let's go sit," I was drawn to the moon-eyed boy, I followed him to the table. He pulled a chair out for me and I sat on it. He smiled at me from across the table.

"How do you drink your coffee?" He asked.

"Well actually, I'd prefer a hot chocolate," I laughed, "I only drink coffee when I'm stressed. What are you getting?"

"I don't drink coffee either, or hot chocolates," he

jack to the guitar and a master to art."

Something about this boy made me want to know him more than I already did. I tried to ask him more questions, some that didn't really matter, others that did, I liked his answers to everything, and I began to realize I loved his soul.

"Do you live here?" he asked, I shook my head.

"No, I travel. I'm a vocalist and a writer, I can't stay in one place for too long. Some people call me Nomad," I sighed.

"But that's not your name," he said, "You strike me more like a dreamer than a nomad." I smiled, he understood me. As Wonder-Lust said, 'You can learn a lot about a person from a first impression.' I felt like Art was the type of person who took the time to figure people out. He was an artist after all. There was mystery behind his moon-eyes, and I wanted to understand him.

But that begs the question, could I truly understand someone else, when I don't even truly understand myself? It's sort of ironic to think that I spend twenty-four-seven with myself, every day I take the time to self-contemplate, to reexamine my morals, and yet I didn't understand myself nearly half as well as I thought this stranger might.

"Your music is incredible," he said, "I loved watching you perform, you were so lively. I can tell you're truly passionate about this," I blushed, "So when can I see you perform again?"

"That depends on whether or not I got the gig at buckle barn's tomorrow. Apparently, it's a pub across town, I'm not too familiar with the area. If I do perform it will be at 10 pm, you should come if you want." He smiled.

"I know of the place you're referring to, and I'll be there," he looked to the stage and say Zephyr setting up, "but let's get out of here, I know this band, they play well but they aren't quite my taste in music."

"Oh really?" I said, "What kind of music do you listen to?"

"Sad love ballads," he said, "Sort of like the ones you sing.

And then I listen to hopeful songs, like the ones you follow your sad tunes with." I smiled, no one had noticed my sad songs before, everyone heard my songs about hope, but they dismissed my sad ones. He heard both, and he liked them.

"Let's get out of here, I have something to show you," I decided to go with him. And he was right, he did have something to show me, it was beautiful, it was called love.

****

V finds this chapter difficult to look back on, not because it was dark, but because it was light, and it dimmed. Day is always followed by night and when V was shaken out of her daydream, it broke her. Looking back on the good memories is harder than looking back on the bad because when they end, it breaks you. V got addicted to sadness. It was her nicotine, poison with honey and cinnamon. V got addicted to the cyclone because for a while it was all she knew. The cyclone broke them both, though I won't spoil it.

V drinks her coffee black now.

She drinks her coffee bitter because Art taught V how to love something more than herself. In doing so she practiced selflessness. She thought he could provide her with stability and so she put trust in him. But then he left, gradually. In doing so, he taught V how to be selfish, independent and cold.

V wanted to be independent together, as all healthy couples do, but Art wanted to be independent alone.

But Art taught V true love, something she did not know before.

Confining her experience to a chapter is impossible. V could write novels about Art, and someday she very well might, but this chapter is painful for V to recount. She cut herself turning the pages.

V loved the tortured artist. He was tortured because he was an artist trapped in the body of a Computer Scientist. All he

wanted was to draw.

V watched Art as his life shifted from a daydream to a nightmare.

V laughed with him.

She wept with him.

She confessed to him.

and when he left,

V cried out for him.

Of all the memories to choose from, V decided to recall the one that was least painful to her. She decided to select a moment of intimacy, of love, of passion to retell. She will bear the pain of recounting this chapter for you, dear reader. Because of all the people V has and will ever love, she gives her soul to the inquisitive, the humanitarians, and the readers. Lovers get her heart, you can keep a piece of her soul, her mind, her thoughts.

This will be both her favorite and most hated chapter of all. Be patient with her, it is short but it is beautiful all the same.

In the Alchemist, the Shepard once stated that every traveler has a person that they would give it all up for. For him, it was the merchant's daughter. For V it was Art. She once thought it was Realist, but that was because she did not know Art.

She dated Art for almost a year. At first, she would take gigs in Toronto intentionally to see him and continue on her life as previously. Eventually, Art convinced her to stop paying for hotel rooms let her move in. Leery loved Art. He took the time to gain her trust, which hurt killed her when he broke it. But, no spoilers.

While V traveled the continent, Leery preferred to stay with Art. So, V left Leery with Art on her travels. Eventually, and very slowly, V unpacked her things at his place, she began to buy more clothes, she even bought twinkly lights to decorate their bedroom. She considered the apartment in Toronto home, because home is where the heart is, and her heart was here.

V stopped looking for gigs in other cities. Part of her wanted

to stay in Toronto so she could be with Art, though she would never admit it. While Art fueled her creativity, she started to limit what she showed to the world.

Their relationship broke because of something called co-dependence. And it hurt them both. Valentine's day was their last night together so that is the night V will recall.

You see reader, love drives passion and passion drives insanity. They lost themselves to the winds of a cyclone. It was neither's fault, but V missed the road. V did not know why, she thought she was done with the roads and the destinations it took her too, but though her soul called to the road, her heart clung to Art.

V wanted to bring Art with her to hear the music, but Art was tied to family. His mother was in this city, his brother was here too. They acted as an anchor pinning him to the ground, and all V wanted was for Art to soar.

Art never respected how quickly V turned to the roads. He did not understand how one could possibly leave their family behind. Likewise, V did not understand how one's family could pin down their child. Abuse them, neglect them, when all he wanted was to soar.

Part of V never understood why Art tied himself to things and people who pinned him to the ground. But she knows he has the strength to break free if he ever wanted to.

Here was the last night of their serenity before he turned cold, and she turned to drink.

****

He traced my bursting star tattoo in the dim-lit room and I blushed. The two of us were lying in bed half-dressed and we were staring at each other, marveling at the different miracles that only we would notice, that only we could see. I traced my hand across the side of his torso, he shivered and pressed himself up against me as I did. I smiled. His hands were wrapped tightly around the small of my back and he pulled me

closer into him. I could feel his breath on my neck, he proceeded to rest his head on my chest and I rested my chin above his forehead.

"I love your tattoos," he said, still tracing the star with his forefinger, it sent shivers down my spine, "Or maybe I just love you."

"And I love your hair," I said stroking his raven feathered hair. It was dark and rich. "Or maybe I just love you." I mocked him, we laughed.

"The bee is for feminism," he said poking the antenna of the symbol hidden behind my back ear. After meeting Able and overcoming my fear of permanence, I decided to get a second tattoo, Art was the only one who knew about it, "and the star, is you!" he pulled me into him and kissed me. His lips were soft and full. He had a beauty mark on his lower lip and whenever I would think back to him while traveling, it would always be the first thing I thought of. Sure, it was a trivial thing to remember, but to me and every inch of him was perfect. To me, it was worth remembering.

"The star is for me," I smiled, "Did I ever tell you about the Shakespeare professor I stood up against?" I said pointing to the bee symbol behind my ear.

"Yes, tell me again though,"

I smiled. "He believed that Portia in the Merchant of Venice was submissive to her husband. Rather than being a hero, she acted only with the intent of rescuing her husband. So, despite her resilience and her ability to dress like a lawyer, cross-dress as a man, and outwit all the men of the play, he argues she is not the heroine but merely being submissive to her husband."

"And then you told him," said Affable, "That he shouldn't diminish the words of the thousands upon thousands of scholars who attest that Shakespeare was a revolutionary writer, and you would not diminish his accomplishments in

simply stating that he would uphold such an outdated view of the role of a heroine. You said there was no reason to study Shakespeare in modern-day if all he did was preach conservative ideologies. You believed he could have been progressive, well, for his time."

"I trained you well," I laughed. He ran his fingers through my hair and pulled me closer into him again, I heard him moan softly into my ear. I told him he was too far away from me and he smirked slyly and pulled me closer if closer was even possible at this point.

"Let's go to Paris," I whispered into his ear, he shook his head.

"No V, I told you my parents need me here."

"They can't stop you from pretending," I said back to him. I stared into his moon-eyes. He smiled.

"Let's go to Paris. I can book myself gigs in Paris. You can work there too. Let's run away together. There is no reason to stay here."

"I could open an art shop," he started and I smiled, "and you can keep booking gigs and when you're famous we can travel the world together on tours and buy a house together in Paris," I kissed him.

"Yes," I muttered, "Art, do you know why I love you?"

"Why?" he kissed my cheek.

"Because you are an artist. Not just because of that, okay let me explain. When you first met me, you illustrated a portrait for me. You made me art. You made *me* art because you saw me as art. When you drew me that portrait, I saw what you saw in me and it was beautiful. When I looked at your portrait of me, I learned to love what I saw. I looked into the eyes you drew me and I saw you and I learned to love them. I looked into the hair you drew on my head; I saw the way in which it spiraled down my cheeks and I learned to love it. You taught me love. Love for myself, and love for you. And

breaks him. That was why my artist had moon-eyes. He watched the city at night and wondered about its mystery.

Art would paint from night into dawn. Whenever I saw his art, I was breathless.

'Wow,' I would think so to myself, 'So, this is how the moon sees the world. The moon's world is so beautiful, it makes me want to live in it.'

All Art did was hold a mirror to the world, he showed everyone that we live in a masterpiece. He saw the art in the world and I saw the art in him, it was beautiful.

"You know what else I wish?" I started.

"What?"

"Two things: I wish you could see yourself from my lens. When I look at you, I see perfection. When I look at you, I see art. Who draws the artist?"

"No one, I never have portraits done of me. I always draw others."

"That's why you are an artist. I wish I could draw, but since I can't, your portrait exists only in my eyes. And you cannot see it the way I do but Art, I promise it is so beautiful. I wish I could show you how beautiful your portrait is. You would draw yourself every day for the rest of your life if you could only see how beautiful you look in my eyes. That is my first wish. I wish you did not see flaws in yourself because they don't exist in my eyes. That would be the first thing I would wish for. The second would be this: I wish you made more art. Your art is beautiful and when you make it, angels smile. I wish you only knew how perfect your artwork was."

"I wish I could make it too sometimes," he admitted, "Art would be a lot easier than Computer Science." "

No baby, you would just be the best in your class. To you, it would be easy, because you're the best. You're my artist." I pulled him closer into me and ran my hands down his back.

"Sometimes I just feel like I'm not enough," he admitted,

but I already knew that, because of the way in which he spoke about himself. I knew he didn't see the portrait in my eye. Even though it was reflected right back at him, like a mirror. A mirror he just couldn't see. He was an angel on earth. His gentleness, his beauty, nothing that could be compared. I wanted him forever. Who wouldn't want an artist forever? Especially one that made art out of you.

"Art, do you love me?" I muttered into his hair.

"Yes," he said

"And do you know I love you?" I asked.

"Yes, I know."

"And I will love you forever," I stated, "So let's make Paris a reality, let's cross the seas together."

"V," Art sighed, "I can't. You know I can't so why..." he trailed off at that.

"Okay Art never mind," I ran my fingers through his hair again as if I was entranced by him. If a drug could be a person, it would be him. I wrapped my legs around his and pulled him closer into my chest.

"Art," I started, "Have you been drawing?"

"I don't have time V, I work." He rolled to his back, "More than what you can say," this stung. Art would never directly say it, but I know he was disappointed in me. I was proud of him though when he was making art. But he didn't make the time to do the things he loved, which contributed to his resistance in traveling with me.

"Art, you are the sweetest man I have ever met and the sweetest man I will ever know," I slide my hand up his spine from his lower back to the back of his neck, "How can I convince you to stay?"

"It's not about convincing V, I have to want it. And I'm not sure if I want it yet. Look I have to go see my parents now," he got out of bed and dressed, he pulled all of the euphoria from our intimacy out of the bed and took it with him.

"But I want you—" I started, but I stopped because he already knew.

"I have to go now V. When we meet again let's get samosa's at the supermarket and watch horror movies in bed."

"Okay Art, and when will that be?"

He didn't answer. He kissed my forehead and walked out of our home.

I didn't deserve an artist like him. Not at this chapter. I know I was immature. I was clingy, I yelled, I got angry, I even insulted him. My artist, I insulted the best thing in my life at the time. The most beautiful person I had ever met. I insulted him out of the petty insecurities, the very insecurities he took so long to distill out of me. So yes, he left me, and my world became very dark and very cold; but it was a coldness I felt I deserved and so I bore it.

There is a special place in hell for those among us who break artists, with hearts as gentle as Art's. Since hell does not exist, I decided to reserve myself this hell on earth. I called it the cyclone and I barely made it out alive.

Passion is enticing on paper, but in practice, it is strong, destructive, and oftentimes dangerous. If I matured quicker, I could have deserved the artist and avoided the cyclone, but instead, I suffered.

He didn't return like he said he would. I slept alone in that cold bed for months. One morning, I took to the road and I knew that this was where the chapter would end, to my dismay.

I looked to the moon and saw his eyes as I drove off into the night.

CHAPTER XI

CYCLONE

"I don't believe in soulmates, but I believed in you." — V

****

V hit the road again. She decided to leave Leery with Art because Leery preferred his company to hers. Leery never did learn how to fully trust V. Possibly because V never really learned how to fully trust herself. V was on the road alone now, and she felt lonely. V booked herself three times as many gigs as she did while living with Art. In fact, V worked herself harder than she ever had before.

V knew deep down that her obsessive work ethic compensated for her loneliness. She was trying to distract herself from the lone road. It had been a while since V last traveled alone. She didn't even have Leery to keep her company anymore.

Despite overworking herself to distract from the loneliness, V didn't entirely oppress her feelings on the road, she had creative outlets to help her cope. Her music was her therapy, and she wrote her fair share of blues. Her songs were meant to call out to Art because she missed him. Every night she requested a seat be reserved for him in the crowd, and while the venue always complied, Art never took his seat.

V booked a number of gigs for herself in Toronto she wanted to be close to Art hoping he might attend her shows. V phoned Art whenever she was in the city to invite him to the show. He never came.

This chapter is about healing and growth. Windstorms kill the weak so that the strong in us may grow. Fear not, dear reader! V is strong and capable of handling herself.

V doesn't endure the cyclone alone, but this time I don't come to her aid, another does. He will help to settle the storm, though I won't spoil it! Read on for yourself.

****

I booked another gig at the venue in Toronto, the one that was attached to the local college. I was eager to perform on a familiar stage again. I hoped this familiar venue would attract the familiar face I yearned for, but he was nowhere in sight. This was my fourth time performing in this festival. To be completely honest, I had outgrown it. I established a large enough fanbase now, and I didn't need the exposure from this organization. I only came back to catch a glimpse of the moon-eyed man, but he never came.

I looked at the display table with my merchandise. The same girl always manned the table. She displayed my merch for potential buyers, the spread included my newly released album, my EP, stickers, and some t-shirts I designed. Now my album had a logo printed on the case, it was an illustration of Leery that Art drew for me. I asked him to draw me something that he felt best represented me, so he drew Leery, I decided to call the album *Dreamer.*

Dreamer was not my name, but it was close. I felt I was getting closer.

The venue opened the doors to the public, and a sea of people gushed into the auditorium. The show was scheduled to start in twenty minutes. I looked back to the seat reserved for my former moon-eyed partner. The seat was empty, again.

The owner of the venue noticed me as I gazed through the crowd, she approached and shook my hand.

"It's a pleasure to have you back, V," said the large woman vigorously shaking my hand. To an outsider, the handshake

might have looked excessive, theatrical even, but I knew her well now. Her personality was larger than life, some found her to be overbearing, but I knew she had a good heart.

"It's a pleasure to be here, thank you for having me back, and thanks for always being so receptive of my new ideas."

"Oh no need to thank me for being open-minded," she chuckled, "I love radical music. Look at *Zephyr*! I invite them back every time their guitarist is in town. Sweet group the lot of them are!" She smiled.

This was only my second time performing in the same festival as *Zephyr*, I hadn't gotten the chance to hear them play last time and I looked forward to hearing their music live today. I turned my attention to the stage and noticed a few of their musicians setting up. I didn't see Wonder-Lust, *Zephyr* swapped out their musicians, the make of the band was dependent on who was in the city and available to play that night. My thoughts lingered back to Art and the night I first met him here, I turned to the manager.

"I have to make a call," I told her, "Will you excuse me?"

"Of course, but make it quick because the show is starting soon," she smiled.

"Do you have a payphone by chance?" I asked, the manager laughed.

"A payphone! Still haven't gotten your own cell have ya?" she chuckled, "You have got to be the only millennial I know without a cell phone. Hell, you might be the only person I know without a cell phone period, I just got my grandmother one last month, she posts on Instagram daily now. Here, take my cell," she tossed me her smartphone. I thanked her and turned to the exit. I was used to commentary, didn't understand how I could live without a cell phone in this day and age, but truth be told I got along just fine. I didn't want to be gotten a hold of. In actuality, there was really only one person I wanted to reach out to me, and he was not interested in returning my calls, that

reason I did, to stay warm.

A man in black pulled a chair and sat beside me and order the same drink as me. It was Wonder-Lust. He smiled at me, and I smiled back. I felt nervous but I didn't know why, I started fidgeting with the zipper on my jacket.

"Are you performing tonight?" he asked, I nodded, and he smiled, "You've been doing quite well for yourself V," I blushed, "I hear your name across the continent now. I've even heard your song on the radio once, have you ever considered taking on gigs in larger cities? I've noticed you play in a lot of local areas. Have you ever considered going abroad?"

"Oh, I don't know," I smiled, "Most of my travel is by car, I don't think I could go abroad right now."

"Oh, you most definitely can," insisted Wonder-Lust dreamy-eyed, "Gigs in the states are incredible. I live in San Francisco for work. If you're ever in the area, you should come visit," I thanked him.

"V, I've got to say I've had my eye on you. You seem to be making a name for yourself, you should be proud. Also, I was wondering, would you maybe want to go on a date sometime? I like hanging out with you and your music speaks to me."

He wanted to go on a date? But I wasn't ready! I wasn't ready to date anyone. I mean, I did like Wonder-Lust, and I thought he was very talented, but I needed more time.

"Can I think about it Wonder-Lust?" I asked, "I just got out of a relationship and I'm not sure if I'm ready to date again. I like you too, but I'm not sure if I'm ready."

"Take all the time you need V," Wonder-Lust smiled. Wait, he wasn't angry? I told him I would.

"You know," Wonder-Lust continued, changing the subject, "I heard you play live last time you performed here. I have to say, you're excellent."

"You heard me? But how? I thought they kept you in the green room before your set."

"They tried to," he admitted, "but I can never pass up on a concert. I was standing at the back. I head your first song, the one about striving for success. The one about wanting to make the future a better place, you really are a visionary V. I can tell by your music."

"My name," I started, wait—was it? Yes, that was it! How could I have been so foolish? I'm a woman who lives in a constant state of trying to make the future the present. It all made perfect sense now. Visionary was my name! "How did you know that was my name? How did you know that was what V stood for?"

"I just listened to your music V, it says more about you then you realize," Wonder-Lust, a band member of *Zephyr*, the boy who wore all black, idolized radical bands, and traveled the continent. Of all the people I had met, he was the only one who had guessed my name. I needed a moment to consider this revelation.

"I have to go now," I started, I jumped up from the table, "I have to prepare for my set," Wonder-Lust smiled and told me to break a leg. I thanked him and booked it to the stage.

The microphone smelt like liquor tonight. I turned to the foggy crowd and set my eyes fixed on Art's seat. It was empty, so I decided to start with a sad song. I looked at the bar and saw Wonder-Lust, he smiled at me from the crowd.

"I wrote a song in the light," I told the crowd, "It's called 'My Artist,' but it's not like my other songs, this one ends on a low note, you see, when something beautiful ends, we're meant to feel sad about it." I picked up my ukulele, and strummed some chords. I started singing Art's song, and the crowd fell silent as I grew numb.

****

Dear reader, the lyrics are reserved for the people present that night. Not to be disclosed for all to hear, but I'll tell you this much about them, the lyrics were perfect and also hopeless. It

was the song for the hopeless romantics, and that is what made it so perfectly sad.

****

When my song came to a close, the audience looked gloomy, but I didn't care. Tonight, I want to be the shot that sobered them.

"This next song," I started, "Is called 'Smothered,' it was written in the dark," I started to sing, and the audience looked even more somber than they did previously, but again, I didn't care. I proceeded to belt out the blues, one sad song after the next, as if they were neighbors to one another in that same dreary town. When I sang my heart dry, I bowed, but the audience did not applaud, they snapped.

'Strange,' I thought to myself, 'They must have mistaken my songs for poetry.'

I blew a farewell kiss to Art's empty seat.

"Actually everyone, hold on a second. I have one more song I want to close the night off with, do you mind if I sing it for you?" the audience hooted and applauded.

"It's called, goodbye," I said, and so I sang, and so I wept.

****

I finished my final song and took my final bow. *Zephyr* was up next. I looked to the right wing and saw Wonder-Lust, I nodded to him, but he looked back at me with a strange look on his face. It was one that I didn't recognize. I passed him in the wings, but before I went, he grabbed my hand.

"V," he said, he looked into my eyes, "You sing sad songs now. Why are they so sad?" I grabbed my wrist back from him.

"Break a leg Wonder-Lust," I said, I brushed my tears aside and whisked myself away from the stage. I jogged to the washroom and looked at myself in the mirror. I could not recognize my reflection. I cleaned the smeared liner from my eyes, my stage foundation started to drip down my cheeks. I took a cloth to my face and wiped it clean. I looked into that

mirror again and I thought back to the mountainside, we never realize we've lost ourselves until we find ourselves again. I looked into the mirror and saw familiar eyes, despite the disheveled appearance that surrounded them, they remained consistent, they remained familiar.

But where was Angel? I looked around the washroom, I checked the stalls, I looked to the ceiling and the floor tiles. Why hadn't Angel come to rescue me? She said she would be there in my times of distress, but where was she now?

"Where are you now, Angel!" I cried to the Heavens, they did not hear me, "Where are you now when I need you most? Where are you now at the peak of the cyclone?" Still, no answer. I wanted to cry, but before I could, a woman entered the washroom. She wore a skin-tight dress and looked a tad tipsy.

"Oh my god!" she exclaimed as I dried my eyes, "You're V, the one who had just performed! I'm a huge fan of your music. I bought your album, and I listen to your covers off of YouTube!"

"Oh yeah, that's me," I smiled.

"You're incredible! I love your music! Please never stop making it, it helped me as I was going through something."

"It did?" I was shocked, I wrote my music so I could heal, I didn't realize I was helping someone else in the process.

"Yes! I love your music, especially the sad songs, they have a weird way of cheering me up. I don't know if that makes sense! But, I love your sad songs! They can get a little dark at times, but I still love them," she liked my sad songs? I know this stranger meant this as a compliment, but I interpreted it as a rude awakening. I didn't intend on being a singer of the blues. I wanted to write cheerful songs, radical political movement songs. Had I gotten weak? Why was I always so sad now?

"Get out there, girl! *Zephyr* is about to start playing now.

You'll love their shit, I'm their biggest fangirl. Swear to god, you'll fall in love with them!" I had never actually gotten the chance to hear *Zephyr* play. All I knew about them was that they were a soft rock, Beatles inspired band that supposedly sang radical and sometimes downright socialist songs. I wanted to hear them for myself. I nodded to the woman and thanked her for supporting my music. I went out to the audience and saw Wonder-Lust on stage tuning his guitar.

The technicians were finally ready and signaled *Zephyr* to start. One the ASM cued the lights, and stage illuminated to a soft red/pinkish color. Wonder-Lust cleared his throat.

"This is a new song, I composed the tune a while ago, but I couldn't find the words to fit it, but inspiration finally hit me tonight as I was backstage just now," he explained. We all listened in silence, "It is called, 'If Only,' and it is dedicated to the visionaries," he made direct eye contact with me.

"Enjoy," the band began to play.

****

The lyrics were meant for V, and V only. It was as if the audience was eavesdropping into their private conversation.

The song was about a broken heart, and a wonder-eyed man's desire to mend it.

V didn't know she needed a song like this until she heard it. In this intimate moment with Wonder-Lust, the cyclone subsided, even if only for a moment.

But when V was alone again with her thoughts, the troubled air resurfaced and thickened around her. The wind tormented her making it a challenge to breath.

The cyclone was at its peak on May 19th... Art's birthday.

****

I decided to get drunk on his birthday.

I couldn't handle it sober. I listened to an Adele song and cried because it reminded me of my last night with him. Now, I don't usually drink alone, in fact, I don't regularly drink period. This said, I definitely don't drink alone, I was warned against it once. Always drink with friends, never alone because when you drink alone, no one will be there to sober you.

Today I wanted to be numb, I needed to be numb.

May 18th, one day before your birthday, two days before we broke up a year prior, I felt isolated, abandoned and betrayed. I tried to think of the negative memories to get over you, all of the times I was stood up, all of the times you canceled last minute, every day I checked to see if you had tried to reach me, and hadn't. Every time we fought, every time we cried. But every time I tried to remember the bad, I was reminded instead of your heart. I thought back to the times I made you cry.

'This love was real,' I thought to myself, 'He cries for me. How could I have made him cry?' or I would think to the way Art wrapped his arms around my torso and pulled me closer into him.

'This love is real,' I thought, 'He pulls me close; I don't think he'll ever let go.'

I thought back to when I made him moan to the heavens and I could see the passion in his eyes, I knew then he would be mine. I would think to myself, 'The sweetest boy I've ever met loves me and wants me, he is the future I want to make the present.'

Some people live in the past, but I live in a constant state of trying to make my future the present, but I don't know how. That is why I wrote Art a love letter, by hand, every week to win him back. It's why I cried at his doorstep after a fight, it is why I reserved him a seat at every show, and it is why I wrote him poetry, even after he was gone.

I was so broken when he left, because I thought he was

perfect, but you deserve someone who is because I think you're perfect," I was sobbing, "Please reach out if you ever need anything. I have my laptop; you can reach out to me online. I won't pressure you to get back together, I'm going to try to move on, but I will always love you, and I will always be here for you should you ever need a friend like me."

I tried to flash him a fake smile through the phone. In my drunken state, I thought if I mustered up a fake smile, I could fool him into thinking I was okay. Thankfully it was a phone call and he couldn't see me; he would have known my smile was fake.

The doorbell rang, it was food service.

"My ice cream!" I exclaimed, I leapt up to answer the door, but the room was spinning. I waited for the room to still, and when I finally got to the door, the housekeeping had already left. They left my tub of ice cream for me on the ground, I was too drunk to be grossed out by this.

'My chocolate ice cream!' I thought to myself, I was ecstatic! I walked back to my bed and began to eat.

'Beyoncé,' I thought to myself, 'Then Selena, then Ariana, then Halsey. I want to listen to them all tonight!" the room kept spinning as I walked to the laptop.

"Oh, no!" I tipsily laughed, "My ice cream is melting!" I laughed so hard at this arbitrary thing.

The room kept spinning as I started to watch music videos on my laptop. They were so funny, well if I were sober, I would not have thought so, but now that I was intoxicated, I found them hilarious. I began to pick out things I did not notice the first time I watched these videos.

'Being drunk is like having a superpower!' I thought to myself.

"Wonder-Lust!" I said aloud laughing. Why exactly I was not sure, I logged into Facebook and I started to message him, "I am slightly intoxicccct," I sent him, with no context. I was

laughing so hard. After listening to some more music, I heard a ping from my phone.

"Intoxicated?" he replied, and I started to cry, without entirely understanding why.

"Yes," I replied, not sure what else to say, he began to message me more. I heard my phone ping several times, I decided not to look right away, I wanted to listen to my music. When I couldn't bear it any longer, I looked at the screen.

"I hope you are having fun," he said, "Are you with friends or alone?"

"Alone," I sniffled, "I am too saaad to have any sun," I started to weep again. I decided to drink more beer to numb the pain. I rechecked my phone, I did not hear it ping, but there were three more messages for me.

"Are you okay?"

"Do you want to talk about it?"

"Is it because of today's date?" Wait did I tell him it was Art's birthday? I guess I did, but he was right, and I was not one to lie.

"Yes," I responded heartlessly. Wonder-Lust responded instantly with two sad-faced emojis. I was not sure how to rectify the situation. I wanted to fix the situation, but I was too drunk to think straight.

"Are you mad at me? I'm sorry, Wonder-Lust. I like you a lot, but I'm still sad. Are you okay?" I waited for the longest minute of my life.

"I'm not mad," he replied, "I just wish I was there to help you feel better." I started crying again but for good reasons this time. I tried to message him and explain that I just had to mourn this year because this year was quite horrible.

"My family hates me Wonder-Lust," I said, I was starting to sober up and so my messages became a little more articulate, "I'm very sensitive about dates and this is a sensitive date. It's the day Art and I broke up, and then my hell began for another six months in limbo," I sobbed into the

phone. He seemed to understand.

"Wonder-Lust," I started, "Do you know why we give roses to the ones we love?"

"No V, I haven't given it much thought."

"It wouldn't be the first time a boy hasn't given it much thought," I said in a drunken slur, "Wonder-Lust, roses need a lot of water to grow and thrive. If you don't water it, the rose withers."

Wonder-Lust asked me for updates on my mood throughout the evening. He wanted to make sure I was okay, I thanked him for messaging. He wondered if he was bothering me by checking in, I said no. His texts made me feel better.

My room smelt like beer and the stench was crowding me.

I considered calling Art again but I decided against it. I decided to send him one last message, it was time to move on.

"Happy birthday, Art. I hope it was a good one," I passed out.

****

I woke two hours later to see my laptop was still on auto play, a 2015 P!NK song was playing.

'I love her,' I thought, 'P!NK doesn't need anyone.' I checked my phone again. Wonder-Lust was trying to message me. I told him I fell asleep and I was sorry for the late reply. He said not to worry and wished me a good night.

"Sleep well V," he said.

But I didn't, because who can sleep in the confusion of a cyclone?

CHAPTER XII

FALLEN STARS

"We collect stardust to remember the fallen stars." — V

****

I was still drunk when I got the call.

It was Sunny, she contacted me through Facebook messenger. I was surprised because it was 3:00 am and Sunny and I haven't spoken since I left the Artistic Alcove in the city of bob cuts.

I debated calling her back the next morning when I was sober, but I figured if Sunny was calling, there was a good reason. It could be an emergency, so I decided to pick up the call.

"Sunny, hi, how are you?" I was trying my best to sound sober, though I doubt I fooled her.

"V, are you sitting down?" she asked me, I could hear her sobbing on the other end.

"What's wrong Sunny?" I had never heard Sunny cry before.

"Why are you talking like that?" Sunny asked concerned.

"Like what?"

"You're slurring your words. Are you drunk?" she caught me.

"A little bit," I confessed.

"I'm assuming you already know. V, that's not the way you should handle grief. There are healthier ways to cope. Who told you? Was it Cheery?" Was she talking about grieving a past relationship? And how was Cheery supposed to tell me anything about Art, he didn't even know him. My mind was fuzzy and I didn't understand what was happening. When I didn't answer Sunny started to sob into the phone again.

"What's wrong Sunny?" I asked, trying to comprehend the situation.

"What do you mean? I lost my best friend V. What do you mean what's wrong?" Sunny started sobbing again.

"Sunny, I don't know what's going on. Cheery hasn't told me anything, I don't understand why you're sad right now. When you're ready, can you try to tell me what's wrong, so I can understand what's going on?" Sunny sniffled.

"Oh V, it's Yippie," my heart sunk in my chest, I felt it might stop beating altogether. Yippie? What happened to Yippie? Were they okay? Was it the cashier of Bill's Boutique? Did she have them arrested for trying on the dress again? Did Yippie go missing? Maybe they wanted to wander the world too, maybe I could find them.

"Where's Yippie?" I asked panicked.

"V," sobbed Sunny, "Yippie is in the stars. They passed away, I found them in the book store sleeping in the backroom. Their body was frozen cold. They died V. Yippie's dead."

I was stunned. Yippie was gone?

"What?" I was heartbroken, "Yippie's gone? How did they die? What happened?"

"People came to inspect their body. Nothing's confirmed but they think Yippie died of an overdose. Mitty just told Cheery and I that Yippie was homeless all these years. Neither of us had any idea, Mitty said they didn't want us to know, but she said that was why they were sleeping in the shop. No one

knew Yippie was using, not even Mitty. V I know you're probably miles away from us, so there's no pressure to come to the viewing, Yippie would have understood, but I just wanted to tell you."

I thought of the cashier, who clearly loved Yippie, despite not wanting to let on. How would they feel about Yippie's death? How did Mitty and Cheery feel? Sunny was clearly devastated. Was it right for me to feel devastated too? I had only known Yippie for two days. Yippie and I crossed paths for only a moment, then we parted ways. Am I allowed to feel broken for losing Yippie, even though I had barely known them?

"Did you tell the cashier?" I blurted out.

"The cashier? What cashier?" Yippie never told Sunny about the cashier? Maybe it was alright for me to mourn Yippie, despite not knowing them for long, after all not even those closest to Yippie ever fully knew them.

"Sunny, in the City Center there is a woman with a bob cut in a prom dress shop. She works as a cashier there, and Yippie was in love with them. She visited her every day and tried on the same prom dress to get their attention. Please Sunny, Yippie would have wanted them at their funeral. Tell the cashier about Yippie, and tell her they loved them more than anything in the world. Yippie had a sketchbook filled with drawings of her, tell her that. Tell her about Yippie, let Yippie live on in that cashier's memory, it is what they would have wanted."

Sunny and I cried together over the fallen star who dreamed of the universe even though it never worked in their favor.

I told Sunny I wouldn't go to Yippie's funeral because that's not how I mourned. I mourned through music.

****

A critique might say Yippie's death was too abrupt, that

CHAPTER XIII

PAPER PLANE

"I fall for shooting stars because they fall for me."— V

****

When you meet a certain type of person, sometimes you hear music. Or you might hear poetry dripping from their tongue as they tell the stories of their day. The inflection of their voice sounds like something out of a symphony, and the meaning behind the things they say are always morally correct. This makes them art because that's all that art and poetry are, morals made accessible.

When one meets a wanderlust, they see something in their smile. It is subtle, not overtly noticeable, but it's there if you look. Wanderlusts roam the earth with their ears a tune to music because it takes them on journeys far beyond what the land they roam could offer.

Now you may ask, 'What does a wanderlust do when they see the world in its entirety? Where do they visit when they've seen it all? The answer is simple, these wanderlusts visit two new destinations: the first they visit is art. Art allows them to travel to unlimited lands. New artists create these ever-expanding realms daily, wanderlusts never tire of art nor new lands. So now for the second destination that they visit when they've seen the world in its entirety, the stars. For the stars are infinite and the possibilities of the expanding universe are endless, and so they look to them and wonder.

Wanderlusts are merely wonder-eyed beings with an affinity for infinity because it is unknown. They are wide-eyed children who analyze the fragments of ever-expanding imaginary worlds. These wonder-eyed voyagers are drawn to people who can show them new worlds, they are receptive to the energy of creatives.

We need people like Wonder-Lust in our lives to remind us to look past the woes we've accumulated when showing the world's wonders to others. V found Wonder-Lust at exactly the right moment. When V lost the ones she loved, she lost her soul to the winds. Wonder-Lust went to retrieve her back her soul from the winds. He is a band member of Zephyr's after all.

When V trusts Wonder-Lust with her thoughts, he takes them with him to new lands. It is frightening to imagine a world without the wonder-eyed. Though I won't glorify the wanderlusts any further, as they, just as everyone else, are not immune to fault. I will say this of them though, wanderlusts are necessary.

V is not a wanderlust, she is a visionary, which makes her just as rare as the wanderlusts, but yet so different from them all the same.

When V sobered up from Art's birthday, when she finished mourning the death of the toxic year preceding the hopeful year to come, she began to message Wonder-Lust regularly. While V worked her local gigs, she kept the idea of traveling to San Francisco in mind. V wondered what it would be like to sing in San Francisco, but she was scared and needed convincing.

****

'The nice thing about cell phones is that there's never any lines at the payphone,' I smirked to myself, 'The bad thing about cell phones is that payphones have become a scarcity.' I was talking into one of payphones in Quebec by the restaurant I just finished performing in that evening. The gig was for a couple's wedding anniversary so most of the songs I sang

tonight were romantic. I dialed up Wonder-Lust's number in San Francisco, he gave it to me earlier that week and we habitually talked in the evenings after or before our booked gigs. When he answered, I told him about my day.

"I signed up to be an organ donor," I said over the phone.

"You did? That's amazing, but should I be concerned?"

"No," I laughed, "I saw a poster. So, I considered it, and I thought, why let my organs die with me when I could house them in another who would put them to better use? If I'm braindead, I my heart won't be much use to me, but maybe someone else can use it. Also, I'm an atheist, which doesn't really matter because religious groups support organ transplant but, if I believe I wither into an abyss after death, why not live, if only partially, through others? I can live forever in memory and my organs can live onward too."

"I don't want to think about you in such a state V, I hope you will never be brain dead."

"Thank you, Wonder-Lust, but these are just hypotheticals," I laughed, "I know it is not an ideal conversation, but I'm sure it is not an ideal conversation for patients on the waitlist to be told they could not find a donor. Also, a donor can save eight lives and improve the lives of up to 75 others."

"You're right, it is important to talk about," he admitted, "V it's amazing you did it. This can save so many lives."

"No, the real amazing people are the ones who donate their organs while they are alive. That is what is really impressive."

"V, I miss you."

"I miss you too Wonder-Lust," I smiled through the phone, I wonder if he sensed it?

"Okay so I know you love performing V, and I was thinking, there is this concert for emerging artists in San Francisco, they host it at a venue a block from my work.

Agencies from LA come down. It's sort of like the benefit concert they hold in Toronto, the one we met at, but this one is on steroids. Want to come? I know the host who does it, they would be down to have you. I showed them your EP, the one with Leery on the cover. Oh, by the way how is Leery?" I shuttered.

"I actually don't have her anymore Wonder-Lust," I admitted, "I left them with my ex. He can provide the stable and consistent home for her that I couldn't."

"Your ex has Leery?" said Wonder-Lust, I could sense he was angered by this, "Well go get her back and bring her to San Francisco, she can stay with me here."

"It's not that simple Wonder-Lust, Leery loves him," I said.

"Well I love Leery," retaliated Wonder-Lust, "Maybe she could learn to love me too."

"I don't think so Wonder-Lust. She doesn't trust easily, she never even learned how to trust me. If I leave her with Art, she might finally be happy. Anyways, Wonder-Lust, I'm not sure if I can come to San Francisco. It's a lot of money and a long flight, plus what would I do with my car?"

"V, you found a parking spot for three months at Heathen's mountainside, remember? You can find a place to house your car for a little while. And if you can't, just sell it. Why tie yourself down to material things? You can come stay with me in San Francisco, I want to show you the world."

"I am not sure Wonder-Lust," I wasn't ready for the world to hear me yet. I was still so young and naïve and my songs were just the same. Who would hear me?

"V, I am here," said Wonder-Lust, as if he was reading my mind, "I want to hear you, and I think you are ready. You keep telling me you don't think you're ready, but I think you are."

"Why don't you perform? If you know the person who runs the venue, why don't you slip them your EP as well?"

"Because V," he admitted, "I don't think I am ready yet either, but I'll tell you what, if you perform, I will too. You just have to fly to San Francisco."

"Can I think about it?" I said, "Or is this offer temporary?"

"It's on the table for when you're ready to pick it up," he smiled and I heard it through the phone, "Noticed I said when and not if? Because this deal really is the best that can be offered." I thanked Wonder-Lust and hung up the phone.

I was starting to get hungry, I reached into my backpack for a snack, but my hands slammed into a solid rectangular shaped item.

"Ouch," I exclaimed, I pulled out the object I saw it was Yippie's journal. The deceased Yippie. The selfless wholesome Yippie who lived for art. I opened it and saw all of the decorated pages and wondered what Yippie would have done in my shoes, Yippie would have gone to San Francisco, and Yippie would have wanted me to go too. I had to go, I was meant to perform for all of the wonder-eyed wanderlusts and LA agents that I could.

****

So, V flew to San Francisco and sold her car. She did not tell this to Wonder-Lust but in seeing she no longer had Leery, she got over her fear of flying and travel.

V was still working out some logistics. She wanted to dedicate a chapter to a character without making it entirely about him and his journey. Instead, she wanted to make it her own.

V decided to sell the car because deep down, she knew that San Francisco very well might be the city she was looking for. The one that's strong enough to carry her dreams, the one she vowed to keep searching for.

Wonder-Lust is a Dream-Catalyst. You see, V had the ingredients inside of her to be a success, Wonder-Lust just helped her realize that there were larger cities out there that she could

fill with her music. Larger cities to hold her dreams.

But don't worry reader, believe it or not, the very character she idolizes in this chapter, the one who helped her heal, he is merely an addition to V's story. This chapter does not deviate from V's story, this is V's story after all, every chapter is her own, she just shares it with other characters. Side characters are merely meant to help V learn, and she teaches them a thing or two in the process.

So, the story continues in San Francisco and it starts with V and Wonder-Lust sharing a bench at a local park. It was early morning still, and this evening the two were going to perform at that concert for emerging artists.

****

"You know what I used to do as a kid?" I smiled, "I made these paper boats. Want me to show you how to make one?"

"Sure," Wonder-Lust smiled, he passed me a napkin and I began to fold it into shape, "I'll make you something too." He took a napkin for himself and began to fold it into a shape as well.

I smiled, this felt childish, I remembered Caprice, this is something she would have wanted to do. I showed him my paper boat and he showed me his paper creation.

"A paper plane?" I laughed, "Everyone knows how to make those."

"Not like me," he said, "I make them the best. I love your boat," he said pointing to my napkin.

"You mean your boat," I put it into his hand and he smiled.

"I love it, will you sign it for me?" I laughed and said I would, but only on the condition he sign mine.

"I feel famous," I laughed, "Want to play 21 questions?"

"Yeah sure, but what is that?"

"Oh, it's what it sounds like, you literally just have to answer 21 questions back and forth and then someone asks,

compatible with and live the rest of your life with them."

"I agree, find your missing puzzle piece,"

"Well no not quite. The missing piece is within yourself. I wouldn't say you need to be complete to be with someone because let's face it, humans have long lifespans. There is no way we could remain complete for the entirety of our lives, rather, we need to find someone who won't try to be the missing puzzle piece either. Instead they need to invest the time and energy into making you check yourself when you lose that missing piece, and they should help you find it again. Do you understand what I mean by that?"

"I do, and I agree with that. That concept is more romantic than the idea of a soulmate."

"Yeah, I know, but some don't see it that way. I try not to tell that to too many people because I don't want to dissuade anyone from believing in anything beautiful and necessary to them. Like religion. I'm an atheist and I don't tell a lot of people that because they seem to care so much about religion. I wasn't always this way though. I met a boy named Heathen; he wasn't worth the chapter I gave him but one thing I was able to benefit from him was that he opened my eyes intellectually. Sort of made me come to terms with reality. Anyways, I'll ask another, if you could choose between having wisdom or knowledge, in assuming they are not one in the same, which would you choose?"

"Wisdom, I want to be known for being wise. People who are wise come up with creative ideas, they're imaginative, and they support others creativity instead of hindering them. I want to be like that, I want to be wise."

"I would also choose wisdom, but I think that goes without saying. I'm a musician after all.

"And a writer," he added, "V, have you written anything lately?"

"I wrote a couple songs," I answered.

"I mean aside from music. Don't let that part of you die, you told me when I first met you that you wanted to write a novel."

"I did say that, didn't I? Let's not think about that now. I have my whole life to write a novel. We only have so much time together before I have to go back to Toronto."

"Back to Toronto? Wait, you're not staying?"

"No Wonder-Lust I paid for a round trip."

"Why don't you just stay with me V, San Francisco has so many gigs for you to play at."

"Yeah, I know Wonder-Lust. I'm just not really ready to settle down yet. In one area I mean. It's a lot of commitment and the majority of my connections and fan base are in Toronto."

"Do whatever you feel like V, but just remember there is an ocean outside of your lake. And they deserve to hear your music too."

"I'll consider it Wonder-Lust, thank you. Anyways back to the game, would you rather be respected by many or loved by a few?"

"Loved by a few. Love is more important than respect. What about you?"

"I agree that love is more important, but I would still choose respect. Reluctantly, but ultimately, I want to be respected, so I can flourish in my career."

"I think that's a good answer too, V."

"Okay last question, love or be loved?" I asked.

"That is a difficult question, ideally I would want to love and be loved."

"Well ideally yes so would anyone, but this is a hypothetical."

"Let me think about it."

"I'm not sure what there is to think about," I laughed, "I already know full well what you'll pick."

"How can you know if I don't know?" he laughed.

"Because sometimes other people see things in you that you don't see in yourself. As an example, a brain won't know its own function, nor what the different areas of the brain are in control of, unless it learns about its function. The same is true for human beings, sometimes we don't know our own function until someone else points it out in us."

"Okay, well here is the concern. Unrequited love can be soul crushing. So, I suppose I would not want that, but then again, loving another requires selflessness. So, I think I would like to experience that. Being loved though is nice. I guess I would choose to love."

"I knew you would say that," I laughed

"How?" asked Wonder-Lust

"Because you're an artist and artists, when given the option, would always choose to feel. I knew a person once, he told me if it came to living life in either extremes or in tranquility, he would choose the consistent option of the two. They picked this option knowing they would never feel true bliss. They chose it even at the risk of feeling numb to the world. You though, I know you would choose to experience the extremes, even despite your calm demeanor, and I would too, and that is why we're compatible. I would also, reluctantly, choose unrequited love over a loveless life. Though neither is ideal, and both are almost equally traumatizing. I've been on both sides of it, and I'd rather be hurt than hurt another. The guilt is excruciating, but anyways love is not important enough to talk about so exhaustively. Love is an addiction and that's why we all crave it. In reality, in the real world, there are more important things to discuss. You probably think I'm a pessimist," I laughed.

"No," Wonder-Lust responded, "Visionaries cannot be pessimists, rather I think you are an optimist-realist. You visualize big dreams, but you put the work into making them

your reality. You don't just sit and manifest them into your life," I smiled and I thanked him, but I knew there was nothing to thank him for. He was right, he was only telling the truth. The sooner I realized that, the better.

"So, you're opening," Wonder-Lust winked, "You're opening again and I just wanted to let you know I hope you break a leg out there. You've definitely got this."

"Thanks, Wonder-Lust, but I'm really nervous,"

"V don't be. You can do anything you set your mind to," this statement was more romantic than the concept of a soulmate, because it meant he wasn't trying to be my missing puzzle piece, Wonder-Lust was trying to help me find my own. "Actually V, I have something to show you."

"What is it?"

"It's something. Follow me." So I followed Wonder-Lust down the park trail and we walked past the welcome sign and the parking lots.

"We're going to do a trust exercise," he said, "You don't have to do it if you don't want to, but I promise the end result will be worth it."

I didn't have Leery with me today. If I did I was certain she would scratch me for even considering following this absurd notion. But even still, something told me Leery would have liked Wonder-Lust, if she had gotten more time to spend with him.

"Are you okay with walking?" he asked and I laughed.

"I'm doing it now aren't I?"

"No," he laughed, "I meant for a long duration, like hiking. Also, are you okay if I cover your eyes?"

"Um, okay one question at a time. Yes, I like long walks," I said, "but I usually like them better if I can see where I'm going."

"How would you know that?" he asked, "Have you ever tried walking without seeing? If not, then how do you know

you wouldn't like it?"

"I guess I wouldn't," I looked at him hesitantly, "Do you have a blindfold?"

"I have a scarf," he admitted, he pulled it out of his backpack.

"Wait," I laughed, "It's July, and you don't wear scarves, you planned this."

"I did."

"So, let me get this straight. You want me to put on this blindfold, and follow you around aimlessly on a long walk. What if I crash into something?"

"You'll be holding my hand, and I would never let that happen. That's the whole point of the trust exercise V. There has to be some trust on your end."

"I don't know Wonder-Lust, I'm clumsy, I'll fall if I can't see where I'm going."

"If you fall, I'll be here to help you up, but you won't fall. Just try this V. You're the type of person who used to travel aimlessly, but you stopped traveling spontaneously. You book gigs in the cities you visit before you get there. You used to just go, but now you plan, I know you're the curious type, travelers usually are. So, let me show you what it's like to be a little aimless. I'll be the cautious one today now that Leery isn't with us."

"I miss her," I admitted, "and Yippie, why do we always lose the good among us?"

"I don't know V. But Yippie would have wanted you to be a little more impulsive. That's how they were weren't they? At least that's what you told me about them."

"Yippie was so unconventional," I thought back to the artist down in the city of bob cuts and impending deadlines. "Okay Wonder-Lust, show me what you see. Pass me the scarf."

He handed me a red scarf and I put it around my eyes and tied it lightly in the back.

"May I take your hand?" he asked, I agreed.

Walking aimlessly was, needless to say, very nerve wracking. I tripped over my own toes and I tried to pull Wonder-Lust in the opposite direction he was taking me, unintentionally. It was almost like I was subconsciously protesting, but he insisted I follow his lead on this journey. Which was an odd concept for me, I was used to leading, I was used to knowing where I was going, but still I tried it. He tried to keep the situation calm by initiating conversation.

"So, you like philosophy," he reminded me, "You told me so once on a phone call. You mentioned it in passing, but still I'm curious. Every philosopher has a philosophy, what's yours?"

"No one has ever asked me that before," I said, "I'm usually the one who has to ask. Well Wonder-Lust since you asked, I believe that humans desire to categorize is detrimental to our progression."

"Alright there Ms. Philosopher, please continue."

"Let's do this Pluto styled, where you just say yes to every question, I ask you."

"I'll try," he laughed.

"Okay so, okay sorry talking about philosophy blindfolded on a walk in a different country is a little hard, let me try to phrase this right... Okay I can do this."

"You can do anything V!"

"Thank you, Wonder-Lust," I laughed, "Okay, so do you believe a thing can define itself? As an example, your brain did not define itself as a brain, nor did it define its own function, you were taught that by others, likely as a young kid in school or by your parents. Yet it took a brain to determine what the function of a brain is, and to define it. I'm not sure if this is making any sense, it's something I've seen off of Instagram, but it's important for my larger point."

"Wait, can I answer with more than just one word?"

continued, "I think if we are honest with ourselves, we can define ourselves."

"True," I replied, "but the question still remains, is it possible to be completely honest with ourselves, without bias? Or is another person more equipped to define us, or will they also have bias?"

"Yeah, that's a question I didn't think about, this way V," he gently tugged my arm to the left again when I started steering off to the right.

"So," I said, I was getting excited, "Can we define anything? That question goes along with my philosophy, that people love to categorize. Innately we categorize. Like countries, religion, major, occupation. You're a coder or an artist, or an intellect or a carpenter, and you must fit certain archetypes, but are you really any of those things? Or did society just define you? We're all good at multiple things, that's why we get so excited about learning new things and starting new projects. It's looked down upon, like you're aimless or directionless for wanting to try new things. For wanting to branch out from your stream, for wanting a qualification that does not assist you in your occupation. Society weans diverse skill out of us. We have to fit in their archetypes and be a productive member of society, a one trick pony. Maybe the trick is that we should be taught how to be more well-rounded and excel in whatever we set our minds to. Why categorize or define if it is impossible without bias?"

"That's a great philosophy V, that's why I like *The Beatles*. They sing about nonconformity. Same with John Lennon, in his song *Imagine*, they teach us to think without borders. I wish there was no such thing as country or categories in general. Then we could all be free."

"You know Wonder-Lust there is a certain thrill of walking blindfolded. It feels aimless sure, but it also feels like, I could be going anywhere. When you take the reality out of

something, you start to feel like the possibilities are endless. I like walking aimlessly, at least every once and awhile."

"Everyone should walk aimlessly. And look, you were nervous before, but you aren't now. Talking helped I'm assuming?"

"It did," I admitted. So, we kept walking but the conversation wasn't nearly as thought provoking and that was okay. Not every conversation needs to be recorded, not every conversation has to be important or come to some sort of revelation. In the end, it could very well just be lighthearted. We were kids after all, and I was walking blindfolded, we were playing games. We didn't have to be mature all the time. We didn't have to know where we were going every step of the way. So, we walked for maybe an hour, maybe two, who knows, I lost track.

We took a break once, I had to eat a snack with the blindfold on. Wonder-Lust wouldn't even tell me what it was. It was gummy bears and a chocolate bar. After we ate, we started up again. My feet hurt, but Wonder-Lust was making me laugh and I was distracted by the discomfort. Just as I thought maybe we should start getting ready for another break, Wonder-Lust gently pulled my arm and asked me to stay where I was for a moment.

"We're here," he said, "Just give me a minute. Can I touch your shoulder? I need you to face a certain direction."

"Yes," I laughed; he maneuvered my torso to face a specific direction.

"Okay," he said, "Take off your blindfold," so I did. I looked up and saw only sky, I looked down and saw the tree tops and distant mountains.

"Wonder-Lust it's beautiful!" I exclaimed, "Are these the wonders you lust for?"

"Yes," he admitted, "This V, is why I wander."

"It's so beautiful," I looked around, "Wonder-Lust you

took me to a mountaintop!"

"It is the highest peak you can get to by foot. I wasn't going to have you rock climb blindfolded," he laughed, "See V, you spent so much time on the mountainsides, you deserved to see the view from the top. I wanted to show it to you, this way, you didn't have to go up through the mountainsides again. You've seen enough of those. Let me show you the world!"

It was then that I realized what Wonder-Lust had meant. Anyone could show me interesting destinations, I could see all the landscapes, and artifacts, and all of the museums of the world. When Wonder-Lust said he wanted to show me the world, he meant that he was going to show me the wonders in the world.

"Dream-catalyst," I muttered to myself.

"What was that?" Wonder-Lust asked.

"It's what you are, a dream-catalyst."

"What does that mean V?"

****

Refer to chapter 1 for the definition of a dream-catalyst. That, or meet a person who will show you the view from the mountaintops. Then you will truly understand.

They stayed the day in the mountaintops, and when morning turned to early evening, they walked back down the path again so they could prepare for their show at the venue. The two didn't suspect that they might just have what it took to get an agent's attention. They walked with confidence. They figured that they just might be enough, without fully realizing that they might actually have what it took to go from stargazing to roaming the universe.

With a universe of visions in her mind, V followed Wonder-Lust to the auditorium, she carried her dreams in her heart and a paper plane in her pocket.

CHAPTER XIV

STARGAZING

"People frequently underestimate me, and I use that to my advantage." — V

****

V has finally reached a point in her life where she can be her own dream-catalyst. After evaluating all of the lessons she had learned from others, V is finally ready to look for inspiration inside herself rather than from others. V has grown, and this chapter is for her. V realizes that while all the other important characters of her life were relevant in their own respective chapters, this is her story. She is the protagonist, this is her legacy, and it's only just the beginning.

At the venue, V and Wonder-Lust were greeted by the owner. She shook both of their hands and directed them to the stage. While the two were ecstatic to finally get the chance to perform, the itinerary for the evening was not exactly what they had originally expected.

****

"They have us performing as one set. They think we're part of the same band. How do we tell him we're both performing as solo artists?"

"We don't," said Wonder-Lust, "I'll accompany you on guitar and sing back-up."

"But no, this isn't what was supposed to happen," I protested, "We were supposed to perform separately, so we

could each perform our own songs. And look, she only allotted 20 minutes, that's not a full set, we'll only have time for three, maybe four songs, this must be some kind of mistake."

"No, V," Wonder-Lust grabbed my arm, "V, it's not a mistake. I'm not performing to represent *Zephyr* tonight, and I don't perform solo at these events. I signed us up together. There are going to be agents here tonight V. No offense, you're good at the ukulele and all, but you need proper accompaniment if you want to get their attention. Focus on your vocals, I already learned the songs from your set."

"You learned my songs? How did you have time to do that? And how did you know which songs I would be performing?"

"V, I asked the host to give me the list of your top ten song preferences. Remember that sheet you had to fill out specifying which songs you planned on performing? I knew she would only allot you twenty minutes because that's just the way this host runs this thing. I memorized the first five songs, and then I got the sheet music for the others just in case. You only need twenty minutes to impress them V, you're really good."

"But what about you? I don't understand, don't you want to get your shot in front of the LA agencies too?"

"Well V, I actually have some news."

"What is it Wonder-Lust?"

"Well I've been thinking about it. I discovered something about myself. I think I know why I like music so much."

"Why is that?"

"Well, it's not for the reason most would think. I like music because it's the purest form of human expression. It helps a lot of people. Sure, people who are going through hard times, they can listen to my music, but it's more than that though. I've always been really connected to radical music. I like the idea of performing songs that inspire civil movements,

inform the people, make others aware of important topics. Well, that's the thing, right? I started to realize that I liked studying music, analyzing art, not because I wanted to be an artist, but because I wanted to be a humanitarian. I want to help people. I've been applying to BA programs; I've been admitted into the Stanford University for Political Science. I'm going to study to be a politician V. That's what I want to do. I will still be part of *Zephyr* and I still want to make music as a hobby, but I want to help people, not just to make them feel better about life, but to improve their lives. I'm going back to school!"

"Wonder-Lust that is incredible! I'm so proud of you, you would make an amazing politician! I couldn't think of a better politician. You can do anything you set your mind to!"

"So, can you V, and I want to be here for you while you launch your career. I want to witness it happen."

"Wonder-Lust that is the sweetest thing anyone has ever said to me. Thank you. I'm so nervous."

"Don't be! You've been performing live shows every evening in various cities across the world. You have a good reputation for yourself, I wouldn't be surprised if these agencies have already heard of you!"

"Thanks Wonder-Lust. Okay, no time for nerves, this is showtime. Okay, so let's get this going," I said pulling out a list I wrote for myself mapping out the songs I wanted to perform, "I have time for four songs on the list, right? I think we are going to perform these three first," I pointed to the list, "and then possibly this one or this one," I pointed to two more on the list, "It'll depend on the crowd and the mood, I guess. I'll announce each song before we start playing, does that work for you?"

"Yes, it does, those are the ones I memorized the chords for. I had a feeling you would play these ones, but if you want to play the others, I have the sheet music so do whatever you

bed in a hospital, that prolonged silence, the anxiousness of the impending goodbye, the melancholy and nostalgia, the discomfort, that would be what Leery's song sounded like. A prolonged sad tune. While I knew Leery was alive and well, leaving her, saying goodbye, it felt like she had died. It felt like this because I knew I would never see her again, despite her being alive and well. Wonder-Lust accompanied the song perfectly. I never thought a man full of wonder could play such sad chords. We moved a few audience members to tears, I allotted a moment of silence for the death of a friendship, and to give the audience a chance to recollect themselves, before I introduced the next song.

I dedicated the song to Wonder-Lust—he blushed—it was called 'My Muse.' Describing music is difficult, you would have to meet Wonder-Lust yourself to hear how it sounds. Let's start by saying it was wonderful and lighthearted, it was a difficult song to play but we made it look easy because that's how Wonder-Lust lived his life. He makes his hard work look effortless.

The last song I played was dedicated to the dream-catalysts. I wrote it for Yippie, and I called it Stargazing. The lyrics were about collecting stardust out of tin cans and cashing them in for coffee, food, and a warm bed. If Yippie could hear the song they would have been proud. So now came the closing song of the night.

"Wonder-Lust got accepted into the Stanford University for Poli Sci," the audience applauded, "He wants to be a politician, and I know he will be a great one, but that means he won't be performing for *Zephyr* as frequently as he once did. So tonight, he will perform the last song of the set," Wonder-Lust was surprised by this, I hadn't told him this was my plan.

'Good,' I thought, 'The art will be more genuine if he's surprised.'

"He will be performing, 'No Borders,'" the audience

applauded him.

"I guess I will be performing one of my original songs," he nodded to me in appreciation, "This song was inspired by John Lennon, it is supposed to be radical and progressive. I hope you can appreciate the meaning," and so he played.

When we finished our set and took our bows we exited into the wings. We were informed by stage management that one of the technicians on headset overheard the agents really liked our set. We asked if we could sneak into the crowd and listen to the next performers and they told us we could as long as we made our way back to the green room before intermission. So we listened to the remaining sets of the first half. When intermission was about to start, Wonder-Lust and I made our way back to the green room to wait there in the hopes that an agent would approach, this was protocol for this venue. Sure enough, the agent that we recognized, the one who only accepted those willing to make hits, entered the room.

"V, Wonder-Lust, you two were incredible. I felt the pain, I felt the loss, I felt the hope, but most importantly, I felt the spirit. I want to represent you two. I think that goes without saying I would be crazy not to, but I just wanted to say, I have not, for a long while, been truly touched by music. That song about Stargazing, I felt that. When I was your age, I was a traveler too, it took me a while to settle. Now I'm here."

"I'm honored to be considered for representation," I shook her hand, "Let's book a meeting to discuss the details. Ms. Altruist. Oh, actually, I beg your pardon, I've heard of you before, I mean it's you, you're Ms. Altruist, you don't really need an introduction, obviously. Sorry I'm rambling, is it okay if I call you Ms. Altruist, or is that too formal."

"Oh yes it's quite alright. I don't go by my first name anymore. I grew out of it."

"Oh, I see," I smiled hesitant if I should ask her what that name was. Fortunately, Wonder-Lust took that opportunity.

"And what is your first name?" he asked.

"Nomad. Nomad Altruist," she winked at me. Oh, so that was why she related to my music.

Ms. Altruist and I exchanged contact information.

"We'll be in touch V," and she left and I knew my career was made.

****

Needless to say, the two celebrated, as youth often do, but this did not need to be documented. Youth should be given the opportunity to celebrate freely without an audience trying to draw meaning out of every conversation. It strips them of their right to be free-willed. We will cut to a conversation the two had before V and Wonder-Lust made their impact on the world.

****

"Stay in San Francisco with me," asked Wonder-Lust, him and I were watching a rom-com on Netflix.

"I can't Wonder-Lust, I need to go exploring. I'm not done just yet, I need to live alone, get my own place. Figure things out."

"Okay, that's fair, I understand," he admitted, "but I'll miss you when you go."

"I'll miss you too Wonder-Lust, but we'll appreciate each other more when I get back. LA is very close to here, I have a feeling I'm going to be in the area quite a bit, and if not, I'll fly out. We'll make things work."

"But where will you go?" asked Wonder-Lust.

"I'll go to New York," I said dreamy-eyed, "I'll go to New York, Ms. Altruist wants me close to the studio, she's having her agency rent out an apartment for me. I'm going to have an apartment in New York City Wonder-Lust! And I'm going to buy a kitten and a puppy to live with me in it."

Wonder-Lust laughed, "V that's incredible, but why are you getting a dog and a cat? Aren't dogs and cats not supposed to get along?"

"Well, I'll need them to keep each other company while I'm at work. I thought this through. Dogs and cats only fight because they're helping each other grow. Growth isn't a bad thing, if I get them young, they'll grow accustomed to one another's differences and embrace them. You see, Aimless would have done much better for himself if he had someone like Leery to precaution him. And Leery, my angel, she would have learned to trust if someone just showed her how to be a little directionless every once and awhile."

"Maybe she just needed someone to put a blindfold over her eyes and show her a mountaintop," he laughed.

"Probably," I admitted, "In fact, I think most people need that. They just don't realize it."

"So, you're going to New York City, then what, when do you start making music?"

"Okay, so I technically could have started whenever, but I actually asked for a couple months to tie up some loose ends. There are a couple things I need to take care of."

"And what's that?" asked Wonder-Lust.

"Just touching up on a few loose ties. Don't worry, it's nothing major. I actually kind of want to get some air, I'm going to go for a jog at the park. I'll be back."

"Okay V, have a good jog!"

"Oh, and before I go," I kissed Wonder-Lust before I left, "Thanks for being a dream-catalyst, and for showing me the mountaintops."

"Of course, V. There's more to see out there, I'm only getting started, I'm going to show you the world."

****

I laced up my red sneakers and ran to the park. I had a feeling this would be the last time I roamed this park unrecognized. Nothing was guaranteed, but I could just sense it. My gut told me I was going to succeed. Just as I looped the bench that Wonder-Lust and I sat on the day of our mountain

date, I saw a familiar face waiting for me by a pine tree. I ran up to her.

"Where were you during the cyclone?" was the first thing I demanded of her.

Angel turned to look at me and I knew I must have crossed a line in demanding that information, still I persisted.

"You told me you would always be there for me in times of crisis."

"I never said that V," said Angel softly, "I said I would be there for you whenever you needed me. You didn't need me."

"Yes, I did. Art and Leery broke my heart, and then Yippie died, I couldn't deal with that violent cyclone."

"But you did, and now you're even stronger because of it."

"You've still got some explaining to do Angel," I mustered up the courage to say. She smiled.

"Okay V, I'll answer whatever questions you'd like, but I won't be here for long so pick the important ones. You see, this is the last time you'll be seeing me."

"What do you mean?" I was shocked, Angel wasn't going to come back anymore? What if there was another catastrophe, another tornado, or a cyclone, she smiled.

"V, you were strong enough to make it out of these situations alone. You don't need me anymore. You know how to handle the storms now; you know how to find the light."

"Who are you Angel?" I asked in a frenzy, "What are you? You came into my life with these familiar eyes, but what does it all mean?"

"Do you want to know the truth or the lie that will keep the story going?" Angel asked.

"The truth," I requested.

"I am the narrator to the story of your life. I don't like watching you go through turmoil alone so I wrote myself in, as a character in your story."

"I beg your pardon?!"

****

Dear reader, forgive me, but I couldn't help poke a little fun and break a fourth wall, but let's revisit.

****

"It was a metaphor V, think about it," Angel winked.

"Who are you?" demanded V.

"V, I am you. I am you; I am a spirit you manifested. Your inner dialogue, that is why you recognize my eyes. You never needed me, not the first time around, nor the second, you always had the power in your own hands. You were always your own dream-catalyst. You just got sidetracked with learning life lessons because you didn't trust that you had the answers within you all along."

"Angel, what now? I'm ready, I'm so ready. Though, I feel like I still have loose ends to tie, and I'm not sure what they are."

"Look deep inside yourself, you'll figure it out. V, I'll give you insight into one person from your past as a parting gift. I did grow quite attached to you, and to your life, it will be a great tragedy for me to disappear into an abyss alone."

"What happened of Art after he left?" I asked.

"You hurt him V, and he missed you. He did, but he's starting to move on. He's still an artist. He got omitted to OCAD, he studies animations and traditional visual arts there now. His heart is still numb, but soon he'll fall in love with his soulmate and they'll treat him like gold. He had a rocky start, but his future is bright. He will be a very successful artist, both in prospects and in happiness."

"Can I know of the others? What about the Artistic Alcove, Angel? What about Leery? Did Caprice have her baby girl? What about Sunny, was her album a hit after all?"

I didn't so much as look away for a second, in fact, I didn't so much as blink, but Angel disappeared. She was gone, and I was on my own now, just like everyone else, I suppose.

my mom a 5.5" x 8.5" package, she examined it and looked back at me.

"What is this?" she asked.

"Open it," I urged, and so she did.

"'Dream-catalyst,' what is this?"

"It's a book I've written about my journey," I told her, "I know I've left you in the dark concerning my life, and I know it hurt you when I decided to leave our yellow house, so I wanted to make it up to you. Open it, I've dedicated the book to you. Anyways, I've been journaling throughout my journey through the streets and mountainsides, I've even seen a mountaintop view. I decided to collect my entries and write a novel; I dedicated the book to you. I want you to see what I went through, I want you to feel like you were there with me, because truth be told, I wanted you there."

"You dedicated it to Zeal too, and who's this boy?" she asked pointing to the last page.

"That's a dream-catalyst I met, his name is Wonder-Lust, he showed me the mountaintops just as I thought the mountainside had finally defeated me. Just as I thought I couldn't climb anymore."

"Oh, he sounds nice. What's a dream-catalyst?" she asked.

"Okay so, I had a dream once, in it I spoke to an angel. She told me that we each have the ability to pursue our dreams, we all have the qualities within us needed to pursue our dreams, but there is a group of people out there called shrinkers, the entirety of their existence is to prove to us that we don't have those qualities within us after all. The shrinkers want to hold us hostage on the mountainsides. Though, every once and awhile, you meet someone called a dream-catalyst, and they help you realize you had the make of your dreams inside you all along. They just help to speed up the process. However, the shrinkers should also be credited for your success just as much as the dream-catalysts are. This is because one day, each

person will overcome enough shrinkers in their life to realize that they were their own dream-catalyst all along. Shrinkers can teach you how to be your own dream-catalyst, and that's what I am now."

"V this sounds like a beautiful book," my mother smiled, "I knew you would make it. I'm happy for you."

"Well that's because you're a dream-catalyst too, when it would have been easier for you to force me to stay, you let me explore the universe, because of you, I am dream-catalyst I am today," I smiled and embraced her. "Anyways, how's Zeal doing? And where's Aimless?"

"Well, Zeal's in school, you know how hard she works. She was omitted to one of the top schools for math and business in the country. She's getting her life together."

"And is she still writing poetry?"

"Yes, she is. She writes every night in that notebook you got her. Sometimes she shares them, sometimes she doesn't. But yes she's been reading and writing poems and taking photos, remember how she used to do that as a kid? She's getting back into it again. She's been keeping herself busy, but I've noticed she started to relax a lot more now that she's been accepted, I think she knows how to turn off work now."

"I'm so glad to hear," I smiled, "Maybe I can visit her when she's all settled into her new school."

"I'm sure she would really like that," she smiled.

"Oh, how's Aimless? You forgot to mention how he's doing."

"Actually V, Aimless is getting older now. He lost his vision."

"Aimless is blind?" I exclaimed in disbelief.

"Yes, but V don't panic. He's doing well, we talked to the vet. It's natural for dogs his age to start losing their sight, but you know that dogs rely heavily on their sense of smell and

their hearing. He's still happy and full of life, it took him some time to adjust, but it's not as large an adjustment for when a dog to lose their vision as it is for a human."

I smiled to myself, something told me Aimless was doing just fine. Nothing and no one could stop that dog from enjoying life and roaming free. In fact, I felt he may have liked wandering best without seeing where he was going anyways.

My mom invited me in for coffee, Zeal was away sleeping over with friends for the night and my dad was working late. He got a promotion at work that kept him busy, but he was doing something he enjoyed so I don't think it bothered him much. I talked with my mom for a few hours, we caught up with each other but I mostly listened to what I had missed. I knew she would catch up with me best by reading my story which she said she was going to do over the next week. I made plans to visit again in a few months so I could tell her about my experience in New York, I told her I would fly her up to see my apartment once my career took off. After the sun set, I turned my gaze toward the window.

"I'm going to go to the ravine now," I said, "Care to join? I want to go stargazing tonight."

"No thank you, but please enjoy the stars," So I went out to the bridge that overlooked the sky and I saw countless stars twinkling back at me. I saw the moon too. Tonight, it was full. I am grateful to say that the sky was transparent tonight. I could see right through the clear air and look out into the starry night.

****

Though one thing never did change about V, as good as she got at maneuvering her future to the present, no matter how experienced or wise she became, a visionary will always be a visionary. V will always look up to the starry nights on bridges overlooking ravines. You can never stop a visionary from stargazing.

The End…

for now …

(but there isn't going to be a sequel, so I guess for you, it is the end.)

EPILOGUE

***** DISCLAIMER FROM THE AUTHOR: This Epilogue is optional, if you can do without it, then close the book. But if you have to have the answers, if you have to look into the future... read on. I can't blame you, I would too. *****

****

Oh, dear reader, I wasn't going to abandon you just yet. V may never get the chance to learn of the future of her friends, but that doesn't mean you don't get to. Not all of life's questions go unanswered. Now, dear reader, I do hate goodbyes, but I am also extremely sentimental so I am at a loss narrating this epilogue, so let's make this quick. I'll try not to get emotional, but no promises. We'll say goodbye to each character one by one, so long! Goodbye! You are loved and will be greatly missed by your sweet narrator. Now, for the questions that do go answered...

Zeal became a multi-millionaire. This was not a surprise, she had the drive, dedication, and heart of a millionaire. Her 4.0 average and her ambition made her extremely competitive to the job market, but she was above that. Zeal started her own company and became a multi-millionaire, though she didn't care much about money and she donated most of it. Despite the rocky days and the hard deadlines, Zeal never forgot herself, and she never lost her zest for life.

Realist became an architect and lived a fairly complacent, and yet sturdy life. He married a woman who taught at the local school, they had three kids together. Realist taught them all how to play soccer, he didn't let them watch TV or waste a sunny day. V's dad got promoted at work, he works at a position he finds

been in NYC. Heathen stayed on the mountainside, and he lived a comfortable life, he played Scrabble recreationally at the board game cafe. Though he and Caprice could never rekindle what they had, he was one day able to meet his son. Heathen meets with H four times a year, he taught him how to play Scrabble.

Art faced adversity early on in life, in fact, life pushed him to the breaking point, and yet he didn't break. This made him unstoppable. He became one of the top animators in the country, he designed cartoons for kids, he did love kids after all. He and Leery got along quite well, they enjoyed solitude together, and eventually, each took large strives in opening up to others. By opening up to each other, they trained themselves to open up to others. V knew the two needed each other.

Wonder-Lust and V visited each other quite frequently. He never lost his spark for life and his eye for wonder. He traveled the world, studied hard, and became a successful politician. Though he never did stop performing, V featured him on a number of her hit tracks, he became a celebrity in his own right, but he never wanted the fame. Nor the prestige, he wanted to make music and he wanted to help people, so he did both. V and Wonder-Lust made things work long-distance for a while, but eventually, V got a second-place in LA, partially for work, but also because she wanted to be near Wonder-Lust, eventually the two lived together there.

So now, for V. Well dear reader, while not all of life's question's go unanswered, some of them do. So V was successful, in more than one regard, but quite honestly, her life is none of your business, nosy reader, no. See, not even V knows what her life has in store for her, she can only reflect back onto the past and look forward to the future, as any visionary does. All V knows is that she certainly got a lot better at making her future the present.

ABOUT THE AUTHOR & UPCOMING WORKS

This is the part where I get to plug my stuff. Did you like this novel? Want to see what I have cooking up next?

****

"For Adults Who Like Fairy Tales," — A short story collection for the adults who need a moral check. A radical, progressive, and magical collection. *LAUNCH DATE: September 1st, 2019*

"Heart Emblem," OR "Black Rose" — A sonnet anthology discussing raw and genuine emotion. Perfect Valentine's Day. *LAUNCH DATE: December 1st, 2019*

****

LET'S STAY CONNECTED:

Instagram: @samanthamirandola

LinkedIn: Samantha Mirandola

Email: samanthamirandola@hotmail.com

Thrive Global Account Contributor: Samantha Mirandola

YouTube Channel: Sammy Mirandola

And hey… thanks for reading my novel

my thoughts. Feminists have better things to do than think of boys; still, I guiltily proceeded. I hoped my innocent age of twenty would absolve me from this charge. This boy was my junior by two years, but I did not care because his soul was my senior. There were billions of boys and millions of reasons to forget any single one of them. However, and to my detriment, once I set fixation on one, it was an onerous burden to push my mind from their focus. I was never sure if it was them that I loved, or rather my desire to grasp complex individuals that attracted me to them. I speculated that lust would reaffirm my desire to know the human condition in them. Rather than inflame the thought of him, whoever he was at the time, I would avoid irritating that infective thought by nurturing it with distractions and songwriting.

Like most people, I was very passionate about studying the human experience. Humankind is narcissistic that way. If I were astute, I would have studied psychology or biology. Instead, I studied the arts though I would hate to define myself by my occupation or discipline of study. I often criticized society's obsession with categorizing one another into restrictive boxes. In my opinion, our inclination to categorize was exhaustive and to our detriment. I considered obsessive categorization and restrictive laws to be a strong indicator of the regression of a society.

I wrote songs by the ravine in the hopes that someday I would become a vocalist. Aside from my desire to sing professionally, I also wanted to write. I was unsuccessful in writing because I approached the craft entirely detached. I needed to write beautiful stories in beautiful places. That was why I came to the bridge at midnight. In the stars, I hoped to find a vision.

Mr. Maverick, a philosopher I adored, correlated corporation headquarters to prison cells because of their

Something noteworthy to mention about me, I am her guardian angel. I pop in and out as a narrator to the story of her life. V and I will meet soon, but our meet will be postponed until a tragedy. She will not undergo turmoil alone this time.

****

As I ran home from somewhere irrelevant to the narrative, thoughts of the boy tickled my mind again. Perhaps that was why I felt light. He was athletic, though I did hate to define others by their hobbies or occupation, his athleticism felt more like a character trait than a hobby when it pertained to him. If athleticism were a frame of mind, this would perhaps be his defining characteristic. However, this was not his name, his name was something else. He was called Realist for reasons I was yet to discover. Realist believed that a day indoors was a day wasted, and I admired that about him. While I prefer cafés to sunlit strolls, he reminded me of the luxury of the expansive grassy fields that lined his paradise. When I spent time with him, I also absorb the outdoors by default. I figured I would call upon him and we could walk our dogs. Realist was always willing to go on walks.

After clambering the hill that led to the cul-de-sac where I lived, I harnessed Aimless–our family dog. Aimless was always eager to see me–or anyone for that matter. Sheep-white and bright-eyed, Aimless always looked forward to walks.

'A sheep, like a dog, will not give life much thought,' I pondered to myself. I instantly recalled, "The Alchemist," and the life it outlined of a shepherd. In fact, a lot of literature talked about sheep. William Blake wrote about them too. The Bible also used these animals as a subject to its parables. What was so appealing of these animals? Was it that they lacked in knowledge where they trusted in abundance? We eat the lambs we fed. Why then do they stay so loyal? Dogs have more

my hair. I just washed it.

"Let me clarify," he said, he pondered for a moment and then spoke, "You once asked me a question. You then answered the question you asked. Your answered assured me my mother was right to call you Nomad."

"Well, what was the question?" I asked. I had asked Realist many questions over the years, which resonated with him so deeply?

"The question was," he started, "If you were to live one of two lives, which would you pick? In the first, you would live in extremes. If you were not in euphoria, you would be in a state of devastation, never placid. Or, you could live in a permanent state of tranquility. You would never feel extremes in anything, not devastation nor bliss, but you would live in a comfortable middle. Which would you pick?"

"I would choose the euphoria," I said without hesitation.

"Even accepting devastation?" he questioned.

"As a consequence, yes," I responded, "Why?"

"Because that's an odd answer. Most would choose tranquility; I would choose tranquility."

There was a pause.

"Opposites attract…" I started.

"Not that kind of opposite," he retorted, his words punched my stomach.

"You know," I began, "Your mother might be wrong. I've never traveled. I stay here in the summers, and I don't have an urge to leave. Also, if I ever were to settle with anyone, it would be with you."

"Oh, okay, well, yes that makes sense. But Zeal, don't you want to go to Texas? I heard Austin, Texas is supposed to be beautiful, and you've never been before, it might be fun to go down and meet new friends with the same interests as you."

"Yes V, I understand that Texas would be fun, but I'm not missing a week of school before exams. I can go to Texas when I graduate."

"You mean later this summer?"

"No, not when I graduate high school! I'm interning this summer V, I already told you. I can't afford to miss a week with this company just to go on vacation. I meant when I graduate University, there are a lot of career fairs in Austin, Texas. I might go down then when I'm looking for full-time work."

"But don't you want to go down and have fun with friends?" I asked.

"I do, but I don't have time V. I'm trying to get into a highly competitive program, I already told you this V. I feel like you never listen to me."

"I'm sorry Zeal, I do listen, it's just that you're always working toward so much it's hard to keep track of what you're prioritizing this week. I didn't mean to make it seem like I don't care about your accomplishments."

"It's fine, I'm not mad, I just can't afford to go to Texas right now."

"I get it," I smiled, "Realist and I just got back from a walk around the neighborhood. Realist says hi, he was asking about you, I told him you were studying."

"How's Realist's dog?" Zeal exclaimed I wasn't surprised that Zeal asked about Realist's dog, Zeal loves dogs, in fact, no

What would you see?"

"Okay fine," Zeal laughed, "but because we're taking double the time we expected, you're buying me two chocolate bars."

"I'll buy out the store for all I care," I smiled, "Look with your lens."

I watched as Zeal explored the open grassy field I took her too. She turned over every rock, searched every leaf, to try to see what I wanted her to see. She took photos of the trees first, then the sky, then some of Aimless and a few of me, she shot some self-portraits, but she couldn't see what I wanted her to see.

"Okay V, I took like a million pictures. I still don't see what you were trying to show me, can you please just tell me what you wanted me to see?" Zeal sighed, "Come on, I have exams V, I need to study. This is taking longer than you said it would, and we still have to stop by the convenience store."

"Zeal, you're so close," I teased, "I want you to take a moment and stop to smell the roses."

"But I did already," Zeal insisted, "Did you not see me taking all of those pictures?"

"I didn't mean that metaphorically," I winked. Zeal thought about it for a minute and scanned the field again one last time, then, just as she was about to give up, Zeal saw it out of the corner of her eye.

"Oh my god, V!" Zeal exclaimed, she ran to the left of the field a few feet from the soccer goal post, "How could I have missed these earlier?" She exclaimed.

"You forgot to take the time to smell the roses Zeal," I

feed on delicious lies. Eventually, they over-indulge.

** The Repressor: They believe themselves to be inferior to those around them. Attempts to alleviate this burden by verbally attacking those of substance. They seem impressive from a distance, but by incessantly attacking others, they deface their own value.*

** The Prejudice: These are the sexist, racist, homophobic people who state obtrusive statements for shock value. They do this because they are subconsciously aware that they are uninformed of culture and art, but do not know how to communicate this due to their own stupidity. These are the lowest amongst the shrinkers.*

V has already defeated the shrinkers of her life, just as a ghost hunter would kill their demons. These shrinkers equipped her with the tools she needs to overcome the tornado. While the tornado tries to kill her, it only elevates her high above the ground-dwellers beneath her. V is now ready to touch the stars.

As unfair or evil as the shrinkers may seem, they are not the true antagonist to this tale. It is both complacency and indifference that play the villain in V's narrative. The shrinkers can do nothing more than push V to her self-defining destiny.

There is one more type of person that should not be forgotten. If complacency and indifference are the villains, then it is the 'dream-catalysts' that play the hero in this, and perhaps all, stories.

**Dream-catalyst: These are the muses, the lovers, the poets, the dreamers, the musicians, the painters, the impassioned. They are the beings who live with the sole intent of pushing others to*

remembering the group, 'Maybe they weren't all shrinkers after all.'

I returned from the pause I deviated into thought from and continued my story,

"My father was screaming. He insulted my mother while driving. He put his foot to the gas and accelerated the car. I asked him to stop. I had asked him to stop multiple times. He refused. Instead of pulling over, he sped quicker. I asked him to pull into a gas station, I explained my rights as a passenger. I explained I felt unsafe. He said no, my mother and Zeal told me to shut up. They were afraid. When we got to the destination, I left. I was called so many names: melodramatic, crazy, I had anger issues, I was a bitch, I was stupid. Every name in the book. When I told anyone, they would laugh. They said if I went to the police, they would laugh at me too."

At times I wished that others could read my mind and feel my pain so I would not have to explain it to them. I wanted to be read. To be understood, but people don't like dirty laundry.

"Is that what happened tonight?" asked the woman.

"No," I said, "Something like it did.' I looking over the ravine's edge, "Sometimes I wonder what it would be like to be a river," I told the woman, "Always flowing. Currents, sharp rocks, it just flows through them. Obstacles mean nothing to the river. Why do they matter than to me?"

"Can I tell you a story?" asked the woman, "It will help to clear the storm." As she said this, perhaps by coincidence, the darkness subsided. I looked to the once starless sky and saw the stars emerging. They winked at me and urged I hear the woman, so I nodded.

> "There was once a group of chameleons who adopted a caterpillar. They liked the caterpillar because she would blend into the leaves of the trees. When she cocooned herself, they liked her even more so because she became a part of the tree. 'A master of disguise,' they thought. All

"V, you're trouble," said my mom quite hurt, "You need to learn how to let go of the past."

She was always telling me to let go. I was never entirely sure what she meant by this. Let go, or what? I lived in the future; I didn't hold onto the past.

I knew she wanted me to learn how to forgive. The problem was, forgiveness only worked when another person has demonstrated some effort to change the circumstance. How could one forgive when another did not show any desire to be forgiven? I never regarded stubbornness as a negative quality. If one were always passive, then nothing would change. I never quite understood why persistence was considered a positive trait, but stubbornness, on the other hand, was considered its negative counterpart. Could one be persistent without being stubborn or stubborn without being persistent? If that were the case, then I suppose I was both. Two sides to the same coin, at least it was a coin of some value.

"Will you be back?"

"Maybe," I saw this did not satisfy her.

"Promise me you will come back someday," she rephrased.

"I promise you will hear from me," I returned, "I promise to write. I'll promise to write. That is all I can promise right now, I will write. When I leave a new location, I'll write, and you can send a letter back to the return address and someday I will go back to pick it up. Better still, I will message you online, I am bringing my laptop."

"If you can't promise to return, I can't promise to write back," my mother said. It was a valid remark.

"Okay," I finally gave in, "I'll come back someday. I'm not sure when, but I will."

She embraced me one last time, and a silver tear slipped from her cheek, "I will miss you."

Leaving the past behind is not easy when you always assumed it would be a part of your future. I never considered myself a Nomad, not from lack of want, but I could never smell the sea salt. I did not realize I was lost in a familiar terrain until the tornado.

When I did mount that red bicycle and cantered it through

"You aren't the first to park a bike by a chattery dog," the woman laughed, "The boy is smart, he brings treats in his pocket to settle them. He isn't popular amongst the people here, but he is definitely appreciated by the local dogs."

"You have an endearing little shop," I said. I examined the space once more. It takes a special kind of person to own a little knick-knack shop like this. I looked at her face again and saw her youthful demeanor. She had rosy cheeks and a cheery smile. Something about her radiated a childish innocence that not many others possessed. I imagined her baby would be mothered well. It took a special kind of person to be own a fairy shop. Even more so, it took a special kind of person to be a mother. Something about her made me believe that she never let her fairy die.

"Well, backpacker, it looks like you are in luck. I need a hand with something, and it looks as though you need a place to stay for the night. Want to pay your wage for a cozy bed and breakfast tomorrow morning?"

I was taken aback by this. Was it that obvious I was on the run? I sniffed my hair; did she smell the sea salt too? I considered her offer. I had not covered as much ground as I intended for the evening. I was troubled by the close distance between this city and the cul-de-sac with the yellow house. Although I had to admit, I was hungry and growing tired. The woman looked kind-hearted, so I felt as though I could trust her. I decided to accept the invitation, but first, I wanted to know why.

"Why are you being so kind?" I asked, thinking back to the elderly man in the white van and all the others who were looking to take advantage of me.

"Because," she told me, "You have familiar eyes. I recognize backpacker-eyes from anywhere. It's rare I see a young woman with those eyes." That statement triggered me. 'I've seen plenty of women with backpacker-eyes.' I thought to

help people discover their dreams?"

"Everyone already knows their dreams, V; I want to help people achieve them! If I was rich, that's what I would do. I would even sell the fairy shop for that dream. Though this would be a disservice to Putter and the others that take refuge in my fairy shop. Someday I'll help them achieve their dreams too. What is your dream, V?"

"My dream?" I asked.

"Yes, what is your dream V, and what have you sacrificed to achieve it?"

"Well," I had to think about it, "I like music. Like, a lot. I sing, and I um, I write too. So, I guess I want to do that."

"Music!" Caprice exclaimed, "What kind of music V, what do you write your songs about?"

"Umm, usually love, or success," I said.

"Do you also write poetry?" Caprice asked, "All singers write poetry."

"Umm the songs kind of are my poetry," I admitted.

"Sing to me V!" I told the woman I couldn't, I just wrote songs for myself.

"Okay, V," said the woman abruptly changing the subject, "Pick something from my home you like and take it with you." I was shocked to hear this.

"What?" I questioned and looked into her eager eyes.

"Take something you like on your journey! Bring anything you like. Just one thing, though, I have a lot of travelers who come and go through here."

"Why would you offer me one of your things?" I questioned, "You barely know me!"

"Pay one forward, and eventually it will be reciprocated," she explained, "All I ask is that you do a good deed for another."

"But Caprice you already did a good deed for me. You offered me a place to stay tonight and some food. Many

buildings were new, differing drastically from the Mennonite town a ways back. There were no rustic old-fashioned buildings here. No straw hats or fairy shops. Instead, there were various tall rectangular buildings, some vertical others horizontal. The sides were built of grey cement. The sheer glass windows that scaled the building sides were also rectangular. Today it was rainy and the sky looked off-white and gloomy. The last day that I had seen the sun peeking through a transparent sky was the day Caprice and I sat together in her baby's sky-fort. While I worked on the interior, Caprice insisted she climb to the top to overlook the view. She was very pregnant and I urged her to reconsider, but she was adamant. I scanned the ground for loose nails or tacks and in seeing there were none, I invited her up. That day the sun was so bright and the sky was crystal blue. If anything, the sun was almost too bright, I had to squint to keep my eyes focused. I thought back to the sky-fort my dad had built me in my childhood. Zeal and I created an imaginary world within it. This was when he was still a dream-catalyst before the shrinkers consumed him.

Ever since that day it had been nothing but off-white skies. Even as the sun was rising, it went from a dark raven black night, to a mystical blue, and finally back to an off-white sky. No sunrise rainbowed the skies to ease each melancholy night into day. I had grown tired of the grey. I wanted warm weather, even if it would drench me in sweat as I traveled on my extensive bike ride. I envisioned pulling over to rest at a beach for a day. I was tempted to soak my feet in the water and lay on the clean sand. I passed a tiny beach on my journey from the Mennonite town to this new city. Perhaps that was why the beach was on my mind. The problem was that it was still so cold that the beach was closed.

I looked around once again at this strange new city. It differed quite drastically from Caprice's fairy shop. This city

shake it.

"I am Yippie. I have purple hair and I read funny books about haunted houses too, just not on paper, I prefer the auditory version. Someday I hope to live in a haunted house because a haunted house is better than no house at all. I am not female, I know I look it, but I identify as a non-binary person. They/them/it, any of those pronouns work for me, but not she. So, if you ever write about me in some book someday you damn reader, you better not call me she!" they said, "I am also a nonconformist. What is your name Reader?"

"My name is V," I said, I hoped they wouldn't ask me what it stood for.

"V?" Yippie asked, "I don't like it, to me you're Reader," they had got to be joking. I began to laugh to myself, "Why ask for my name if you don't intend on calling me by it anyway?"

"Probably the same reason why I'm stealing this book from you even though I hate the cover and I won't read it," they responded, "I like knowing what something thinks it is before I decide what I think it is. You think you should go by V because it's the name your parents gave you, and I think you should go by Reader because it's what you actually are. "Wuthering Heights," thinks it should have a haunted house on the cover because of some publishing house, but I think it should have something else. I'm not sure what, but something else," I didn't know how to respond to this lunacy.

"You know," I decided to change the subject, "I once tried to look up the synonym for nonconformist, I write songs, I was writing about a particular person, but when I looked up the synonyms for nonconformist they all had negative connotations to them like; violent, dissident, freak and dropout. I found this offensive because I think I just might be a nonconformist too."

"You know why I said 'I think I like you' instead of saying 'I like you?' I said that because you consider all of those things

why they all gathered here but not in the city square until I noticed a few elderly locals emptying bird seeds from their pockets. The birds crowded around them and ate them from their hands. It reminded me of something you might see in a movie. It was only then that I realized how kind-hearted bird feeders must be. Birdfeeders gave others substance without expecting repayment. All they asked for in return was their company.

I also saw vendors in the street, but they were not pushy vendors like I've seen in other large cities in the past, the people of these vendors were reading or sketching or listening to music. Some even turned on their speakers and played indie music for those who bypassed their vendor. The contents of the vendors were just as romantic as the marvelous shops in Caprice's town. One vendor sold stickers and compliments. It, quite literally, had a sign hanging from the booth that said "Stickers $1, sneakers $10, compliments FREE. One vendor was an artist trying to sell his paintings. They were rather good; he painted the birds on the street feeding off of the local's hand across from him. This entire street seemed very colorful. Though I much preferred sunny days to gloomy ones, I felt as though if I lived on this street, I wouldn't give the bleak skies on rainy days much thought at all. Yippie walked me up the steps to a purple building that matched their hair and nails. I wondered if it was an inspiration to them. Yippie opened the door and it chimed; they gestured for me to walk in ahead of them.

"Oh," I said aloud, "You wanted to take me to a book shop?" I looked around, the books all looked tattered and half read. There were classics like "Sense and Sensibility," and "Jane Eyre," on the walls. I looked at the counter and noticed the others in the shop. Just like Yippie, they also had colorful hair. One had pink hair, another yellow and another a red updo. So, this is where Yippie spent their days.

backward. Let me tell you something, isn't it a little backward that we all read about our life lessons when we should be going out and living them?"

"Yippie, I get what you're saying, but sometimes one just wants to learn from books. The just don't resonate with you the same way that they do with others do," retorted Mitty.

"Yes, and all is well when one learns from books, and music, and dance, and paintings. But further, still, I wonder, is their art to be found in the artist?"

"There is an artist to be found in the art," answered Sunny, "So by that logic, yes there should be art in the artist."

"Then why don't we see it?" Yippie asked.

"I see it," Sunny explained.

"Well, yes Sunny you're different. You hug strangers on the subway when they look like they're in a bad mood. And everyone in this city is in a bad mood so you give out a lot of hugs. That's not the point Sunny, I don't mean you. You are the artist, of course you're going to see the art in the artist. You see the art in everything. I mean this, why don't the people with bob cuts listen to the advice of the artist, unless they see the artist in the art?"

"Some people need a little extra help seeing art in everything," Sunny responded, "We just help them."

"Interesting," returned Yippie, "See Reader, not all life's questions go unanswered. Sometimes you don't even have to read to find those answers. Alright, kids, it's time for me to go collect stardust, I am off. But, don't peddle off until I get to see you perform Reader, then I give you permission to fly the coop." Yippie left the bookstore and the bell chimed as they left.

****

Yippie is a lovable person. That is clear to anyone who meets them and truly gets to know them. Yippie is quite loveable because they love everyone. Even when they are snubbed by the

CHAPTER VI

SILVER SUNSET

"He got angry at the alarm he set." — V

****

Mitty offered to let me sleep in the shop that night and so I did, Yippie didn't stay. I did not know at the time that I was taking their bed by agreeing to sleep in Mitty's back room for the night.

I left early the next morning. Mitty left me breakfast in the break room of the shop before closing. She asked me to wait until noon before leaving the next day. She said she had a present for me and wanted to say goodbye, but I couldn't wait. I was itching to get back onto the road; mostly because staying in one location for too long unsettled me, but also because I hated goodbyes. Yippie asked Mitty to give me the parting gift last night. Now that it was noon and I had already peddled a great distance from the City Center and the Artistic Alcove, I understood why Yippie persisted in pushing Mitty concerning the parting gift. Yippie knew I wouldn't stay.

I realized for the first time during my stay in the city of bob cuts that I wanted to continue performing my songs in front of people, like, a lot of people. Sunny taught me something about the value of performing original works. She was right, the artist is in the art; and Yippie was also right, the art is in the artist. People were listening to me and, for perhaps

honest. If you weren't, you would've run off with the car already."

"I didn't notice that the keys were in the ignition," I admitted.

"Because you're honest. A dishonest person would have checked first, hoping to luck out so they could make a break for it," he reaffirmed.

He walked me over to the car, he was right, the keys were indeed in the ignition. I insisted he let me start the car first to ensure it ran before I handed him the necklace; this took some convincing, but his objection eventually subsided. He permitted me to start the engine.

"Are there ownership papers I can sign? How can I be sure you won't call the police insisting I stole your vehicle?" I asked once I handed him the necklace. Someone like Sullen might be capable of that remorseless betrayal.

"Well, 'cause it's a piece of junk," he said snatching the necklace from my palm, "Besides, what's that gonna do? I call the police, tell them you're in a red beat up car in the next town over, they get it back to me, and I'm stuck with this lemon. And then they remember I haven't paid a couple parking tickets and charge me for them. You're assuming you're worth the headache. This cat and mouse game don't all that much interest me. Once you leave, I'm gonna have a smoke and maybe go hunting this afternoon. My gun don't have a permit neither, another reason I can't be bothered to call the cops."

"Alright Sullen," I said, inching my hand toward the PRNDL switch, "I suppose that was a fair trade, enjoy the necklace. It will look charming on you," he groaned. I scooted the seat forward so I could reach the foot pedals. I had to readjust the mirrors, I looked back at Sullen, he was examining the necklace and watch.

"You know Sullen," I said startling him, "I bet you could

the cover was drawn in vivid detail. I initially glossed over that sketch, but when I looked at it a little closer, I noticed a house on the cover. The word 'W. Hights' was etched into the front. Yippie couldn't read, so that would have meant that they were trying to copy the shape of the letters on the book's cover page by memory. So, the cashier once had my exact same copy of "Wuthering Heights," and Yippie remembered them reading it on the subway when she still had long hair and a joyous demeanor. This was why Yippie took so long to examine the cover of my book! Yippie wanted to give the book to the cashier. My heart melted, there was still love in the world after all. A loud tapping on my window woke me from my wake-dream.

"Excuse me!" exclaimed a high-pitched voice from the window, "Do you have a cat?"

"A cat?" I asked, I looked to the window and saw a middle-aged woman and a girl standing beside her, the girl was holding a fluffy skirt, she must have been a dancer.

"No," I responded, I then rolled down the window and let the woman explain herself.

"Sorry to bug ya," said the cheery woman, "but I think I hear a cat in your car."

"I don't have any cats," I said, then I realized what was happening. Maybe this woman knew the source of the squeaking.

"My husband grew up on a farm," she exclaimed, "He used to tell me that a lot of stray cats would crawl into the engine of their pickup trucks. They think it's nice and cozy in there, but they can't stay there for too long otherwise they overheat," explained the woman, "May I check under your hood?"

"Of course!" I exclaimed; though now that I knew that the origin of the squeaking was a cat, I was worried that it might be hurt, I had been driving for a little while now. "Do you think the cat is ok?" I asked.

had in my purse. $18.00 could cover some cat food, maybe a toy, but the carrying case would cost more. I was not sure I could afford it. I looked back at Sullen and his beady eyes.

'I'll figure it out,' I thought, 'I'm a clever girl, clever girls are resourceful.'

"I'll take her," I said, Ami smiled, Sullen groveled.

"She can't keep it! That's my damn cat! I pawned her off fair and square, she's mine!" Sullen began to make a scene, the rest of the shelter was staring now. He began to bang on the tables and throw a tantrum. "The. Cat. Is. Mine!" He chanted, two security guards noticed the fuss and stood on either side of Sullen.

"We're going to have to ask you to leave," said Ami, I smiled. Sullen left without another word.

"So," began Ami, "Now comes the time to naming the cat."

"Well," I began, "In all honesty, I've never had a cat before, I think the first step is to get her some equipment."

"Well sweetheart, what's your budget?"

"$18.00," I said ashamed, "That's all I have right now. The kitten will be spending a lot of time in there," I admitted gesturing to my car through the window. "I suppose I can't let her sit free in the car, can I?" I was used to Aimless, and he would have no problem sitting passenger without a crate. Though, I suspected I could not do the same with a kitten.

"Well, I'll tell you what," Ami said, "For $18.00 you can get a decent sized bag of cat food. I can throw in a carrying case, litter box, and a couple towels for you as well. It'll keep the bottom of her crate nice and soft for her," Ami disappeared behind the counter. I was shocked, Ami was about to give me over a hundred dollars' worth of equipment for free? Why would they do such a thing? Ami came back out with my silver tabby in a large crate. It would have comfortably fit a tiny dog; it had a small litter box in it too, and the bottom was lined with towels. Ami placed the crate on the counter and went into the

cars would whirl past. The few that did zoom by had drivers who seemed distant and uninterested in communicating with pedestrians. I walked further up the route, and if it were not for the electrical wire above me, I would have feared the entire location was vacant and uncivilized.

Leery looked cold, and I felt terrible for her. She looked as though she wanted to exit her enclosure and escape, so she could find a warm recluse on her own. Though I admired Leery's sense of adventure, I figured it best to keep her safe in the tiny enclosure. I knew she would be most comfortable with me in the long run, despite her desire to travel alone.

After only ten minutes of wandering the open trail, I noticed a small plaza up ahead. It was nothing fancy, but it looked as though it had a few activities. From where I stood, I could see a few commercialized fast-food restaurants, a small post office, and several cafés. I figured this plaza was likely the primary source of entertainment for locals. Aside from this plaza, the town seemed rather empty. I wandered through the town square and noticed something intriguing, a board game café. Board game cafés were typically located in small neighborhoods. They would serve as a source of entertainment for the locals; a board game café also suggested a dense population of youth. My curiosity overwhelmed me, I decided to venture into the café.

I walked to the door. The building had large windows on its side and on the glass were painted several cartoon and anime characters, some of which I recognized from my childhood. I decided to walk in. To my amazement, I saw a wall of board games along the back of the café. It was a fascinating sight, indeed! I went to the back wall and examined the tower of games that quadrupled my height.

"Excuse me," exclaimed a female voice from behind me, I turned to see a sour looking lady that reminded me of the cashier from Yippie's city, though she did not have a bob cut or

'I must find her a permanent home,' I thought to myself.

Heathen made his way to the table, Leery moved to the back of the cage and eyed him with the intense glare she welcomed him with previously.

"Congratulations," I nodded, impressed with his collected demeanor.

"Yeah," he said nodding, "That guy comes here all the time, he's not my main concern."

"He did well in his first few moves," I suggested, Heathen shook his head.

"Not really, he always does decently at the start, but he's inconsistent. Always makes risky moves. Silly mistakes. Amateur stuff. There's another woman who comes in. She's not here yet, she's usually late, but she's excellent."

"Oh, is she," I started, "How long has she played?"

"Her whole life. Her mother was an English major, got her into it when she was young. She came in first for several national spelling bees. She started doing scrabble instead because it was more fun, I guess."

"Is she your age too?" I asked.

"No. Couple years older. I'm the youngest one here. Well, aside from you," he looked over at me.

"Oh, I'm not actually here for the Scrabble," I admitted, "I don't play. Well like I've played a couple times, but I usually lose. I just do it for fun, not competitively. Actually, it's kind of cool that you play Scrabble, I didn't think you could play competitively."

"Oh yeah. It's a thing," Heathens said sarcastically. I smiled.

"Do you want a coffee?" he asked me.

"Oh, sure, thanks," I usually would have declined, but the barista kept wandering to the table and eyeing Leery who was causing a nuisance in the board game café.

"Cool, I'll go get it," he said, "How do you drink your

"Thank you," chuckled Elfin, "I do it for fun now. But I love beating Heathen, it irritates him," I laughed.

"Hello, V," the boy with the cartoonish jacket extended his hand, "I'm Staid."

'Staid,' I chuckled to myself, 'I've never met a serious man in a cartoonish vest.' Though now that I did give it some consideration, he did seem rather formal in his persona. Perhaps not his outward appearance, but maybe he was trying to compensate with a more outlandish physical presence to make up for his more stoic demeanor. Perhaps the purpose of his more flamboyant appearance was to appeal to an onlooker so they would not initially judge him to be too serious.

"Hi, I'm Dote," smiled the woman with long hair, "and this is Apt," the blonde woman in spectacles smiled and shook my hand.

"Apt, do you play?" I pointed to the board.

"Oh no, I would do quite terribly if I played," she chuckled to herself.

'I see,' I thought to myself, 'She is apt but humble, sort of like the man Heathen competed against.' This always seemed to be the case. Some of the smartest people I've known would always self-doubt their aptitude. They would frequently fail out of programs and score poorly on tests. While the inept found their way to the very top. I took this evidence as proof that the correlation between success and intelligence was nothing more than a façade. Hard work also didn't constitute success. I know a lot of hard-working unsuccessful people. What was it then that made these inept few so successful? It was the self-doubt of the intellect. Something told me if Apt played, she would win.

"Elfin, V," called the barista loudly from behind our table. I jumped. Oh no. I did sign up to play, hadn't I? Why would they put the newcomer at the end of the chain? I was going to fail miserably. I looked to Elfin, and she flashed a genuine smile at

and they think they are discovering a glimpse of that person's third face, but maybe they did not truly discover a glimpse of anything special. Maybe they just discovered a secret, something the writer was trying to shield from them to protect their feelings. And, maybe the writer was too influenced by the emotions caused by the event that tainted their perception of their subject to accurately portray their true feelings toward them, without bias. Maybe for one to truly discover something about a person's third face, they would have to read a fictional piece of theirs. Something that removes the bias."

"Oh, I see, so that they might grasp a glimpse of their subconscious by reading a writer's work of fiction," considered Elfin, "Okay, I see what you're saying. So maybe someone is not fully capable of revealing their third face because they aren't entirely sure of what it looks like in the first place. Their third face is their subconscious."

"Yeah, exactly," I agreed, "Maybe that's why people are fascinated with stories about mermaids or vampires or wizards. The author can express their third face, their subconscious, through these fictional characters. They aren't exactly a reflection of reality, nor are they a tactile object of any sort, but they share just enough similarities with human beings—just enough shared experience—that the author's subconscious can truly be expressed."

"I like you, Philosopher," Elfin smiled, "You would be fun to get high with," she said, I laughed.

"I've gotten that before," I admitted, "I don't smoke though. But yeah, I like talking about philosophy I guess, I mean why waste energy discussing reality? The abstract is so much more fun."

"Do you have any tattoos?" Elfin asked.

"Oh no, I'm too chicken for that," I laughed.

"I'm surprised. For someone so interested in revealing their third face, you sure do take extra precaution to hide it

Elfin offered to go get me some water, but I tried to reassure her I was okay. I tried asking her to elaborate on her environmental projects, but I knew very well that my efforts to appear sober were in vain. Elfin was sweet about continuing a one-sided conversation, as I was in no state to provide an adequate response. After several minutes of dialogue, Elfin insisted, despite my request that she retrieve a glass of water, and a bag of chips for me. As she got up to leave, Heathen, who was sitting to my left, put his right arm around me and pulled me into his chest. I got a whiff of his musky cologne and the stench of cigarettes on his breath. His breath smelt like rum, and I could bet his fingertips smelled of marijuana.

'This poor distressed boy can't stay sober,' I thought to myself. In my muffled mind and buzzed state, I imagined the deranged past that caused such a perturbation in this boy, which made him feel so broken that he had to resort to mood altering substances. The story I mustered up of what I considered to be his troubled past was alluring, and his eyes, just as in the board game café, were piercing. Even more so in the night than in the day. My drunken mind played out an array of jumbled scenarios as I considered what his troubled past might have been, all in which left the boy a tortured messed. I liked to imagine some sick glorified tragedy that left him aloof. Maybe his soulmate cheated on him, and perhaps this left him in a disheveled state.

No, it was that he had to leave his family just as they discovered they needed him most. Was it an ambition that drove him to drink? Perhaps he realized a falter in his ambition to pursue his true passion, maybe he needed to sacrifice his dreams for another's sake, and this left him feeling hopeless and broken.

'He must be some tortured, selfless genius,' I fantasized to myself. I saw him looking off in the distance, and I wondered what he was searching for.

succeed. We would all be entirely self-sufficient."

"You know, you may have a point. AI is some of the most intelligent software we have existing to date. But, would you like to know about another creature that entirely lacks empathy and does not mourn its loved one's Heathen?"

"Who?" he asked.

"Apes, Heathen. Animals. There's a widely accepted misconception that it is our empathy that holds us back from achieving success. Though those same individuals fail to acknowledge that it is our empathy, our passion, that differentiates us from the apes. Without it, we would be no better than them. The idea of robotic superiority is a facade." I think I made my point loud and clear.

Elfin burst into the room in a frenzy. Heathen and I looked at each other.

"What's up Elfin?" Heathen asked.

"V, I'm so sorry. I placed Leery on the ground for less than a minute, I just needed to go bring Dote some water, and now she's gone. I don't know where she went, I'm so sorry."

"Leery!" I exclaimed, "Where's Leery?"

"Relax, we'll find her," Heathen reached into his pocket and pulled out a cigarette, he lit it after placing it between his teeth. "You can sleep here until you find her if we cannot find her tonight. In fact, I insist on it. I don't want this cat turning up a week from now with you a hundred miles from us," he exaggerated, "Then, I would have to take care of the damn thing."

"I thought you said you liked cats," I spoke up.

"I do, that was called sarcasm, look it up. Could get you eleven points in scrabble."

"Yeah well, you know what Heathen, calling you a prick scores me thirteen points," shouted Elfin, "So, I guess you lost this round." Heathen didn't dare talk back to Elfin. She had passion in her voice that I could tell she was mustering up for

was not all that bad," I smiled.

"No, I am not yet finished; this is certainly not meant to be a compliment. I was going to bite my tongue about this, but I wished someone shook me out of this before I fell into the same trap, you're falling head first into. I want to do this for you goddammit. I still don't like you; V. I mean the real you. We became friends because I started liking the person you became. You are familiar now."

"What are you saying?" I asked her, "You don't want to be friends anymore?"

"That is exactly what I'm saying, but not in the way you think. Okay, how do I explain this? Here," she pulled up her three-quarter sleeves and revealed her forearm to me. Like Elfin, it was covered in tattoos. Though I occasionally saw the barista's tattoos when she would roll her sleeves up to mop the floors or clean the counters, she never did showcase them to me. Once I asked her about them, and she brushed me off rather curtly.

"Alright, here," she pointed to a tattoo of two masks, the symbol for theatre, the emblem for emotion. I began to understand now.

"You're an actress?" I asked her astonished.

"Not everyone involved in theatre is an actress V," the barista rolled her eyes shrewdly.

"Director?" I asked again, she shook her head.

> "I did the set design. And I was good at it. No one cares much for the actors V when the set is lacking. I was the set designer, and I was good. I was projected to design for Broadway, all of my professors said so. Nearing my graduation, I applied to several different theatre companies. All of which my profs referred me to. I mailed out the letters, and I received word from one, I was ecstatic to find that my top choice, a theatre company known to work intimately with Broadway set designs,

and cried.

****

There is a well-known superstition that when one breaks a mirror, they suffer seven years of bad luck. But what about those who break a heart? What do they suffer?

Well, dear reader, they suffer something worse than bad luck. They bear the loss of their brokenhearted lover. You see when one gives you their heart, and when they permit you to break it, that person truly did love you. In losing them, you are missing out on a particular type of love that you might never find again.

Heathen lost V. Someday he'll think back to her as he sits alone in his living room.

V will not go through this trauma alone, this time she has me. Let us not comfort V, instead, let us teach her how to comfort herself.

****

"V, stop crying," a voice said to me, I looked up to see Angel, the woman I met at the ravine on that starlit night. Overjoyed, I reached out to her and tried to hug her, but she was transparent, and I felt nothing, nor did she.

"Angel," I sobbed, "Heathen and I..."

"You need not say a word V, we have all been listening to your tale. I think it is safe to say Heathen is to blame. Even if Elfin did fall victim to his cunning tricks."

"Angel, he gave me love like no other," I was beginning to sob, "Sure he poked fun at me, at my ambition, but he was never serious. Angel, he was always there, he was always present. Whenever I needed him, he was there to hear me out. He gave me constant attention, he introduced me to his friends..."

"V," began Angel, "He stole your heart, and he broke your trust. He may have been sweet, but you were sweeter. Heathen took a bite out of your heart, and then Heathen left you. He left

procured with Heathen and the others as the conversation continued.

"Your novel has shifted V," said Able, I did not understand, but she continued, "You have wasted so many pages on others advice. From what you've been telling me, your first few chapters discussed your own philosophies of the world. Remember? Now read your more recent chapters. They consist of mostly dialogue. You quote those from your past. You insist they can offer you wisdom. Though you fail to see that you've possessed this wisdom in your heart all along."

"I'm not writing a novel," I started.

"Exactly my point, you are a writer V, and a songstress. Yet, I have trouble believing you as you just now told me you are not writing a novel. Have you written or performed any music recently?" she pressed.

"Not since the Artistic Alcove in the city of bob cuts. I haven't performed music since then," I signed.

"V, darling, when you do not pick up the pen and tell your own stories, your novel consists solely of other stories, not your own. What is your story, V? What is your legacy?" I knew Able was right even though I did not want to admit it.

"I am scared Able," I admitted looking into her eyes, "I am scared I will lose myself again to the mountainsides."

"Mountaintops are lovely and worth the clamber V but don't lose yourself again to mountainsides. Mountainsides belong to the half-hearted. Those who started on their hike to reach the mountaintops, but then quit, and decide to reside in the towns on mountainsides instead. It sounds as though you spent enough time on the mountainside to recognize the land of the half-hearted. Your concerns are valid. They are valid because we have all, at one point or another, found ourselves caught stuck on a mountainside with strangers who disempower us."

"Why did I give them such a large chapter Able? An

tracks on YouTube, she filmed herself off of her laptop. When V was not performing, she spent the remainder of her time scouring the web, booking herself gigs in the cities she wanted to visit. The prospect of an upcoming gig in an exciting new city kept V going. It also forced her to keep moving forward. Whenever she became too comfortable in one location, V would book herself a gig in a new city.

Now, for the sad truth. This beautiful chapter pains V when she recalls it to memory. Not because it's unpleasant, but because it ends. V could write an entire novel on this chapter alone, and she very well might someday, but for now, she will keep it concise. It will save her a great deal of heartache to keep this chapter short.

I only wish that V could have read this chapter on the night of the cyclone, but I won't spoil the story for you. Let's draw our attention back to V and her sassy kitten.

****

"We're in Toronto baby!" I exclaimed to Leery, she looked back toward me discontented by my outburst that woke her from her nap. Judging from her disdainful reaction to my enthusiasm, I gathered that Leery was not particularly enthused with our new location. In all honesty, I think Leery just wanted to get out of the car.

During those six months that I traveled the continent, strangers had begun to recognize me on the streets. Booking gigs became easier with every new city I traveled to, I wondered what Toronto had in store for me. When I traveled through the cities in the northern states, I played at gigs hosted in bars and pubs. I had access to the equipment at each venue, and I got discounts on food. The owners of the pubs I performed at would give me the names of local studios I could rent out to record my album. I had already recorded an EP in one studio owned by a woman that I had met at one of the venues I performed at. She let me use her recording studio on

YouTube," I said, "I'm not sure if you noticed, but I'm sort of a starving artist. Paying for music is a bit of a foreign concept to me right now."

"I'm just teasing, I haven't heard any of your music yet either. Anyways, do you like The Beatles?" he asked.

"The Beatles? Yeah, they're good. Are they your muse?"

"Not just my muse, my inspiration in life. I love them, their music inspires me. I even have a tattoo quoting them, want to see it?" He took off his leather jacket and exposed his inner forearm. There was a 'let it be' tattoo inked onto it.

"It's beautiful!" I replied, "Is that your favorite song by them?"

"No," he admitted, "I like their song, 'Across the Universe,' better, this one serves as a personal reminder, to let things be as they are."

"My mom always told me I needed to work on that," I admitted, "She's constantly telling me to let things go. But anyway, what's your secret? How do you keep calm in calamity?" I teased.

"I just try to remember that nothing matters in the bigger picture. The living can't control life, and that's okay. When I feel overwhelmed, I look to my tattoo and I listen to The Beatles. If that still doesn't help, I try to put my problems into perspective by looking up at the stars. There's a whole universe out there and everything we do here is so insignificant when you compare it to the ever-expanding universe. The universe doesn't need us, we need it. Once you accept that you can't control anything, nothing can control you. Sorry, I went on a bit of a tangent there, what's your name by the way?"

"I'm V," I introduced myself, I prayed he wouldn't ask what it stood for.

"Cool, nice to meet you V, I'm W.L."

"W.L. wait what does that stand for?" I said without

admitted, "I guess I'll try a hot chocolate too," he smiled. I offered to pay but the boy insisted and walked to the concession stand. I looked around the room, Zephyr was setting up their instruments on stage and Wonder-Lust was tuning his guitar. He looked busy. I turned back to face the moon-eyed boy. Why did his eyes look so familiar? He was an artist of South Asian descent with raven feathered hair and chocolate eyes. He must be a local, I wonder if he came here with anyone tonight. He came back to the table with the beverages and I smiled because he asked them for in-house cups instead of the disposable single-use ones.

"So, Art," I began to sip on my hot chocolate, "What do you do?"

"I'm a Computer Scientist," he explained, "I develop software programs for corporations."

"No Art," I laughed, "I didn't ask about your occupation, I asked you what you do. What are you passionate about? You told me you were an artist."

"Yes, I am an artist," he smiled and my heart melted, "I make animations and do self-portraits. Actually, here let me show you," he pulled out his phone and showed me his illustrations. "This is my uncle, and this is a celebrity my friend likes, I drew him for her." The portraits were gorgeous! They had impeccable detail; I was astonished by his skill. Then he showed me his animations. He showed me the logos he created for video games and children's books. It was then, as I looked at his children's storybook illustrations, that I saw it. It wasn't his skill that made him an artist, it was his warm heart. I marveled at his art for a while, he was very talented and I told him so.

"I want to be a jack-of-all-trades and a master of a few," he said, I smiled, I found that clever. "I am a master of art and software development, but I want to learn other skills. I also play the guitar," he started, "but I am not a master at it. I am a

you showed me love is gentle. You taught me selflessness. Both because I became selfless for you, and also because you became selfless for me. You taught me gentle love, which does not involve screaming or shouting or broken hearts. You are so gentle to those you love, it made me gentle too."

"V, I love you too."

"And something further," I started, "You cried for me, you cried to me. You showed me your soul, your heart, and it was so beautiful and gentle. And you hold me like you don't want to ever let go. You taught me to be gentle, to the world, and to myself. Without you I would be a storm, you showed me the light in the weather. You brought the sun out."

"That's what artists do V," he pulled me into him and I felt his chest against mine. I heard his heart beating softly. I never wanted to leave.

"V," he sighed, "Why do we have to die? I want to live forever, without physical ailment. Without sickness or pain. I'm going to build us a machine that will allow us to live forever. I want to live young forever with you."

"Me too Art," Art was the type of man who loved ideas. His favorite quote was by Eleanor Roosevelt, "Great minds discuss ideas; average minds discuss events; small minds discuss people," and he lived by it.

He had a great mind, but sometimes men with great minds suffer the most. Our society is not built for great people, just as the farmer said.

They do not always fit into the society, not because they are not enough like they convince themselves to be the case, but because they are above the society in which they live. They are meant to shape the society, not fit into it. Because of this they often struggle. They struggle when society tries to rip them apart, but great people do not realize that society rips them apart because they are strong enough to put themselves back together again. He is strong enough to build a society that

person was Art. Aside from him, I did not want to be contacted. This was an abstract concept for some to grasp, but I just didn't enjoy permitting others to maintain open communication with me 24/7. It was an annoyance most dealt with as a consequence of the demanding and expanding world of technology and workplace expectations. Everyone felt entitled to my time. Everyone. Making them realize that they are not, in fact, entitled to my time was a challenge...

I froze. Perhaps this is how Art felt when I tried to contact him, did I smother him the way I feared the world would smother me?

I walked to the back alley and phoned up Art, my artist. He didn't answer, just as I expected, but not what I had hoped for. I waited for the machine and left a message.

"Art, hey. I'm performing tonight at Hagey Theatre, you know, that venue we met at? Can you please come? It's the last time I'm performing before I leave the city for a month. I have a gig in Niagara Falls after this, and I really want to see you. Can you please just come tonight? I perform soon. If you miss my performance it's fine, I just want to see you. I'll buy you a drink or something. Oh, wait, shit, you don't drink. I forgot, well, they have bubble tea across the street, I know you like that. I'll get you bubble tea. Can you please answer my messages?" the call ended. I called back again, hoping for another result, but when I got the voicemail all I could mutter into the phone was, "I love you," I hung up. Maybe he would come tonight, perhaps he just couldn't get to the phone. Maybe he couldn't answer the phone because he was driving over.

I decided I needed a drink. Just one, I didn't want to get wasted before the show. I just needed to take the edge off. I ordered a rum and coke because it was the only thing I liked, even though I was not a fan of coke, it diluted the rum nicely. I often wondered why people drank before I started drinking more frequently. Then I realized that they did it for the same

perfect, I knew you were beautiful. When I saw Art, I saw love, I saw kindness, and I saw a gentle-hearted man with a difficult life. All he wanted was to tend to a flame that burnt him one too many times before, it left his hands smoldered. Without Art, who tended to the flame, it got out of control. The flame threw fits, burning down the forests because all it wanted was for him to return. The flame needed Art to tend to it, but he became ice cold. On paper, fire and ice sound lovely, but in practice, one melts, and the other mourns his loss. I was drunk, I blasted sad music, the tune tickled my eardrums.

My motel had a phone, I dialed up Art.

"Art, I just wanted you to know that I worry about you a lot. I care about you so much and I know I'm not with you now, but I love you and I want you back. You were supposed to be my future, but then we both let pride and passion get in the way of that. I am a poet, and I write sad poems with you and sad poems without you. I can't breathe without you, and I can't imagine a future without you either. Every time I think of my future, I see you there with me. I don't believe in soulmates, and I know I was terrible for you, but I loved your heart and your mind, and your soul, if souls exist anyways.

"I love your art, and I want it back in my life. I can't imagine a future without you. I would wait in empty coffee shops for the rest of my days if I was certain that someday he would sit across my table, and hold my hands again. Now I have to move on, and it hurts. You left me, and I knew you were right for doing so. I know it's probably tough on you too. Man, losing the one you love, it's horrible. It's like a cyclone but even more chaotic," the voice memo ended. I cried again and called one last time:

"Art, I love you so fucking much it breaks me to see you don't want to talk anymore. I really want you, but if I can't have you, I hope you find someone who loves you and appreciates you the way you deserve to be loved. I wasn't

it didn't contribute to the story. It was random, unnecessary to the plot. Well, that's kind of the point.

See dear reader, in real life, sometimes there isn't some greater purpose to catastrophe. Sometimes the good among us will die, there is no rhyme or reason to it. Trying to contextualize Yippie's death, finding the inner meaning in it, analyzing their life, trying to understand why they got the short end of the stick... doesn't that sound familiar? Doesn't that sound like the real world?

Yippie died and lived by unfortunate circumstances contributed by a failed corrupted society. Just like the farmer, Yippie didn't value the society because the society didn't value them.

****

My heart ached for two now, while one was living, and the other had passed, and I knew I would never see either again.

When stars fall, they don't break, but the hearts of those who loved them do.

who do you like, then the game awkwardly ends. You didn't play it as a kid?"

"No, I haven't," he admitted, "But let's play."

"Do you believe in fate?" I asked him, he considered it.

"Yes and no. Sometimes I do, other times I don't. For instance, I think its fate that we met, because we both live in different countries, we both play very different genres, I almost didn't perform the night we met. I was originally planning on performing in Vegas, but there was an issue with the rental car, I tried booking a flight, but there weren't any flights heading out that would get me there in time. I was bummed because I wanted to perform, then I remembered there were some *Zephyr* band members performing at a venue in Toronto. Initially I was not going to go, but they told me they were down a guitarist and they said they could use some vocals so I said screw it. Then I met you. How could I not believe in fate?"

"You make a compelling argument Wonder-Lust, though I'm not sure about fate. I think we make our own fate. Everyone always thinks I'm a pessimist for saying that, but I think they're being pessimistic for not seeing the beauty in that. They think making our own fate is a bad thing. Of all the options, of all the people you could have chosen to meet, of all the places you could have chosen to go, you chose here. There is something beautiful and special in that. Every person in your life you chose to let in. I think that's better than fate, because you made a decision, and you make that decision over and over again every day."

"That's different," considered Wonder-Lust, "but I like the way you think. It's my turn, right? Do you believe in soulmates?"

"No, but I do believe in love. I think there are a combination of different people you can meet and fall in love with. The trick is to fall in love with someone you're